LITERARY CRITICISM AND CULTURAL THEORY

OUTSTANDING DISSERTATIONS

edited by
William E. Cain
Wellesley College

A ROUTLEDGE SERIES

OTHER BOOKS IN THIS SERIES:

THE MAKING OF THE VICTORIAN NOVELIST

Anxieties of Authorship in the Mass Market

Bradley Deane

Routledge
Taylor & Francis Group

NEW YORK AND LONDON

Published in 2003 by
Routledge
711 Third Avenue, New York, NY 10017

Published in Great Britain by
Routledge
2 Park Square, Milton Park, Abingdon, Oxon OX14 4RN

Routledge is an imprint of the Taylor & Francis Group, an informa business

First issued in paperback 2013

10 9 8 7 6 5 4 3 2

Library of Congress Cataloging-in-Publication Data

Deane, Bradley, 1971–
   The making of the Victorian novelist : anxieties of authorship in the
mass market / by Bradley Deane.
       p. cm. — (Literary criticism and cultural theory)
   Includes bibliographical references (p.) and index.
   ISBN 0-415-94020-6 (hardback)
   1. English fiction—19th century—History and criticism. 2. Authors
and publishers—Great Britain—History—19th century. 3. Literature
publishing—Great Britain—History—19th century. 4. Authors and
readers—Great Britain—History—19th century. 5. Fiction—Authorship—
Psychological aspects. 6. Fiction—Authorship—Economic aspects. I.
Title. II. Series.
   PR871 .D36 2002
   823'.809—dc21
                                                      2002010034

ISBN 13: 978-0-415-94020-7 (hbk)
ISBN 13: 978-0-415-86700-9 (pbk)

Contents

Acknowledgments

Victorian novelists liked to use their prefaces to affirm their warm fellow-feeling with their readers, frequently thanking them for their steadfast friendship. While the professional model of authorship through which this book will be perceived prevents me from expressing a similar optimism, I may at least take this opportunity to thank the many friends who have already read and contributed to these pages. This project began as a doctoral dissertation for the English Department at Northwestern University, where the intellectual community allowed me to see how hollow the Romantic claims about writing as the work of solitary genius can really be. Betsy Erkkila graciously agreed to read a dissertation outside of her field, and while I have greatly benefited from her insight, I am more thankful still for her generous encouragement and intellectual enthusiasm. Christopher Herbert challenged me to confront the sort of daunting questions from which I might otherwise have shied away, and helped me to answer them with his equally daunting expertise in Victorian culture. It is to Jules Law, though, that this work is most indebted. His contributions at every stage of the project are greater than I can adequately acknowledge here; suffice it to say that the most interesting and important elements of this study are the ones with which he was most directly involved. Of my other friends and colleagues at Northwestern, I want to thank Wendy Wall, Jeff Masten, Jay Grossman, Chris Lane, and Matt Frankel for their advice, encouragement, and the kind of sympathetic bonhomie that the Victorians liked to imagine of their audience. My wife Jennifer, finally, helped me more than she will admit, giving me both invaluable scholarly criticism and the confidence to proceed when I needed it most. I dedicate this book to her with gratitude, affection, and admiration.

Introduction

A specter haunts literary criticism—the specter of the nineteenth-century author—and not even the alliance of all the formalist challenges of a hundred years have managed to exorcise it: not T. S. Eliot's assertion in "Tradition and the Individual Talent" that artistic progress necessitates the extinction of the author's personality, nor Wimsatt and Beardsley's more fundamental defiance of authorial intention as a critical criterion, nor even Roland Barthes's provocative proclamation of the death of the Author-God who tyrannizes over the potential plenitude of textual signification. A creditable history of twentieth-century critical schools, in fact, could be pieced together entirely from each generation's distinctive methods for announcing the author's interment. Yet the legacy of the nineteenth-century author refuses to be laid to rest. In the twenty-first century literary marketplace, authorial cults of personality continue to drive production and consumption: we continue to encounter that old authorship in the photographs on dustjackets, in online chatrooms and innumerable fansites, in the unremitting stream of promotional book tours. At academic conferences, too, and in the pages of course catalogs across the country, we find that the largely uninterrogated category of "the man and his work" is as ubiquitous as ever. In this sense, Mark Twain's joke about the wide exaggeration of the rumors of his death has taken on an ironically persistent afterlife.

This is a study of the origins of nineteenth-century authorship in Britain, and more particularly of the social, economic, and aesthetic transformations that allowed it to achieve its almost unassailable hegemony in popular culture and professional criticism alike. My approach to authorship thus arises not from the purely formalist tradition, which dismisses authors as (at best) extra-literary distractions, but from the perspective of literary sociology, which investigates authorship as a historically variable and culturally influential dimension of the practice of making literature.

The goal of this latter field of inquiry is not simply to browse biographies of writers in search of new ways to reveal their intentions or the inspirations behind their writings—a project to which the formalists compellingly objected—but to uncover socially specific assumptions about authors that shaped the practical implications of literary culture. Barthes is right about the extent to which authorship has governed our understanding of literature over the last two centuries, but this seems to me all the more reason to recover the precise grammars of authorship through which writers and readers have historically made sense of one another; to put it a bit crudely, if we want to understand the stakes of *Middlemarch* for its original readers, we shall also have to explore the cultural embeddedness of "George Eliot." But this is not to concede, as Barthes suggests, that writers themselves have exercised divine authority over their texts, or even over their own public identities. A society's ideals of authorship are constructed collectively rather than individually, and they coalesce at the nexus of a wide array of public discourses and material practices, so that writers can be as constrained by authorship as readers.

Writers may be individual human agents who set pen to paper to make a living, but *authors* are the products of ideology. I use this last term in the sense suggested by Louis Althusser, who treats it as the way in which people imagine their relationship to the fundamental social conditions that actually structure their lives. I share Althusser's sense that we should not regard ideology merely as political deception or the self-serving doublethink of false consciousness, but, more profoundly, as the set of axiomatic propositions through which individuals experience their social lives, and I also follow Althusser's example in treating ideologies as broadly determined by a society's distinctive configurations of legal codes and economic institutions, even though, as he pointed out, this determination is not always efficiently immediate or even easily traceable. But I have also adapted Althusser's general formulation of ideology to the specific concerns of this project: I treat the ideology of authorship as the imagined relationship of writers to the conditions of production and circulation in which they worked, so that it is shaped not only by writers themselves, but also by publishers and printers, book buyers and periodical readers, reviewers, circulating libraries, bookbinders, literary agents, and legislators. I have also departed from the general use of "authorship" to denote the characteristics shared by writers in all genres, which would be too abstract a meaning to do justice to the complexities of nineteenth-century print culture. It may be that in earlier periods, to be "a man in print" might have meant much the same thing whether one wrote poetry, drama, criticism, or all of these, but, as I emphasize in my first chapter, by the beginning of the nineteenth century these different genres were associated with different audiences, different modes of production, and, in effect, different authorships. The study of nineteenth-century authorship must therefore begin with the recognition that, in practical terms, no such monolith existed.

Of the different authorships produced in nineteenth-century print culture, this book focuses on those that shaped the social history of the novel, asking what it meant—and what it could have meant—to be a Victorian novelist. The novelists of nineteenth-century Britain were the first writers to experience the full industrialization of literary production, and they stood at the center of an sustained debate over the cultural transformations brought about by mechanical production, new techniques of distribution and circulation, and, above all, the staggering growth of reading audiences. Authorship, it bears repeating, is as much a public concern as an individual one, and novelists were thoroughly embroiled in the momentous restructuring of the Victorian public. And since fiction was altered more than other literary forms by the growth of the market, the social status of novelists across the nineteenth century was both more mercurial and more controversial than that of writers in any other genre. Easily dismissed at the beginning of the century as hacks who pandered to the ignorant or indolent, novelists by the end of Victoria's reign could be esteemed among the greatest of artists. Between these extremes stretches a century of ideological contention between alternative representations of authorship, and traces of these struggles remain legible in the themes and forms of the novels themselves.

This project examines a sequence of literary crises in order to offer an original narrative of the antagonistic proliferation of representations of novelists, the figures onto which Victorians projected the hopes and anxieties of their transforming society. The particular crises I examine all find their epicenters in the upheaval of nineteenth-century print culture: these include new modes of production, arguments over copyright legislation, and revisions of the criteria of periodical criticism, all of which are linked by anxieties over the exponential expansion of the literary industry. The striking growth of the reading public serves as the engine that drives my narrative, as it provides, in real, quantifiable terms, an explanation for the practical changes that gave nineteenth-century fiction its characteristic properties. An exceptionally popular novel in the Romantic period might have circulated 10,000 copies; by the beginning of Victoria's reign that figure had quadrupled, and twenty years later a popular novelist might expect to address an audience in excess of 100,000, a number which, relative to population, would still seem remarkable. And the new readership was not only quantifiably different; it was increasingly perceived, for reasons that introduced new cultural anxieties, as being qualitatively different as well. The powerfully influential emergence of what we would now call a mass market was not understood in strictly numerical terms since the "mass" of this market is necessarily relative: though it implies particular methods of production and pricing, it also depends on a *perception* of textual circulation that trangresses the traditional boundaries of class. In this way, what we might call mass-market anxieties historically precede a measurably democratic (or, as some writers feared, anarchic) access to literary culture. And it is this specter, one closer to the original Marxist specter to which I alluded at the outset, which haunted nineteenth-century authors themselves.

My narrative divides the century into a four-part historical frame, each part corresponding to a crucial phase of conflict over the potential consequences of the widening sphere of fiction's reach: the post-revolutionary concern with literary popularity during the Romantic period's skirmish of genres; the advent of serialized fiction and other early-Victorian experiments with mass-market publishing; the mid-Victorian explosion of the periodical press and the panic over sensationalism; and the late nineteenth-century contest between best-sellers and classics. The particular debates in each period gave rise to new images of the novelist—the impersonal public servant, the sympathetic friend, the professional storyteller, and the proto-modernist artist—which encoded distinct ideological assumptions about the growing public's engagement with literature. The level on which these ideological clashes occurred was largely rhetorical—their chief weapons were metaphors, analogies, and symbols—and their influence on the mediating tropes of authorship remains especially apparent in the pages of popular novels. For each major transition in print culture, therefore, I have provided a reading of a popular novel that encodes and rewrites the keywords of authorship's rhetoric. But I have also explained why the persistence of certain elements of authorship's vocabulary should not be taken to mean a smooth continuity in definitions of the novelist. For instance, the connotations of "sympathy," a central term throughout the century, were virtually antithetical for Elizabeth Gaskell and Henry James. What seems at first to be a relatively stable vocabulary, one that seems to demonstrate the endurance of Romantic ideals in particular, was in fact subject to a richly complicated set of contradictory inflections.

The first chapter revisits the most influential of the Victorian novelists' precursors in the Romantic period, reading their competing constructions of authorship as responses to the unprecedented potential for circulation revealed by the success of Walter Scott's *Waverley*. Beginning with the familiar rhetoric of Romantic authorship articulated by William Wordsworth, I outline the ways in which the glorification of the autonomous, prophetic genius of Romantic ideology was enabled by a staged rejection of the growing audience, and explore Wordsworth's use of his marginality in the marketplace—partly strategic and partly thrust upon him—to justify a form of authority that could reject popularity as a yardstick of literary success. I then contrast Wordsworth's author-centered aesthetics with the relatively neglected model of authorship associated with the "Great Unknown," Walter Scott. Scott's emphasis on the social utility of fiction as the privileged measure of literary merit led him to de emphasize his authority as a writer, and to defer instead to the diverse tastes of the large readership he courted. Insistently anonymous and, as he put it, "impersonal," Scott likened novelists to postmen rather than to prophets, suggesting that writers should be regarded as civil servants to be judged only by the immediate instrumentality of their productions. My reading of *Waverley* points to the narrative fissure brought about by the strain of appealing to readers who had previously been thought to belong to incompatible audiences, while the ambivalence of his discussion of authorship likewise underscores his obsessive regard for the public reception of his work. In emphasizing the profound discontinuities between Scott and Wordsworth, this chapter establishes the mixed heritage from which novelists would derive their rhetoric of self-representation and their uncertain sense of their relationship to the literary market.

The second chapter traces the ironic emergence of early Victorian representations of novelists as sympathetic, intimate, and friendly—in terms, that is, closer to those of the marginal William Wordsworth than to those of the popular Walter Scott. As the reading public continued to expand, popular novelists enjoyed greater leverage in the relations of literary production and the economic demands of wider publication presented them with new incentives to foreground their personal presence as the creators of their work. Synthesizing the disparate values of Scott and Wordsworth into an ideology I call Industrial Romanticism, they formulated a version of personalized authorship that could address the pressing social concerns of class antagonism and alienation at the same time it enhanced their prestige and justified their demands for greater remuneration. I analyze these transformations as they were expressed in the copyright reform debates of 1837-41, and in the most astonishingly popular novel of those years, Charles Dickens's *Pickwick Papers*. *Pickwick* is a notoriously loose and baggy serial novel produced over the two years in which the copyright movement gathered momentum, and by its conclusion it had become a very different book. I read in the novel's formal and thematic metamorphoses the hidden narrative of Dickens's emergence as a sympathetic friend to his readers, a paradigm of authorship that would dominate the Victorian imagination for decades. But *Pickwick* also provides a record of the traditions that were repressed to create the familiar "Dickens," including the trope of editorship and the possibility of a relatively anonymous, collaborative model of literary production.

Chapter three turns to the decline of the friendly novelist in the 1860s, a period that saw explosive growth in the periodical industry, and one which would produce—not coincidentally—both the derided "sensation novelist" and the forerunners of the modern literary critic. I argue that anxieties over the mass-market weeklies and illustrated newspapers spurred reviewers associated with the new "higher journalism" to contend that the reading public could no longer be counted upon to distinguish good from bad, or to save themselves, in Matthew Arnold's terms, from cultural anarchy. They reimagined the universal immediacy of sympathy as the potential for epidemic decay, and in making the case for their superior taste, they conjured the image of a menacing "sensation school" of novelists as their dark antithesis. Wilkie Collins, whose extremely popular *The Woman in White* was one of the first novels to be branded sensational, suffered at this moment a precipitous decline in his reputation among reviewers. His novel reveals that he, too, was concerned about the influence of a broad new readership, which he called the "Unknown Public," though his response was different from his critics'. His novel thematizes the breakdown of sympathetic relations as a foundation of identity in the public sphere, and its fascination with legal discourse in the story and its narrative frame exemplifies the rise of a professional model of authorship.

By the last decades of the century, ideologies of authorship had grown strikingly diverse; Collins's rhetoric of professionalism, now formally adopted by a new Society of Authors, was only one among many contending models. The Society's most celebrated antagonist, Henry James, took a contradictory position, and during the "art of fiction" debates of the 1880s he asserted a construction of the novelist as an artist who transcends the more worldly considerations and social duties of professionalism. James's novels at the time sold relatively poorly, but rather than support the common view of James as a victim of an increasingly fragmentary reading public, the fourth chapter emphasizes his impulse to embrace and reinforce the audience's new divisions. James found in the balkanization of the Victorian market the chance to preserve writers' cultural distinction from the threat of a leveling mass-market consumerism (a fear some contemporary writers felt was confirmed by the appearance of a new literary category, the "bestseller"). And in developing an authoritative image of his integrity and mastery, James contributed to a construction of literary value that perceived the ultimate aim of reading as an individual appreciation of a novelist's unique artistic vision. Along with this increased stress on communing with an author's sensibility, James pioneered in *The Princess Casamassima* an impersonal narrative style that further mystified the work of writing. His alienated "vessel of consciousness" technique and his understanding of the novelist as the invisible deity reigning over the meaning of his fictional world mark the demise of the Victorian paradigm of sympathetic novelists and heralds the advent of modernist literary authority.

The final chapter is organized differently: it is designed to fill in gaps in the narrative of the first four chapters, but also to give more careful attention to the particular concerns of women writers as they addressed the changing market for fiction. After discussing the methodological dilemma of treating the work of women novelists as either a wholly separate tradition or as indistinguishable from the ideologically feminized work of men, this chapter offers an analysis of the representation of domesticity as a field in which the private experiences of women intersect with public constructions of Victorian novelists' authority. Drawing on the fiction and criticism of two writers, Elizabeth Gaskell and George Eliot, I explore the range of women writers' modes of engaging audiences, while maintaining my more general argument that changing perceptions of the reading public structured their divergent authorships. While I feel that Gaskell and Eliot's contrasting tactics of self-representation usefully inform our understanding of the distinctive predicaments of women writers, it is also possible to regard their respective accomplishments in the larger narrative frame I have provided: the section on Gaskell's *Mary Barton* could be productively read between the chapters on Dickens and Collins, while Eliot's *Middlemarch* records the beginnings of an ideological transition that would ultimately lead to James's position as it is described in the fourth chapter.

The individual chapters are designed to serve as significant interventions in the criticism of the particular novels they address, but my project draws its greatest strength from the combination of these chapters into a sustained narrative of considerable scope. Taken together, these historical junctures begin to suggest a general trajectory of novelistic authorship, especially in what would become its most canonical tradition. As authorship was granted increasing importance as a locus of literary value, novels themselves moved toward a self-reflexive appreciation of forms of consciousness. And as novelists turned from earlier models of public utility, their work became in practice, as well as in theme, less overtly political, less comprehensive, less socially engaged. This may seem to us like a natural evolution since it is the story that late-Victorian novelists retrospectively advanced, in various coded and allegorical ways, as their tradition. Yet I emphasize that these changes were not inevitable or even predictable. By focussing on moments of intense ideological friction, I have attempted to record a history of plausible alternatives to familiar representations of the novelist.

My argument depends on many of the sophisticated recent advances in the field of Victorian publishing history, but its theoretical origins might be better understood by its complicated relationship to the work of Michel Foucault and the many studies he has inspired. His influence over the pursuit of exciting new dimensions in the study of authorship over the last two decades can hardly be overemphasized. I share his sense of the fundamental importance of the question posed by his classic essay, "What Is an Author?", and also his belief that the answer does not lie solely in intellectual history, but in the complicated interaction of institutional imperatives and psychologistic displacements of the techniques of cultural power. More importantly, I share his interest in what he calls the "author-function," the mediating influence that forms of authorship exercise over particular discourses. But Foucault tends to assume that the social consequences of authorship, while historically variable, are at any given time static and monolithic, and studies that have followed in his wake often understand authorship merely as an inadvertent epiphenomenon of a society's legal code or of its processes of production or circulation. While my attention to the growth of the market offers a similar grounding in material practices, this project reveals constant conflict between multiple author-functions, so that in my account, writers, publishers, and reviewers become agents in an ongoing struggle, rather than passive functionaries of society's deepest and most inescapable structures of power. Authorship thus becomes a field of contention at the intersection of the Victorians' complicated literary legacies and the new political and technical developments that continued to reshape notions of novelists' work. The story I will tell is about authorship's constant mutability and the incessant struggle to mold its contours to fit the diverse needs of a turbulent society. The story of authorship in the nineteenth century has valuable lessons to teach us still, because it is the story of how authorship itself came to eclipse other ways of imagining literature's social purposes.

The Making of the
Victorian Novelist

CHAPTER ONE

Dueling Authorships in the Romantic Period:
The Author of *Waverley* and the Great Unknown

Captain Clutterbuck, an amateur antiquarian of some minor repute in literary circles, vividly remembered a winter day in 1821 when he encountered an apparition. His account of this incident begins with his visit to the shop of a bookseller in Edinburgh—probably John Ballantyne's publishing house—where he is welcomed as a friend and former associate. Taking advantage of his host's good favor, he decides to explore the inner regions of the building, a dark, labyrinthine network of narrow passages, "obscure recess[es]," and "crypts." As he wanders through the eerie, book-lined corridors, Clutterbuck becomes unnerved: he writes of his creeping feeling of "holy horror," and his dread of stumbling onto something "unmeet for mortal eye." His fears are realized, in part, when he finds himself in a vaulted chamber "dedicated to secrecy and silence," at the center of which sits a cryptic figure, "closely veiled and wimpled." But though he cannot make out any of its features, Clutterbuck senses at once that the apparition he beholds is "the person, or perhaps I should rather say the eidolon, or representative vision, of the AUTHOR OF WAVERLEY!"

Like his story, Captain Clutterbuck is a fiction, an imaginary character who relates his supernatural experience in the "Introductory Epistle" to Walter Scott's *The Fortunes of Nigel* (1822). Clutterbuck belongs to that imaginary gallery of editors, introduction writers, and collectors of tales in whom Scott delighted when composing the prefaces to his novels, and like the rest of them, Clutterbuck's function is to prepare the reader for the story that follows. We might think of him as a rhetorical gatekeeper, a figure designed to mediate the relationship between the culturally determined expectations of Scott's audience and the text of the novel: Clutterbuck sets the tone, advises readers about the nature of the discourse to follow, and suggests to them—directly and indirectly—discursive forms alongside of which Scott's production is best understood. At a time when the cultural value of novels was still a subject of regular debate, Scott's interest in suggesting to readers the terms in which his work should be received is readily understandable. What may seem less obvious to us is the analogous function performed by another imaginary construct, the "Author of *Waverley*."

Though now our immediate impulse is to associate this title with Walter Scott, it is worth remembering that Scott did not publish novels under his own name until the twilight of his career. His original readers would have met, like Clutterbuck, only the mysteriously concealed "Author of *Waverley*" on the title pages of these books. This does not imply that readers knew nothing about the nameless Author—on the contrary, his particular opinions, philosophies, and merits were discussed at length in Scott's introductions and in contemporary reviews—but that they knew him as a textually constructed public figure rather than as the biographical individual Walter Scott. The distinction is crucial because it allows us to separate the writer from "authorship," the socially constituted ideology through which his work is understood. It allows us to see more clearly, in other words, one dimension of what Michel Foucault has called the "author-function." As Foucault explains, ideologies of authorship are "tied to the legal and institutional systems that circumscribe, determine, and articulate the realm of discourses," and are thus "not defined by the spontaneous attribution of a text to its creator, but through a series of complex procedures" (130). While not free of its own ideological baggage, Scott's whimsical metaphor of the ghostly author in the publishing house underscores both the actual impersonality of authorship and its institutional locus, while the "Introductory Epistle" itself participates in the "complex procedures" to which Foucault alludes.

Scott's dogged insistence on anonymous publication earned another nickname for the Author of *Waverley*: the Great Unknown. And to a great extent, the version of authorship endorsed by Scott and shaped by contemporary forms of production and circulation remains unknown today. Scott has in this regard been overshadowed by a retrospective critical assessment of his period that focuses on Romantic poetry, a discourse distinct enough from Scott's novels and produced under such different conditions that it was grounded in a contrary set of ideological principles. This other representation of what authors do and how readers should approach their work, especially as articulated by Wordsworth and Coleridge, is more familiar to us today, largely because we continue to live under the shadow of the Romantic ideology of authorship that they helped to establish. Their idea of an autonomous, original creator pervades popular representations of artists, it forms the basis of our copyright laws, and, in literary criticism, it has given rise to a tenacious understanding of literature as an expression of the soul of a genius. Because of the Romantic model's lasting influence, historians of authorship have tended to describe an organic, continuous hegemony of this ideology, a narrative which typically credits Wordsworth with originating an understanding of authorship that we have lived with ever since.[1]

If such accounts portray the dissemination of Romantic authorship with an air of inevitability, they can do so only by effacing its historical struggle with competing ideologies under changing relations of literary production. They thus unconsciously recapitulate Wordsworth's mystifying formula of literary achievement: "every author, as far as he is great and at the same time *original*, has had the task of *creating* the taste by which he is to be enjoyed: so it has been, so it will continue to be"("Essay Supplementary" 100). Despite such claims and the tendencies of modern criticism to agree with them, Romantic authorship was not from the outset some enduring intellectual monolith ushered into England by Wordsworth as if by divine fiat. It was mostly limited, at first, to an unpopular and rather experimental species of poetry, and thus contended with other possible conceptions of authorship from the beginning. Moreover, it was consolidated alongside a mode of production that had little use for the quickly growing numbers of British readers in the early nineteenth century, and indeed, it made a virtue of its social marginality. Wordsworth, in short, would hardly have seemed a likely candidate to suggest the template of a new and widely influential author-function.

The relatively neglected representations of the Author of *Waverley* offer a striking contemporary counterexample to the Romantic refashioning of the poet, and the history of the Victorian novelist must begin by outlining both of these influences. Even though Wordsworth would eventually (and ironically) supply later writers with much of the symbolic vocabulary they employed to conceptualize their work, Scott's achievement transformed the institutional and ideological structures through which novels were produced, circulated, and evaluated. *Waverley* (1814) itself had appeared to immediate critical acclaim and a degree of commercial success that, as Richard Altick puts it, "marks a new era of fiction" (379), and the novels that followed continued to set new standards in practices of publishing and circulation, even as they helped redefine the cultural status of the novelist. Restoring both Wordsworth and Scott to their historical and material contexts, this chapter will examine not only the social stakes of their competing constructions of authorship, but also the different modes of production and relationships to the emerging market out of which they arose. Taken together, Wordsworth and Scott suggest the complexities of the struggle to define authorship in the Romantic period, and so provide us with a valuable record of the Victorian novelist's ambivalent parentage.

THE PROPHET MARGIN

Traditionally, the advent of Romanticism in Britain has been bound to the publication of *Lyrical Ballads* in 1798, but the Romantic *author* arrived—a bit tardily—with Wordsworth's "Essay Supplementary to the Preface" to his 1815 edition of *Poems*. Given Wordsworth's experiences between the publication of these two texts, the lag of seventeen years is telling. Not only had his youthful political radicalism ebbed, he also found himself, as a writer, in a far less prominent position than he had expected; the revolutionary promise of *Lyrical Ballads* had evaporated, and despite that volume's relatively encouraging sales, Wordsworth's subsequent reception had proved disheartening. At the same time, the enormous successes of other poets and unprecedented achievements of novelists—of whom the Author of *Waverley* was the most conspicuous example—offered a sense of what "popularity" might come to mean in British print culture. It is in the "Essay Supplementary" that Wordsworth first thoroughly articulates the fundamental characteristics of Romantic authorship: the author is a mystified genius, an autonomous creator of original works, doomed to be isolated by greatness and misunderstood by his contemporaries. Bitterly slashing his way through literary history, Wordsworth casts the work of one poet after another onto a critical bonfire intended to illuminate his own genius all the more brightly. Angry at the "unremitting hostility" with which his own poems had been received (100), Wordsworth is particularly severe to writers who had been the popular darlings of their day: Congreve and Macpherson, Pope and Dryden, and a dozen more beside are consigned to the pyre. He scorns the sort of writer willing to "accommodate himself to the likings and fashions of his day" (95), and struggles to liberate writers from what he perceives to be the consuming public's tyranny of mediocrity: "Away, then, with the senseless iteration of the word *popular*, applied to new works of poetry, as if there were no test of excellence in this first of the fine arts but that all men should run after its productions, as if urged by appetite, or constrained by a spell!" (105). Wordsworth's first extended attempt to redefine authorship in relation to readers and society is driven by precisely this concern, a desire to provide some "test of excellence" other than that threatened by the growing dependence of writers on the court of popular appeal represented by the market.

Wordsworth's solution—his emphasis on the sensibility of writers themselves as the test of excellence—tempts us to assume that he was merely suggesting some alternative by which his own work would not be found so egregiously wanting, that he decried popularity simply because his poetry was unpopular.[2] But this assumption underrates the significance of the alternative he constructed. Authorship itself becomes, in Wordsworth's aesthetics, the alpha and omega of literary meaning; the poet is the prioritized, singular source of textual creation, and is thus, from the perspective of the reader, the key to a text's meaning and value. As the foundation for an emergent conception of authorship, these notions have implications that reach far beyond whatever form of personal self-aggrandizement Wordsworth may have had in mind. They should be understood not simply as a rejection of outdated aesthetics, but as a negotiation of the profound developments through which the eighteenth-century "crowd" gave way to the modern notion of a "public."[3] The primacy of the figure of the poet, along with its associated virtues of originality and creativity, suggested ways to conceive the proprietorship of textual productions, appropriate modes of circulation among this new reading public, and a different basis for literary authority. Wordsworth's understanding of authorship is in fact a shrewdly strategic reaction to changing conditions of literary production and to the readers responsible for the ongoing transformation. For Wordsworth, "popularity" is shorthand for an eighteenth-century paradigm of literary value that could no longer be trusted. His ideology offers a method of cultural management through the control of discourse, particularly by shifting the locus of that control from its previous basis in reception to production, from social consensus to individual sensibility.[4]

Despite the assured and sometimes bombastic tones in which Wordsworth makes his case for a new understanding of the poet, the fragility of his position is everywhere betrayed by its hostile denial of other models of literary authority. His description of an authoritative *writer* standing in relation to readers as a leader bringing followers to some intellectual "advance" or "conquest," for example, is explicitly contrasted to the image of an authoritative *reader*, "stretched on his palanquin and borne by slaves" ("Essay Supplementary" 104). The doubts that lurk behind Wordsworth's defensiveness indicate that the eventual acceptance of Romantic ideology was far from inevitable; in fact, as I shall emphasize here, the Romantic construction of authorship was born out of the experience of marginality under changing relations of literary production. The targets of Wordsworth's invective, the book-buying "PUBLIC"—as opposed to the abstract "PEOPLE" ("Essay Supplementary" 108)—and the "frantic novels, sickly and stupid German tragedies, and deluges of idle and extravagant stories in verse" that they prefer to read ("Preface" 11), suggest that he was not inattentive either to the widening circle of readers or to the force of their demands. What he insistently and repeatedly attacks is the notion that the growing literary marketplace would be the authoritative arbiter of literary merit, that the "test of excellence" would be consumption. Marginality could become, in response, not simply a condition thrust upon Wordsworth by forces frustratingly beyond his control, but a privileged position outside the corrupting influence of the marketplace.

Wordsworth was by no means the first to contend that the sphere of genius existed outside of the world of commerce. His emphasis on the organic nature of original genius may be traced to Edward Young's *Conjectures on Original Composition* (1759). Young's metaphors first provided the terms with which the Romantics would eventually define authorship: "An original may be said to be of a vegetable nature; it rises spontaneously from the vital root of genius; it grows, it is not made; Imitations are often a sort of manufacture wrought up by those mechanics, art and labour, out of preexistent materials not their own" (qtd. in Parrinder 178). Young's argument depends on an imaginative fissure between natural production and human or social production, and his description of the latter (suggesting manufacture and mechanical work) could easily be metonymically extended to encompass the sphere of trade and the market, especially after more thorough industrialization made commerce increasingly synonymous with mechanized manufacture. Although the "genius" that Young exempts from relations of production is still an abstraction, with the internalization of the term—the growing sense of genius as an intrinsically personal attribute—artists themselves could be similarly differentiated from workers. There remained only a short step for Wordsworth to apply this hierarchy of production to the producers themselves.

Still, Young's ideas failed at first to attract much attention in Britain, and a gap of half a century stretches between his work and its Romantic elaboration. The delay, for which intellectual history seldom accounts, is less a matter of Young's argument gradually creating the taste by which it would be appreciated than of audiences creating a set of conditions under which other writers would come to find its ideological value. In Germany, by contrast, Young's appeal was more immediate, and his book quickly went through several editions. Martha Woodmansee's materialist analysis of late eighteenth-century German aesthetics helps to explain this discrepancy. Woodmansee contends that because of the peculiarly difficult circumstances that obtained for German writers at the time (e.g., the relatively late emergence of professional writers, their difficulties in supporting themselves on token "honoraria," and rampant piracy exacerbated by the legislative independence of the hundreds of German states), they were enthusiastically receptive to ideas that, like Young's, helped them claim ownership of their work and a privileged role in the production of books. With the notion of original genius, the Germans writers could combat either the prevalent construction of authorship, in which writers, like craftsmen, used established conventions to represent ideas that were freely available to anyone, or the economic view that writers contributed only one small portion of the work necessary to produce books, the finished products of an entire branch of manufacture. While striving to protect their own material interests, especially in their efforts to secure copyright protection, these writers consolidated the modern social and juridical meaning of the "author," which characterizes the writer, as Woodmansee puts it, as "an individual who is solely responsible—and thus exclusively deserving of credit—for the production of a unique, original work" (*Author* 35). Wordsworth, adapting the German experience to his own disheartening situation, applied the same valorizing principles to his work, pushing the priority of authors so far that he would represent them as outside, or rather above, any other agents in the relations of production or reception.

Woodmansee's work suggests that these arguments over the status of authors must be seen against the background of a contemporary movement to redefine the social implications of art more broadly. As the number of readers grew and the public market began to supplant patronage as the primary source of support for literature and sustenance for writers, the old order was overturned. Not all writers greeted the new market conditions with equal pleasure. Those, like many poets, who fifty years earlier might have won wealth and prestige under the patronage system, found that the nascent mass market had little use for them The writers who were excluded by new market forces sought to justify their work in a way that would not rely on public approval of—or even public interest in—their productions. Yet to suggest such a perspective they would need to challenge the accepted notion that art was to be judged precisely by its relation to reception. As Woodmansee summarizes, "the arts up until this time had been perceived as intervening directly in human life—as imparting and empowering beliefs, as communicating truths (and of course falsehoods) in a pleasing form—and their value and excellence as works of art had been measured, *instrumentally*, in terms of their success (or failure) in serving these broad human purposes" (12).

Instrumentality is a slippery criterion, of course, since use-value is more an object of ideological contention than a quantifiable absolute. But the significance of the reversal Woodmansee describes may be measured, in the British context, against the doctrine of "utility," which had more specific aesthetic implications. In eighteenth-century Britain, as Raymond Williams has shown, utility had become a "primary test" of literary value:

> It was a sharp tool against definitions of social purpose which excluded the interests of a majority of people, or in one sense of all people, such as definitions of value in terms of an existing social order, or in terms of a god. The test of value was to be whether something was useful to the people, and specifically, as the idea developed, to the majority, 'the greatest number.' (*Keywords* 327)

To the limited extent that Wordsworth argues that poetry should have such a broad social effect, its impact is indefinitely deferred until some hypothetical future audience, conceived in the image of the poet's own sensibility, becomes capable of appreciating its true power. In the meantime, however, the opinions of the majority are absolutely not to be trusted. Wordsworth's rejection of popularity constitutes a radical break from this prevailing ideal of utility. Like those of the Germans before him, Wordsworth's aesthetic priorities may be shown to derive from the experience of marginality, the marginality of poor sales and public indifference, and that of inadequate remuneration under the system of literary production. In the first case the problem to be addressed is one of reception, in the second it is one of production, but in both cases the new ideological response would be to defy the swelling market, to sever writers and their products metaphorically from economic relations, and, in effect, to imagine marginality as a form of privilege.

Wordsworth's celebrated portrayal of the poet as a man "possessed of more than usual organic sensibility" first appears in his preface to the second edition of *Lyrical Ballads*, where he begins to illustrate what this sensibility entails. In response to the general question "What is a Poet?",

Wordsworth provides the following definition: "He is a man speaking to men: a man, it is true, endowed with more lively sensibility, more enthusiasm and tenderness, who has a greater knowledge of human nature, and a more comprehensive soul, than are supposed to be common among mankind" (18). Poets therefore stand out among other people as different in the degree of certain human virtues they possess, and not, significantly, because they actually *do* anything unusual. One recognizes poets by their souls, by their particular knowledge, or by their sensibility, but not because they write poetry. The actual work of composition is here entirely effaced; the poet is "a man speaking to men," and this single action that Wordsworth allows poets is insufficient to distinguish them from anyone else. Indeed, by stretching this formulation, he both elides the activity of writers and suggests that poetic discourse occurs outside the division of labor attendant on the specialized industrial economy; Wordsworth quickly adds that poetic discourse gives pleasure to a "human Being," considered "not as a lawyer, a physician, a mariner, an astronomer or a natural philosopher, but as a Man" (21; see also "A Poet's Epitaph"). Just as Young had contended that original composition took place outside the realm of work and manufacture, so Wordsworth—even in his earliest and simplest descriptions of the authorial genius and "organic sensibility"—abstracts the poet from the divisive world of labor. For the Romantics, the author was to be not a kind of worker, but a kind of person.

It is because the poet lives outside of the fragmented world where "Getting and spending, we lay waste our powers" that poetry remains particularly powerful ("The World Is Too Much with Us" 36). Free from the division of labor, the poet's soul remains integral and organic, and therefore has privileged access to timeless human verities that transcend the ephemeral world of the market. As David Riede shows, Wordsworth's claims for authority are thus grounded in "His wholeness of mind, his sanity, [which] betokens a harmony with eternal principles, with truth."[5] Wordsworthian authority is justified by a particular construction of the poetic self, in other words, and it becomes necessary to assert this self repeatedly in defense of poetic authority. Again and again in his poetry, the poet's sensibility becomes the subject of his own verse,[6] and the very object of reading such poetry is a sort of communion with a great and original soul. But this personal relationship of poet with readers must assume that their communication is unmediated, that the materiality of texts and publishing is no impediment to being a "man speaking to men."

For all of Wordsworth's self-revelation, he tells us little about the extent to which he himself was involved in getting and spending. But like the Germans before him, the structures of valorization he asserted for authorship were entirely consistent with his material interests in publishing. His desire to see poets recognized as solely responsible for the creation of unique works is undoubtedly linked to his long obsession with copyright protection and ownership of intellectual property. In a letter to Thomas Noon

Talfourd, who championed copyright reform in Parliament during the late 1830s, Wordsworth advises that if copyright were extended, "Authors as a Class could not but be in some degree put upon exertions that would raise them in public estimation—And say what you will, the possession of Property tends to make any body of men more respectable, however high may be their claims to respect upon other considerations" (qtd. in Erickson 60). Likewise, Wordsworth's evocation of the Miltonic "fit audience let me find though few!" ("Recluse" 245) has a corresponding material basis in his typical publishing strategy of printing a relatively small number of books at a high—even luxurious—cost to consumers. Lee Erickson summarizes Wordsworth's strategy as follows:

> His books sold steadily to a few who could afford them. Wordsworth wanted to be read by more people, but he felt that while it would be better if the prices of his books could be lower, he would rather have a good return from those books he sold than reduce the percentage of his returns [. . .]. Wordsworth recognizes a trade-off between the price of a volume and its circulation but clearly considers 'reasonable pecuniary return' as his final publishing criterion. (68)

Here again Wordsworth's arguments about authorship remind us that the ideology he proposed was not so much a rejection of the growing industrial market as a strategic negotiation with market forces staged as a rejection. "Do you know the reason why I published *The White Doe* in quarto?", Wordsworth asked at a party in 1820 about his expensive edition; "To show the world my own opinion of it" (qtd. in Rowland 55). His prophecy that works of genius would find only minuscule audiences was fulfilled in part by his decision to publish his works at prices that would be out of reach for the majority of readers. The isolated, original genius at the center of Wordsworth's doctrine of poetry, in other words, is as much a publishing strategy as an aesthetic criterion, as much a way of controlling the circulation and interpretation of discourse in the market as a transcendent ideal of human expression.

Frank Lentricchia has commented that "a respectable generalization about romanticism would emphasize the obsessive dualism of its way of looking at the world" (210). I have touched on some of the relevant binary oppositions in Wordsworth's thought here (e.g., timelessness/temporality, artist/craftsman, originality/popularity, creation/manufacture, the people/ the public), and attempted to show that this dualism is heightened to Manichaean absolutes by Romantic writers' rhetorical rejection of an emerging market in which they occupied a marginal position. This rejection had all the fervor of theological divisions between right and wrong: as Percy Shelley puts it, "Poetry, and the principle of Self, of which money is the visible incarnation, are the God and Mammon of the world"("Defence" 134). This fictional opposition became the prerequisite for the Romantic version of literary authority, an argument for detaching literary value from its social foundations and transferring it to a tiny group of enlightened prophets. But though we can historicize Romantic authorship in this way, literary criticism continues to have trouble imagining alternatives. Lentricchia has shown that even anti-Romantic, structuralist attempts to evade the idea of a unique and autonomous creator often make assumptions based on the Romantic model, and more recently, David Riede has argued that "Literary authority [. . .] remains grounded in Romantic valorization of the imagination and ultimately in the Romantic conceptualization of the self" (9). Authorship continues to imply authority along the lines that Wordsworth suggested, with the effect that we tend to assume that it was always desirable to be an "author," that to take up a pen was always in some measure a sort of Wordsworthian will to power. In the remarks on Scott that follow, I will try to show a less dualistic construction of authorship, one that does not oppose one kind of authoritative selfhood with another, but which disperses authority across the ostensible barrier between art and the market.

"THE ORDINARY BUSINESS OF THE WORLD"

Walter Scott's understanding of authorship is firmly rooted in the Augustan tradition of utility that the Romantics challenged, and he viewed their celebration of individual genius with suspicion. In a letter to Shelley, Scott counseled the younger writer

> against an enthusiasm which while it argues an excellent disposition and a feeling heart, requires to be watched and restrained, tho' not repressed. It is apt, if too much indulged, to engender a fastidious contempt for the ordinary business of the world, and gradually unfit us for the exercise of the useful and domestic virtues, which depend greatly on our not exalting our feelings above the temper of well-ordered and well-educated society. (qtd. in Sauders 187)

The danger Scott finds in the Romantic exaltation of authors is that they will become less "useful," and for him such usefulness presumes writers' respect for the society in which they write and a contiguity between the work of writing and the "ordinary business of the world." Within the ideological frame Scott inherited, he would explore potential (and sometimes inconsistent) relationships of authors to modes of production and circulation, but the Romantic theme of a polarizing struggle between art and the market or the artist and the public is noticeably absent. Asked whether he is willing to trade lasting fame for immediate popularity, for example, the "Author of *Waverley*" responds that "it has often happened that those who have been best received in their own time, have also continued to be acceptable to posterity. I do not think ill enough of the present generation, as to suppose that its present favour necessarily infers future condemnation" ("Introductory Epistle" 55-56). It should perhaps come as no surprise that the writer who was both the most critically venerated and the best-selling man of letters in the Romantic period should view this choice as grounded in a false distinction. Scott's self-representation—especially as a novelist—was shaped by the importance he accorded to a broadly social utility; his work would emphasize a deference to public opinion and a corresponding personal restraint of the sort he found lacking in Shelley.

Before *Waverley* was published, Scott was already one of the most famous, popular, and esteemed poets of his day. His subsequent shift to writing novels at the age of forty-three, along with a thorough revision in the ways he represented the work of writing, thus constitutes what Jane Millgate has called "one of the most amazing right-angled turns in literary history."[7] The rupture between the two phases of his career instructively reminds us of the different possibilities of authorial representation presented by distinct genres. Scott had described the work of poetry in terms of aristocratic (and even feudal) patronage: poets wrote—or minstrels sang—to immortalize the exploits of their masters and the clans to which they claimed personal affiliation, and they advanced their own fame in the process.[8] In keeping with this model, Scott's poetic career was generally characterized by an aggressive courtship of fame and literary reputation. Effacing the collaboration of the many antiquarians and scholars who had helped to collect and authenticate ballads for *The Minstrelsy of the Scottish Borders* (1802-1803), Scott presented the work publicly under only one name, "Walter Scott, Esq., Advocate." Later he was to plagiarize the meter devised by Coleridge for the still unpublished "Christabel" in his *Lay of the Last Minstrel* (1805), and then accuse another poet of having stolen it from *him*. In short, Scott lost no opportunity to commend his own work to the public, as in his anonymous review in the *Edinburgh Annual Register* that proclaimed "the three most successful candidates for poetical fame" to be Robert Southey, Thomas Campbell, and—last but not least—Walter Scott (qtd. in J. Sutherland, *Life* 148).

Yet Scott found the prospect of becoming famous as a novelist much less appealing. In his 1831 introduction to *The Abbot*, for example, he qualifies his pride in his success by admitting his subordinate position among types of writers: "though it were worse than affectation to deny that my vanity was satisfied at my success in the department in which chance had in some measure enlisted me, I was nevertheless, far from thinking that the novelist or romance-writer stands high in the ranks of literature" (163-64). Writing in this ostensibly lesser form, Scott would suggest that to be personally identified as a novelist would be neither necessary nor desirable, and he explored the possibility of publishing as an anonymous or—to use the term he preferred—"impersonal" author. The "Author of *Waverley*" would exempt himself from the poet's desire for personal recognition, particularly the centrally important pursuit of personal literary reputation: "Let fame follow those who have a substantial shape. A shadow—and an impersonal author is nothing better—can cast no shade" ("Introductory Epistle" 47).

The sudden and unexpectedly successful appearance of a nameless new novelist in 1814 stirred eager curiosity in the literary world. Even those readers and critics who suspected that *Waverley* was the work of Walter Scott were nevertheless at a loss to explain why the writer they began to nickname the "Great Unknown" might avoid his reputation as the most emphatically *known* man of letters at the time. Critics today are less interested in the question than they were in the Romantic period,[9] but there was clearly more at stake for Scott than the whimsical perversity implied by the typical critical dismissal of the problem. Anonymity was important enough to Scott to go through the trouble of having all of his manuscripts copied out in a different hand before he submitted them, and important enough that he continued to publish as the Author of *Waverley* even after bankruptcy forced him publicly to acknowledge his productions. There was only one aspect of his career that he treated with comparable secrecy, and the parallel is no coincidence.

Scott's other great secret, of course, was his clandestine involvement in the publishing and printing businesses of the Ballantyne brothers. After 1802, when Scott began to invest heavily in James Ballantyne's printing business, he signed a series of secret contracts which effectively made him an unnamed partner in that business (1805), and later the senior (but still silent) partner in the press and in the new publishing firm of John Ballantyne & Co. (1809). Astute observers may have guessed that Scott was enmeshed in the commercial aspects of book production—just as they might have guessed that he was the Author of *Waverley*—but Scott refused to admit to either until the crash of 1826 forced him to reveal both. Scott had enough of a bourgeois background to take advantage of commercial opportunities but too much aristocratic pretension ever to do so under his own name, and his reluctance to associate himself publicly with the Ballantyne businesses or other publishing ventures testifies to his anxiety over being unmasked as some sort of tradesman.[10] Scott's unwillingness to confess his production of the novels was closely related to just this anxiety.

Regardless of his purely personal motivations for keeping his name hidden, Scott's use of anonymity is effectively consistent with a version of authorship that defers personal authority. Foucault has usefully distinguished the symbolic function of authors' names from the general use of proper names, and he demonstrates that while a proper name "moves from the interior of a discourse to the real person outside who produced it, the name of the author remains at the contours of texts," where it "serves as a means of classification" (123). According to this formulation, once Scott's novels began to appear under the sobriquet "The Author of *Waverley*," they were not, strictly speaking, anonymous. This designation, like "the author of the Scotch novels" or "the Great Unknown," is sufficient to allow critics and consumers to identify and classify his work. But in contrast to Wordsworth's painstaking project of grounding his literary authority in his extratextual humanity by eliding the gap between Wordsworth (the individual denoted by the proper name) and "Wordsworth" (the authoritative speaker constructed in the texts), Scott refused to provide readers with a proper name to point anywhere outside of his novels. The Author of *Waverley* thus remains hovering at a level of pure textuality, knowable only through the texts that bear that name, and open to judgment only through the products of his labor, rather than through a particular kind of human sensibility perceived as anterior to them.

In the "Introductory Epistle" to *The Fortunes of Nigel*, his most complete statement on the nature of his work and his relationship to the public, Scott emphasizes the textual limits of the identity of the Author of *Waverley* by staging an imaginary dialogue between the Author and one of his textual children, the character Captain Clutterbuck. We have seen already that the vision Clutterbuck encounters in the bowels of the publishing house is pointedly impersonal, a specter whose features are hidden behind a veil. During the ensuing conversation Clutterbuck relates news of criticism from the world beyond those book-lined corridors—where, presumably, the eidolon of the author cannot go—and attempts to learn more about the author's identity, but is rebuffed each time. Altogether, the effect is playfully overdone: the Author's existence is confined to a publishing house, he will reveal nothing of his history, and even his ghostly eidolon is disguised. The Author of *Waverley* can be known only as an author, only in his capacity as a writer, only at the level of the text, just as he becomes a character in his own fictions.

Clutterbuck poses a number of criticisms (asking him why his work is so sloppily constructed, why he publishes with such rapidity, if he writes only for financial motivations, why he refuses to curtail his productivity, etc.), to which the author offers a surprising number of ambivalent responses. Ultimately, it is Scott's attempt to define the interaction of the novelist and the reading public that yields his most fascinating and insistent representation of the author's impersonality:

> To the public, I stand pretty nearly in the relation of the postman who leaves a packet at the door of an individual. If it contains a pleasing intelligence, a billet from a mistress, a letter from an absent son, a remittance from a correspondent supposed to be bankrupt,—the letter is acceptably welcome, and read and re-read, folded up, filed, and safely deposited in the bureau. If the contents are disagreeable, if it comes from a dun or from a bore, the correspondent is cursed, the letter is thrown into the fire, and the expense of postage is heartily regretted; while all the time the bearer of the dispatches is, in either case, as little thought on as the snow of last Christmas. The utmost extent of the kindness between the author and the public which can really exist, is, that the world are disposed to be somewhat indulgent to the succeeding works of an original favourite, were it but on account of the habit which the public mind has acquired; while the author very naturally thinks well of *their* taste, who have so liberally applauded *his* productions. But I deny there is any call for gratitude, properly so called, either on one side or the other. (48)

Scott's striking postman analogy reveals the imaginative contortions he would go through to preserve the impersonality of his novels' authorship. His association of novels with letters seems reasonable enough; we can readily infer a certain degree of distance between the author of a letter and its recipient, and we can see how a letter, like a novel, might be received according to whether it was judged to be written by a bore or someone with some "pleasing intelligence" to convey. But Scott does not imagine the author as a correspondent. The novelist is to be found at one more remove as the "bearer of the dispatches," the agent of circulation rather than production, who comes in direct contact with neither the sender nor the receiver of the letters, and who will be quickly and completely forgotten. Scott then goes on to drive home the separation of the writer and public by rejecting the necessity of any personal relationship—such as that implied by "gratitude"—existing above and beyond the simple transaction he describes. Like most of the pronouncements in the "Introductory Epistle," Scott's point seems on the surface coolly practical and free from the "cant" he hopes to dispel, but the urgency of his desire to allow only the most impersonal authorship remains evident in the awkwardness of his metaphor: if the author is merely delivering the letters, who wrote them?

Underlying this ambiguous metaphor there is a certain authorial passivity which may recall other metaphors of authorship as diverse as Coleridge's Eolian harp and the platinum filament catalyst of T. S. Eliot's "Tradition and the Individual Talent." Still, Scott's metaphor needs to be considered in its own terms: the Author of *Waverley* is not passive in relation to cosmic winds of transcendent truth or in relation to the chemical combination of ideas in the creative process, but passive in relation to the circulation of texts among readers. It is not a passivity that authorizes writing by imagining that the writer is a representative of some greater force, but which defers authority to readers who may decide, according to their judgment of a text, whether to treasure or destroy what authors bring them. For this reason the question of who wrote the letters may be bracketed in favor of the more important question of whether or not the reader finds that the letters convey pleasing intelligence. In keeping with this emphasis on readerly authority, the author does not appear as an Eolian harp or platinum filament, but as a civil servant.

The "expense of postage" in Scott's metaphor gestures toward the novelist's engagement with the literary marketplace and his concern throughout the "Introductory Epistle" with describing this relationship. Later the tax on postage is refigured as the "voluntary tax" readers pay for their books: Scott's "emolument is the voluntary tax which the public pays for a certain species of literary amusement; it is extorted from no one, and paid, I presume, by those only who can afford it, and who receive gratification in proportion to the expense" (53). The writer thus appears as though an agent of the state in the service of some general public desire, a desire that is not created or "extorted" by anyone. As for the money he receives in the process, "it is won by my toil, and I account myself answerable to Heaven only for the mode in which I expend it" (53). As far as we know, none of Scott's critics had actually chided him for the way he spent his money; this odd defensiveness suggests some anxiety about the extent of his sales, and it shows again that in response to such anxiety he implies that though his texts are subject to public scrutiny, he himself is not. It is enough to know that the public gets what it pays for.

The Author also describes his relationship to the market more abstractly, not in terms of civil service or taxation, but according to the esteemed principles of Scottish enlightenment economics that might be expected to exclude his contribution:

> I do say it, in spite of Adam Smith and his followers, that a successful author is a productive labourer, and that his works constitute as effectual a part of the public wealth, as that which is created by any other manufacture. If a new commodity, having an actually intrinsic and commercial value, be the result of the operation, why are the author's bales of books to be esteemed a less profitable part of the public stock than goods of any other manufacturer? I speak with reference to the diffusion of the wealth arising to the public, and the degree of industry which even such a trifling work as the present must stimulate and reward, before the volumes leave the publisher's shop. Without me it could not exist, and to this extent I am a benefactor to the country. (53)

Answering Adam Smith's distinction between the unproductive work of men of letters and the more directly beneficial products of other branches of manufacture, Scott contends that books should be considered functionally equivalent to other commodities, and that writers are therefore entitled to the same respect that Smith's doctrines accord other producers of public wealth. In effect, Scott claims that as a novelist he advances the public good merely by generating commodities, a consideration that comes even before the public good reflected by the use-value of his circulating productions. Kathryn Sutherland has noted that Scott is actually claiming two different roles in the production process here, both master-manufacturer and workman.[11] To these two models of labor we might add, as we have seen, civil servant and collector of voluntary taxes, and—before he finishes—lawyer, soldier, physician, and clergyman, these last four serving as examples of men of dignified professions who nonetheless accept the money to which their work entitles them (54). None of these examples disguise the Author of *Waverley*'s commercial interest in his productions, though cumulatively they leave no clear idea of exactly where the novelist stands in the relations of production.

In other passages Scott approaches a more Romantic definition of his work. He claims, for example, that when he tries to write according to a strict plan, his "imagination" suffers, and his thoughts become "prosy, flat, and dull": "I am no more the same author I was in my better mood than the dog in a wheel, condemned to go round and round for hours, is like the same dog merrily chasing his own tail, and gamboling in all the frolic of unrestrained freedom" (49). The use of such terms as freedom and imagination in the composition process, along with the suggestion of spontaneity in creation, are reminiscent of Romantic descriptions of the genius at work. Likewise, we hear Wordsworthian echoes in Scott's declaration that even if he were not well remunerated for his work, he would "probably continue it merely for the pleasure of playing; for I have felt as strongly as most folks that love of composition which is perhaps the strongest of all instincts, driving the author to the pen, the painter to the pallet, often without either the chance of fame or the prospect of reward" (54-55). Here composition seems less like the "toil" he earlier described, and more like, as the Romantics tend to put it, a natural and spontaneous expression of self.

The difference between the Author of *Waverley*'s position and the Romantics', of course, is that he combines aspects of their way of thinking with other priorities—especially the market—that they despise. He can claim a semi-Romantic understanding of composition and still write that, nevertheless, he is not "hypocrite enough to disclaim the ordinary motives, on account of which the whole world around me is toiling unremittingly." Indeed, for all of the many incompatible metaphors he suggests here—postman, laborer, lawyer, even gamboling dog—he never really sacrifices the idea that he is, ultimately, writing in a commercial market and for a public of readers who will judge his work rather than directly judging his "sensibility." The approbation of this authoritative public, represented by continuing popularity of his books, is all he ultimately needs to justify his participation in the mushrooming literary market: "When they dance no longer, I will no longer pipe" (55).

THE USES OF *WAVERLEY*

Waverley; or, 'Tis Sixty Years Since was warmly greeted by its original critics, but not, pointedly, because its author laid bare his soul or exhibited oracular insight. Although Francis Jeffrey, reviewing the novel for the *Edinburgh Review*, does not doubt "the author is a person of genius," he writes that "the secret of this success" is not only the power of the author's mind, but also the restraint that the writer shows in "content[ing] himself, even in the most marvelous parts of his story, with copying from actual existences, rather than from the phantasms of his own imagination" (208). Jeffrey praises this novel precisely because it is not wholly a product of the writer's fancy, because it is as much "copying" as creation; later Jeffrey further qualifies his interest in the author's genius by specifically objecting to the "passages in which the author speaks in his own person" (242). Like Jeffrey, the first critics of *Waverley* were less interested in the author's sensibility than in the novel's usefulness. John Croker's assessment of the novel in the *Quarterly Review* opens with a brief history of the genre of the novel, which he concludes by claiming that "so far as utility constitutes the merit in a novel," recent books like *Waverley* clearly indicate an advance on the work of earlier novelists (355). Utility is the primary concern of *Waverley*'s reviewers, just as it is for Scott. In defending his novels' failure to meet high standards of composition, he contends that his clumsy execution should be excused by the merit of having written "a few scenes which had sufficient interest in them to amuse in one corner the pain of body; in another to relieve anxiety of mind; in a third place, to unwrinkle a brow bent with the furrows of daily toil; in another, to fill the place of bad thoughts, or to suggest better; in yet another, to induce an idler to study the history of his country; in all, save where the perusal interrupted the discharge of serious duties, to furnish harmless amusement" ("Introductory Epistle" 45). What ultimately matters, to Scott and to his reviewers, is whether his novels fulfill an instrumental function; in the terms of Scott's postman analogy, the bearer of the letters is less important than the extent to which the letters have some "pleasing intelligence" to convey.

This is not to say that all readers would necessarily find novels useful for the same reasons. Even within the category of utility, various interpretations of usefulness competed for attention. As we have just seen, the Author of *Waverley* lists several functions his texts might perform, most of which relate to the relief of toil, pain, or "bad thoughts," and which are then subsumed under the primary objective of granting the reader some "harmless amusement." One function, that of inducing "an idler to study the history of his country," stands out in his list as having more to do with edification than amusement, and it therefore seems somewhat out of place. But this is exactly the potential use for which *Waverley* was most praised by its critics. For them, the distinguishing aspect of this novel was its historical content; it was not merely entertaining but also factual and accurate. Jeffrey applauds the novel's "fidelity and felicity" and its "perfect accuracy" (210). Croker finds that the "interest and merit of the work is derived, not from any of the ordinary qualities of a novel, but from the truth of its facts, and the accuracy of its delineations" (377). The *British Critic* goes even further, writing that "We are unwilling to consider this publication in the light of a common novel [. . .] but as a vehicle of curious accurate information upon a subject which must at all times demand our attention—the history and manners of a very, very large and renowned portion of the inhabitants of these islands." This reviewer also points directly to the pragmatically political value of that information: "If the history of those bloody days, which is embodied in this tale, shall by an early and awful warning inspire the nation with a jealous vigilance against the very first symptoms of their recurrence, we shall consider that not even the light pages of fiction have trifled in vain" (qtd. in Hayden 68-69). Scott may have thought that amusement was the chief benefit to be derived from fiction, but as Ina Ferris has summarized, the critics saw *Waverley* as "speaking to the serious political concerns of the age, a point underscored both explicitly through direct commentary and implicitly through the way in which it merges with respected genres of nonfiction" (84-85).

The same accurate historical content that the critics found so appealing in *Waverley* also contributed to the book's great sales. The combination of genres attracted readers who might not otherwise have trifled with novels. Readers of fiction were typically assumed to be young women or indolent men with nothing better to do with their time, but the respectability of Scott's historical fictions would interest a wider and more diverse circle of readers. Thomas Love Peacock writes that in their mutual interest in the *Waverley* novels, "the scholar lays aside his Plato, the statesman suspends his calculations, the young lady deserts her hoop" (qtd. in Hillhouse 120). A contemporary American critic makes much the same point, claiming that the "astonishing popularity" of the *Waverley* novels is manifest in the way that they have "worked their way in a few years from the lady's work table and the lounger's parlor window to a temporary fellowship at least with the dusty corpuses of the civilian and the ponderous polyglots of the divine" (qtd. in Hillhouse 9). *Waverley* itself anticipates the function of history as a discourse appealing to diverse readers in an early encounter between two of its characters, Edward Waverley, reader of poetry and romance, and the classically-educated Baron of Bradwardine, who prefers "simple prose":

> he sometimes could not refrain from expressing contempt of the "vain and unprofitable art of poem-making," in which he said, "the only one who had excelled in his time was Allan Ramsay the periwig maker."
>
> But although Edward and he differed *toto coelo*, as the Baron would have said, upon this subject, yet they met upon history as on a neutral ground, in which each claimed an interest. The Baron, indeed, only cumbered his memory with matters of fact; the cold, dry, hard outlines which history delineates. Edward, on the contrary, loved to fill up and round the sketch with the colouring of a warm and vivid imagination, which gives life to the actors and speakers in the drama of past ages. Yet with tastes so opposite, they contributed greatly to each other's amusement. (57)

The "neutral ground" that Waverley and the Baron find in history is suggestively analogous to the neutral ground that critics and readers found in Scott's historical romance. Indeed, this passage's productive combination of tastes—of cold, dry facts and imaginative, dramatic coloring, along with the distinctive (though mutually supplementary) kinds of amusement they bring—reads like a recipe for the entire novel. But as the tastes of Waverley and the Baron are "opposite," there remains within this synthesis the strong possibility of conflict. *Waverley*'s critics, though sensitive to the useful combination of historical fact and vivacity of romance, nevertheless tended to prefer the factual historicity of the stories to their imaginative components.[12] Scott, on the other hand, usually privileged the amusing powers of romance over the instructional value of historical fact. The question of whether Scott uses history in the service of romance or romance in the service of history has been central in the evaluations and reevaluations of his work for two centuries, ultimately proving little except that his use of history operates less as "neutral ground" of consensus than as a no-man's land of considerable contention.

In the last forty years, no single aspect of Scott's work has drawn as much critical attention as its juxtaposition of romance and history, and this criticism has largely been divided between two camps: the first, whose most prominent representative is Georg Lukacs, downplays the elements of romance in the novels to discuss, for example, how Scott's historical imagination contributed to the development of realism, or to contemporary debates about historiography (see *The Historical Novel* 19-63); the second camp, notably championed by Alexander Welsh, emphasizes the romantic and imaginative features of the novels, usually in order to analyze Scott's imaginary resolutions to his contemporary problems (*The Hero of Waverley* 1-20). More recently, critics such as James Kerr have attempted—more productively—to study the complex (or even dialectical) interaction of these terms. Kerr tells us, for example, that "If history subverts romance, then romance, in turn, alters history, not merely softening and blurring its harsh outlines, changing its colors slightly, but actually reinventing the past, making a new story out of history" (17). It is not my purpose here to offer any resolution to this ongoing debate, but merely to suggest that if we want to understand the original historical relevance of this tension, we should examine it in the terms that Scott and his critics first framed it, that is, as a question of textual utility. It is in this framework that we achieve the clearest image of the Author of *Waverley* as a novelist: not an already authoritative creator or the founder of a branch of historical inquiry, but as a deferential writer trying, with contradictory results, to entertain and instruct an audience. When Kerr claims, for instance, that the "motives of Scott's revisions [of romance and history] can only be understood against the story of his life," and that the "modal tensions of the Waverley novels can be traced to Scott's conflicted sense of his own historical position" (9), he proposes an author-centered explanation that presumes an authoritative author behind the text rather than, as Scott's contemporaries thought, a text whose authority needs to be measured by its social or political value. I want to demonstrate that much of the tension between history and romance in *Waverley* is directly related to questions of utility, and that the uneasy combination of varieties of utility finally leads to ambiguous versions of authorship in the novel.

The story of Edward Waverley begins by establishing his character with reference to his education and the formation of his character, which is in turn shown to be the product of the kind of books he reads. Young Waverley had been left to choose any books from the "large Gothic room" that served as the family library (13), and, predictably, he selects books that have much in common with Gothic novels (even though the story is set before the vogue for Gothic fiction): from English literature he prefers "poets who have exercised themselves on romantic fiction," and he reads Italian *novelle*, French military romances, and Spanish "chivalrous and romantic lore" (14). In short, choosing books by the sole criterion of "amusement," Edward seeks out romances, fictions set in the past but without any educational or historical value. His reading, therefore, has "evil consequences, which long continued to influence his character, happiness, and utility" (13). The specific consequences that the novel traces are his "wavering and unsettled habit of mind" (31), and more importantly, his tendency to invest reality with meaning derived from his own Romantic imagination. This last consequence is evident early in the novel, as Waverley imagines scenes from his family's history and, "like a child amongst his toys, culled and arranged, from the splendid but useless imagery, visions as brilliant and fading as those of an evening sky" (18). The fault, according to the narrator, lies with his guardians, Sir Everard and Miss Rachel, who both "held the vulgar doctrine that idleness is incompatible with reading of any kind, and that the mere tracing of the alphabetical characters with the eye, is in itself a useful and meritorious task, without scrupulously considering what ideas or doctrines they may happen to convey" (13). From the start, then, *Waverley* is directly concerned with the practical effects of forms of reading. Waverley's preferences, chosen for amusement, are not only themselves useless, but also affect his own "utility," which in turn causes him to produce his own "splendid but useless" interpretations of history and the world around him.

The narrator has cautioned the reader not to expect his own historical romance to be of the same sort that Waverley so perniciously devours. He points out in the first chapter that he has not called the book "'Waverley, a Tale of other Days,'" in which case "every novel-reader [would] have assumed a castle scarce less than that of Udolpho" (3). *Waverley* is, of course, a tale of other days, but of a different kind; it will include something besides the merely amusing historical romance associated with the Gothic. The readers are also warned not to expect, as one might given the introductory chapters on Waverley's education, that this novel will imitate Cervantes: "My intention is not to follow the steps of that inimitable author, in describing such total perversion of intellect as misconstrues the objects actually presented to the senses, but that more common aberration from sound judgment, which apprehends occurrences indeed in their reality, but communicates to them a tincture of its own romantic tone and colouring" (18). If the protagonist in this alternate tale of other days "apprehends occurrences indeed in their reality," there is sufficient difference to distinguish this novel from both Cervantes and from other historical romances: this one will include reality, that is, real history. But real, instructive history, as Waverley's reading habits have shown, fails to amuse. Since Scott wants to amuse and to relate history at the same time, Waverley becomes the ideal protagonist: through his eyes the readers will see historical fact adorned with "romantic tone and colouring," thus enjoying the pleasure of amusement without the uselessness of *mere* amusement. Waverley's adventures generally fulfill this formula. His journey to Scotland invokes the great theme of romance, the voyage into the unknown, while all along the narrator offers comments that deflate Waverley's Romantic perceptions and provide historical background and explication about the people and places Waverley encounters. These two perspectives constitute a double journey into romance and history, the imaginary and the real.

An early address to readers represents the novel's narrative structure in a similar way. The narrator "beg[s] pardon, once and for all, of those readers who take up novels merely for amusement, for plaguing them so long with old-fashioned politics," but excuses the dullness of this historical exposition by asserting that "I cannot promise them that this story shall be intelligible, not to say probable, without it. My plan requires that I should explain the motives on which it proceeded; and these motives necessarily arose from the feelings, prejudices, and parties, of the times" (24). Here again, though more explicitly, is the claim that the value of the novel does not reside entirely in "amusement" and the implication that what keeps it from being so is the presence of history. Without this historical background, in fact, this particular story would be unintelligible. The narrator goes on to describe the nature of the journey the readers have embarked on in this narrative, a movement which parallels Waverley's own:

> I do not invite my fair readers, whose sex and impatience give them the greatest right to complain of these circumstances, into a flying chariot drawn by hippogriffs, or moved by enchantment. Mine is a humble English post-chaise, drawn upon four wheels, and keeping his majesty's highway. Those who dislike the vehicle may leave it at the next halt, and wait for the conveyance of Prince Hussein's tapestry, or Malek the Weaver's flying sentry-box. Those who are contented to remain with me will be occasionally exposed to the dullness inseparable from heavy roads, steep hills, sloughs, and other terrestrial retardations; but, with tolerable horses, and a civil driver, (as the advertisements have it) I also engage to get as soon as possible into a more picturesque and romantic country, if my passengers incline to have some patience with me during my first stages. (24)

Dismissing the fantastic forms of transportation associated with romance, the narrator describes the movement of the plot in the realistic terms of everyday travel. At the same time that the narrator apologizes to readers who expect romance, however, he promises they will reach "romantic country" after all, if only they bear with him. In this curious gesture, the narrator attempts to have it both ways. History is both the condition of intelligibility for this story and that which disrupts (as a terrestrial retardation) the story's progress. Romance, on the other hand, is both what the novel refuses and what it strives to be. Only the "first stages" of the narrative movement, it would seem, will be characterized by the realistic tedium of political history; the real trajectory of the plot, we are assured, is towards amusement and romance.

But here the journey of *Waverley*'s readers diverges from the journey of the protagonist. Waverley begins from a position of reading for amusement and of pure romance, but he is no Don Quixote: Waverley will come to learn what his early reading left him ignorant of, that which "adds dignity to a man, and qualifies him to support and adorn an elevated situation in society" (14). Waverley's socialization follows the template of a typical *Bildungsroman*, a kind of socialization which, as Franco Moretti points out, depends on stabilizing the protagonist's Ego in accordance with the Freudian reality principle (11). Waverley's internalization of the real is depicted as the result of a struggle with history; that is, not only the real history of political actions and their palpable consequences (with which he must learn to replace the solipsistic false history of his romantic reading), but also the real history of the Jacobite uprising of 1745. It is as a result of his involvement in the '45 that he learns that his Romantic inclinations have dire effects for his family, just as, on a larger scale, the whole Romantic enterprise of capturing the throne for the dashing Pretender has threatened the social order. Edward's progress, unlike that of the narrative post-chaise (which wants to be a flying sentry-box despite itself), proceeds from initial stages of romance to an engagement with history.

The two conflicting trajectories clash in a remarkable moment which is at once a turning point in the novel's plot and a culminating moment in Waverley's *Bildung*. During the skirmish at Clifton, in which Fergus and his company of highlanders are defeated, Waverley alone escapes, and he manages to convince a local farmer to conceal him. During his protracted stay at the farm, it becomes clear that the Stuart cause has become desperate, and Waverley begins "devoutly" to hope "that it might never again be his lot to draw his sword in civil conflict." Having thus reconsidered his participation in the rebellion, he begins to dwell on the consequences of the '45:

> his mind turned to the supposed death of Fergus, to the desolate situation of Flora, and, with yet more tender recollection, to that of Rose Bradwardine, who was destitute of the devoted enthusiasm of loyalty, which, to her friend [Flora], hallowed and exalted misfortune. These reveries he was permitted to enjoy, undisturbed by queries or interruption; and it was in many a winter walk by the shores of Ulswater, that he acquired a more complete mastery of a spirit tamed by adversity, than his former experience had given him; and that he felt himself entitled to say firmly, though perhaps with a sigh, that the romance of his life was ended, and that its real history had now commenced. He was soon called upon to justify his pretensions to reason and philosophy. (283)

According to the framework of Edward's development, this passage represents the definitive shift in his life towards socially condoned maturity. He has seen the consequences of his misguided Romantic ventures, his spirit has been tamed, and he no longer desires to contribute to any civil strife. Fully socialized and rendered a docile subject of the state, Waverley decides to return to London, thus spatially doubling back on the Romantic journey that led him into misfortune. In keeping with the symbolic logic of the novel, the culmination of his education is fittingly described as a movement from "romance" into "real history." At the same time, however, this passage marks the *end* of real history in the novel and in its protagonist's life. The actual historical events of the '45 will now recede into the background, from which they will surface only occasionally through second-hand reports. Moreover, the skirmish at Clifton and the various "strange concealments [. . .] and hair's-breadth 'scapes" are the last incidents in the story that the narrator will claim to be based on fact (341, 340). The plot is now free to roll—or fly—on, unimpeded by reference to history: it has moved into purely fictional history, which is to say, romance.[13]

The narrative structure's remarkable chiasmus reveals the extent to which the two kinds of utility Scott discusses—history as amusement ("romance") and history as education ("real history")—do not coexist as productively as the happy encounter of Waverley and the Baron Bradwardine on neutral ground suggests. They seem almost to cancel each other out, and in fact, the narrator suggests such a cancellation in an early passage where he questions the ultimate value of teaching through amusement, even going so far as to repeat in miniature the same gesture of chiastic negation:

> There wants but one step further, and the Creed and the Ten Commandments may be taught in the same manner, without the necessity of the grave face, deliberate tone of recital, and devout attention hitherto exacted from the well-governed childhood of this realm. It may in the mean time be subject of serious consideration, whether those who are accustomed only to acquire instruction through the medium of amusement, may not be brought to reject that which approaches under the aspect of study; whether those who learn history by the cards, may not be led to prefer the means to the end; and whether, were we to teach religion in the way of sport, our pupils might not thereby be gradually induced to make sport of their religion. (12-13)

Waverley, I have tried to suggest, is a text deeply concerned with the utility of reading, both as it is thematized in relation to the education of its protagonist, and, more directly, in its eagerness to offer its own readers something they want. It is at the same time profoundly ambivalent about the effectiveness with which kinds of utility can be combined. The yoking together of history and romance, or instruction and amusement figured as types of historical romance with different emphases, gestures towards an accommodation of diverse readerly tastes (as the "neutral ground" analogy implies), and *Waverley*'s critics suggest the novel's success in this regard. But the same integration of discourses that ensured the novel's unprecedented sales left it scarred with ambiguity and contradiction.

These are nowhere more evident than in the novel's frame, the two chapters that are expressly and exclusively concerned with authorship. In the first chapter, "Introductory," the "author" (as the first person narrator identifies himself), playfully lists the other subtitles he might have chosen for the story, each time implying a different variety of novel (e.g., the Gothic, the novel of sentiment, the novel of fashion) before dismissing it. The effect, as in choosing the "uncontaminated name" Waverley, is to establish the originality of his own text by emphasizing its difference from its predecessors. The author proceeds to relate that the "object of my tale is more a description of men than manners" (4), which is to say that what he attempts to describe is the fundamentally human, "those passions common to men in all stages of society, and which have agitated the human heart, whether it throbbed under the steel corslet of the fifteenth century, the brocaded coat of the eighteenth, or the blue frock and dimity waistcoat of the present day" (5). History here takes a subordinate role to the transhistorically human, so that the distance between particular eras makes little more difference than changes of costume. As he reiterates, "It is from the great book of Nature, the same through a thousand editions, whether of black letter or wire-wove and hot-pressed, that I have venturously essayed to read a chapter to the public" (5). These statements to some extent approximate Wordsworthian themes (originality, the transcendence of Nature, the importance of the permanent over the temporal), though the author will also differ from Wordsworth in subordinating all of this to an immediate didactic purpose: he claims that the illustration of "moral lessons" is "the most important part of my plan, although I am sensible how short these will fall of their aim, if I shall be found unable to mix them with amusement" (5).

Yet the last chapter, "A Postscript, which should have been a Preface," reverses the expectations of the first. Now the author is less playful, and writes in the somber and grandiose language of contemporary historiography: "There is no European nation which, within the course of half a century, or little more, has undergone so complete a change as this kingdom of Scotland [. . .]. This race [of Jacobites] has now almost entirely vanished from the land, and with it [. . .] many living examples of singular and disinterested attachment to the principles of loyalty which they received from their fathers, and of old Scottish faith, hospitality, worth, and honour" (340). Instead of originality, the author now stresses his debt to the historians, eyewitnesses, and other writers who inspired his project or confirmed its historical accuracy. Indeed, factual accuracy becomes important enough that he claims "the most romantic parts of this narrative are precisely those which have a foundation in fact" (340). But the most significant reversal is the inversion of the opening chapter's men-over-manners formulation. The author here describes his "purpose" as the preservation of "some idea of the ancient manners of which I have witnessed the almost total extinction" (340). Thus, while the first chapter dismisses "manners" because they are ephemeral, in the last chapter they become the *raison d'être* of the novel, but still because they are ephemeral. The degree of contradiction between these two presentations of authorship is startling—original and imaginative on the one hand, scholarly and collaborative on the other—though it takes little effort to imagine how the disparate authorial images are functions of the split between the different kinds of utility on which they base claims for *Waverley*'s value. Still more striking, ultimately, is the gesture by which Scott tries to combine the two descriptions, in a sense, by making *both* of them the preface. Jon Klancher has written of the early nineteenth-century periodical market that attempts to reach an increasingly diverse readership resulted in a newly polyphonic prose style and greater breadth of cultural reference: "When 'crowd' becomes 'audience,' it must be quieted, the dialogic murmur of its innumerable voices displaced by proxy of the mass writer himself" (80). Though in Scott's case there is little sense of an attempt to "quiet" the audience in any authoritative manner, Klancher's point suggests how the ambivalence of Scott's construction of authorship was inflected by his interpretation of the audience for which he wrote.

Many readers have examined *Waverley*'s first chapter and have seen Scott claiming authority as a novelist by mocking his predecessors. Others have looked at the last chapter and seen Scott asserting his authority by demonstrating his scholarly mastery of the period's history. Both of these positions are supported by textual evidence, but both overlook a more interesting and important issue. The crucial question of utility, which so confuses Scott's presentation of authorship, extends well beyond the narrative frame to become one of the central problems of the entire novel. And this schizophrenic concern about utility says less about the authority of the writer than it does about the authority of the audience that the writer is trying so deferentially to serve. For decades after the publication of *Waverley*, Scott's reputation rose and fell according to the general sense of whether or not he had accomplished anything useful with his novels. His first readers thought he had, even if they did not entirely agree upon the usefulness he had achieved. But with the onset of the Victorian period, Scott's criterion of utility was absorbed into the broader ideology of Utilitarianism, which later novelists would define their work against. Though Scott was still generally admired, Victorian writers turned away from his impersonal construction of authorship to embrace an ideology that depended more than ever before on the palpable and legible presence of a writer behind the text. Scott's novels—indeed his very soul—would ultimately be scrutinized from a perspective that, as a novelist, he could never have anticipated, a perspective suggested by the work of his relatively obscure contemporary, William Wordsworth.

CHAPTER TWO

Making Friends:
Dickens, *Pickwick*, and Industrial Romanticism

Charles Dickens recalled the genesis of his first novel, *The Posthumous Papers of the Pickwick Club* (1836-1837), as a writer's triumph over the opinions of his meddlesome illustrator and publishers. Approached with a request to supply copy for a series of comic illustrations, Dickens successfully pressed his own vision for the project, and set to work only after his authority was recognized: "My views being deferred to, I thought of Mr. Pickwick, and wrote the first number" (44). Despite its appealing simplicity—here is the future literary lion, unfettered and inspired—this account so wildly reinvents the novel's collaborative origins that it belies even Dickens's own earlier accounts: the novel's original preface has him, contradictorily, "deferring to the judgement of others" (41). Dickens's disingenuousness on this point may be understandable given the centrality of this story in the origin myth of his own career. Still, his depiction of a single instant of authoritative artistic creation offers little help in tracing the production of this notoriously fragmentary book. After all, the Samuel Pickwick whom Dickens conceived for the serial's first number resembles the character whose adventures conclude in the twentieth installment only in his most superficial outlines. The Victorians' beloved sentimental hero, whose "countenance lighted up with smiles, which the heart of no man, woman, or child, could resist" (895), first appears as a figure of ridicule who inspires suspicion and even violence, and whose two most visible symbols, unfashionably superannuated gaiters and unreliable spectacles, suggest an insulating alienation rather than contagious warmth. Pickwick's puzzling metamorphosis is complicated by the parallel change in the narrator's tone, which fitfully abandons its initial irony and sarcasm in favor of an earnest moralism and humanistic optimism. But the novel's most consequential transformation lies in its representation of literary labor: at the outset of its serial publication, *The Pickwick Papers* announced itself as having been "edited by Boz," and only with the text's final installment was it instead described as authored by someone named "Charles Dickens." The great value of *Pickwick* lies in the sensitive record it provides of the contest through which this familiar "Dickens" was produced. Like Pickwick, Dickens would arrive not in a flash of inspiration, but out of a protracted struggle to seize the new opportunities of early Victorian print culture.

Dickens admits that Samuel Pickwick "becomes more good" (45) over the course of the novel, but fails to note the extent to which this is also true of his narrator, or indeed, of the way he represents himself. The movement from anonymous editor to personalized author indicates Dickens's increasing concern with intimacy and sympathy, the qualities that would become hallmarks of early Victorian novelists. As in *Pickwick*'s case, sympathetic friendship became a typical way for these writers to describe their relationship with their characters, but it also came to serve as the dominant metaphor of the relationship between novelists and their readers. "No one thinks first of Mr. Dickens as a writer," explained a critic in the North American Review. "He is at once, through his books, a friend" ("Charles Dickens" 671). Dickens himself represented an extreme case of this relationship—the reading public's *best* friend—but he was more unique in degree than in kind. In *Pendennis* (1850), Thackeray similarly described novel writing as "a sort of confidential talk between writer and reader" (33), and a decade later Wilkie Collins wrote of his pleasure that characters of *The Woman in White* (1860) "have made friends for me wherever they have made themselves known" (32). In slightly varying ways, this perceived personal intimacy characterized the work of most acclaimed novelists of the first decades of the Victorian period: a defensible list might also include Charlotte Brontë, Kingsley, Gaskell, and later Trollope and Eliot. It would be under the aegis of this particular form of friendship—private, confidential, domestic—that novels would continue their climb to respectability and prestige. Novels could literally be welcomed, as their authors figuratively were, into every household. But the price of their entrance into the friendly, domestic sphere was a staged denial of the public world of the market, or more specifically, of the increasingly industrial relations of production and circulation that actually dictated the relationships of textual circulation.[1] Such an ideology de-emphasized the real work of writing, and in presupposing an immediate, personal, and non-alienated connection between writer and readers, it even denied the materiality of textual communication, imagining books not as the marketable products of writers' labor, but as mystical portals of sympathetic bonhomie; thus "no one thinks first of Mr. Dickens as a writer. He is at once, through his books, a friend."

The seemingly innocuous metaphor of friendship masks the emergence of a momentous reconceptualization of authorship and—through authorship—of the cultural and political stakes of Victorian literary production; as Foucault has observed, the characteristics we attribute to writers are "projections, in terms always more or less psychological, of our way of handling texts" (127). Indeed, this personalizing metaphor for novelists offers insight not only into changing relationships in Victorian print culture, but also into the gradual rise of authorship itself as a central criterion of the novel's literary value. The sympathetic friendliness attributed to novelists was not perceived as an end in itself, but as the fountainhead of a great current of social sympathy, which would in turn work to promote public stability and naturalize class divisions. The emerging focus on novelists as personalized, affective subjects is unmistakably a shift towards the author-centered aesthetics elaborated by the Romantic poets, though the novelists were thought to wield a degree of immediate and pragmatic social influence with which the Romantics, in even the most charitable view, could not be credited. The ideology symbolized by friendship, which fused together in the person of the author the instrumentalist benefits of wide circulation with Romantic artistic priorities, might properly be called *Industrial Romanticism*, or Romanticism retooled for the mass consumption.

Dickens's investment in an intimate, personalized paradigm of the work of writing may be traced back in his career as far as *The Pickwick Papers*. Published with the final installment of the text, Dickens's original preface provides some sense of what authorship had come to mean over the course of the novel:

> The almost unexampled kindness and favour with which these papers have been received by the public will be a never-failing source of gratifying and pleasant recollection while their author lives [. . .]. If any of his imperfect descriptions, while they afford amusement in the perusal, should induce only one reader to think better of his fellow men, and to look upon the brighter and more kindly side of human nature, he would indeed be proud and happy to have led to such a result. (42)

This is a familiar Dickensian account of the circulation of kindness from the author through the novel to the public and ultimately back to the author, the friendly figure who presides over this limitlessly proliferating economy of symbolic exchange. As early as 1838, the *Edinburgh Review* noted that the tendency of Dickens's work was to make his readers "practically benevolent—to excite our sympathy in behalf of the aggrieved and suffering in all classes" ("Dickens's Tales" 42), and throughout his career, Dickens never tired of persuading his readers to regard his work in exactly this way, or of emphasizing the role of his own sentiment as the basis for its effect. The 1848 Preface to *Dombey and Son*, for example, slightly refines this dynamic while leaving its fundamental premise essentially intact: "If any of [my readers] have felt a sorrow in one of the principal incidents on which this fiction turns, I hope it may be a sorrow of that sort that which endears the sharers in it, one to another. This is not unselfish in me. I may claim to have felt it, at least as much as anybody else; and I would fain be remembered for my part in the experience" (41). This revolutionary formulation of friendship was compellingly suited to alleviate anxieties about the burgeoning literary marketplace. A wide readership, especially one which extended into the working classes, could prove that the novel was performing its imagined effect of alleviating alienation, self-interest, and class antagonism. The developing friendship between Samuel Pickwick and his servant Sam Weller—founded on a mutual regard that transcends any merely economic relationship—is thus merely one thematic corollary of the novel's lofty cultural ambitions.

Kathleen Tillotson's work has established the standard genealogy of the novel's conquest of the incipient mass market: "It was Scott more than any other novelist who had been responsible, and through the breach rushed Dickens" (15-16). We should not assume, however, that Dickens's rush through the breach implies an imitation of his predecessor, or that what he found on the other side of the barrier was the same public that had greeted the Author of *Waverley*. When Dickens announced in 1842 that he would "rather have the affectionate regard of my fellow men than I would have heaps and mine of gold" (qtd. in Welsh, *Copyright* 31), he spoke in terms that typified the emerging image of Industrial-Romantic novelists, terms that Scott, twenty years earlier, would have found outlandish. Not only had the Author of *Waverley* freely joked about his economic interests, but he also persistently insulated himself from any sort of personal relationship with his readers, claiming that

> The utmost extent of the kindness between the author and the public which can really exist, is, that the world are disposed to be somewhat in-dulgent of the habit which the public mind has acquired; while the author very naturally thinks well of *their* taste, who have so liberally applauded *his* productions. But I deny that there is any call for gratitude, properly so called, on one side or the other. ("Introductory Epistle" 48)

The ideological gulf that stretches between Dickens's priority of "affection-ate regard" and the dry, transactional logic of Scott's sharply limited "ut-most extent of kindness" represents a woefully neglected chapter in the history of authorship, a rupture every bit as revolutionary as Samuel John-son's repudiation of patronage or Wordsworth's preface to *Lyrical Ballads*. The presentation of the work of writing that Dickens ultimately espoused was not founded on Scott's, even though at the time he started writing there was no more illustrious novelist than the Author of *Waverley*, nor any contemporary writer more unanimously judged—by any criterion—to be successful. Instead, Dickens and his novelist cohorts, the darlings of Vic-torian readers, embraced a creed previously associated only with a clique of marginally popular poets and abstruse German philosophers. Just at the moment when their books began to dominate the shelves of booksellers, these novelists developed a personalized conception of their work that owes far less to Scott than to Wordsworth—even though Wordsworth had singled out novelists as a particular nemesis to his artistic ambitions, and in spite of his suspicion that popularity was the irrefutable hallmark of aesthetic inferiority. That the early Victorian novelists should turn from Scott and bring the rhetoric of Romanticism into the mainstream of the swelling literary marketplace is one greatest ironies in the history of authorship.

Friendship and sympathy had been keywords for the Romantic poets long before they began to appeal to novelists.[2] Coleridge, to cite an obvious example, chose to name one of his short-lived periodicals *The Friend*, while Wordsworth argued tirelessly and vehemently for the model of personalized and non-alienated authorship epitomized by his famous definition of the poet as "a man speaking to men." But as novels continued to climb to prominence in the years before Victoria's accession, the practices of literary production and circulation in which the Romantics had worked altered substantially. The widening circle of readers that had so alarmed Wordsworth continued to grow, and the acceleration with which it expanded was without precedent. The number of Coleridge's "friends" might have been reckoned by the hundreds, Dickens's by the tens of thousands,[3] and as the audience changed, so too did the implications of friendliness with one's readers. While the Romantic poets had imagined authorial intimacy as an ideal with which to condemn the industrialization of the literary market and the vulgarity of popularity, Victorian novelists found in the same metaphor a way to justify popularity and make a virtue of mass consumption. What Dickens rightly called the "almost unexampled" success of his novel with the reading public is a token of how dramatically that public—and its influence—was growing. As an emerging metaphor for authorship under these new conditions, friendship represents one response—and a particularly influential one—to the rapid changes of the literary industry. Composed during a period when authorship was under particular scrutiny, *Pickwick* clarifies the political and cultural stakes of the quintessentially Victorian ideal of authorial friendliness, and reveals the particular anxieties in which it would become further entangled.

EDITING AUTHORSHIP

The abrupt reversal that led authorship of novels to be valorized in increasingly Romantic terms could not have occurred—or at any rate could not have been sustained—without significant transformations in the environment of Victorian print culture; in other words, it took substantial changes in the production and circulation of novels for this ideology to thrive as it never had before, for this strikingly new way of perceiving novelists to seem plausible, desirable, and—ultimately—self-evidently true. And the most marked changes in early-Victorian practices of reading, writing, and publishing all centered on the vast and sudden expansion of the market for print. The politically tumultuous days of the Reform movement in the early 'thirties had encouraged the British to read with an increasingly urgent desire for news and opinion that reached even beyond the growing middle classes to attract new readers from among politically engaged workers. At the same time, technical innovations in printing (including the steam press, stereotyping, and cheaper, mechanically produced paper) combined with the proliferation of circulating libraries and the new possibility of national distribution by rail to enable the wide distribution of affordable books. Taken together, such developments fostered an embryonic mass market for print that not only radically increased the pool of potential consumers but also ushered in new groups of readers with different priorities and distinct tastes. Towards the end of the decade, the entire climate of print culture was changing, and the instability of the transition opened up the door for profound reevaluations of the value of reading and of the author's place within those systems of valuation. In *Pickwick*'s fitful movement towards the image of the friendly novelist we may read traces of these transitions, particularly in the competing ideologies, metaphors, and constructions of literary value that Dickens came to repudiate. In a novel so strikingly supersaturated by diverse expressions of print culture, alternative models of the work of writing are abundant: from the mock parliamentary report of its opening chapter, the story meanders through an elaborate compendium of early nineteenth-century discourses, gleefully assimilating the work of antiquarians and folklorists, travel writers and amateur scientists, lawyers and politicians, Romantic poets and newspaper editors.

Pickwick was not, as I have mentioned, a novel written by "Charles Dickens" as it first appeared; it was only over the course of the story's publication in monthly parts (from April 1836 to November 1837) that intimations of a personalized authorship began to surface, and it was only in the final number that Dickens discarded the pseudonym "Boz," published his name, and suggested that his work should be considered a novel.[4] That Dickens had at first introduced himself as "Boz," the "editor" of *Pickwick*, is well known. In fact, many literary historians and biographers are quite fond of the story, since the young Dickens's pseudonymous editorial facade adds a certain piquancy to the story of his rise, during the production of *Pickwick*, from a hack writer hired to supply copy that would accompany Robert Seymour's illustrations to the phenomenally successful star of Victorian literature. It is as though Dickens's future stature as the most prominent novelist of his day is thrown into still greater relief by contrasting it with this relatively humble journalistic posturing, or as though the seemingly inevitable fame of "Charles Dickens" lends a retrospective charm to the first tentative ventures of "Boz." The "editorship" of the *Pickwick Papers*, in short, makes for a good joke—in the text and out of it—though the conceit was perhaps already a tired one. It had been used frequently by eighteenth-century novelists, by Scott, and even more recently in Carlyle's *Sartor Resartus* (1833-1834). The trope outlasted *Pickwick*, too: *Jane Eyre*, to cite a well known example, was originally "edited by 'Currer Bell.'" Still, the very familiarity of the editorial trope should alert us to something more serious about Dickens's joke. Its frequent recurrence in relation to fiction but not in, say, contemporary poetic or dramatic contexts, implies that the novel was somehow less of a uniformly "authored" discourse, or that, at any rate, fiction evoked different standards of originality, intentionality, or of production more generally.

In other words, if we dismiss the editorship of *Pickwick* as a simple joke that would inevitably be abandoned, we forget that the trope had a traditional association with the novel, and that it suggested particular ways of thinking about the work of writing. Moreover, Dickens's use of an editorial facade at the outset of *Pickwick* certainly seemed to its first readers to make as much sense as any other description of what "Boz" was doing. Early reviewers called "Boz" the "arranger" of the *Papers,* thus following his lead without any sense of irony.[5] Dickens also became more literally the editor of *Bentley's Miscellany* at the beginning of 1837, while *Pickwick's* serialization was still in progress.[6] Given Dickens's involvement in the periodical press and the considerable confusion over the unusual serial format of *Pickwick's* publication, his ultimate claim to be the author of a novel was actually less intuitive than his initial editorial posture. In such a context, the question is not why Dickens would portray himself as an editor, but why he would depart from this representation. The appeal to novelists of the editorial metaphor, particularly its role in enhancing the illusion of fiction's realism, was beginning to dwindle. It suggested anonymity and a corporate rather than an individual authority (epitomized by the use of the editorial "we") at a time when writers were becoming aware of the new power that mass-market production, with its insatiable need to predict popularity, could accord to established authors. In the social turmoil of the 1830s, moreover, editorship's association with journals and newspapers evoked the antagonistic factionalism of periodical publication, which supplied each political perspective or religious persuasion with its own organ. The rhetoric of editing could neither allow Dickens to articulate his triumph over his publishers nor assist him in appealing to the sentiments of a reading public radically reconceived as a harmonious totality.

Pickwick itself provides some clues to the more specific implications of the editorial trope at the moment of its production. In the second number, the narrator helps to clarify what editing means in the novel:

> Many authors entertain, not only a foolish, but a really dishonest objection to acknowledge the sources from whence they derive much *valuable information.* We have no such feeling. We are merely endeavoring to discharge, in an upright manner, the responsible duties of our editorial functions; and whatever ambition we might have felt under other circumstances to lay claim to the authorship of these adventures, a regard for truth forbids us to do more than claim the merit of their judicious arrangement and impartial narration. The Pickwick papers are our New River Head; and we may be compared to the New River Company. The labours of others have raised for us an immense reservoir of *important facts.* We merely lay them on, and communicate them, in a clear and

gentle stream, to a world thirsting for Pickwickian *knowledge*. (115-6, my emphasis)

Editorship is not creative or original; instead it culls and arranges "valuable information," "important facts," and "knowledge" that have been established by others, with the ultimate goal of disseminating this knowledge to the "world." It is also, as the New River Company analogy suggests, both a mechanical and commercial activity. And though editing may appear less glorified than authorship (which would be an object of "ambition"), it is nevertheless somehow more honest, and its "regard for truth" makes it (by these criteria) more useful. All of this bears more than a little resemblance to instrumentalist models of literary value, including its suggestion of the modest extent to which writers should be esteemed. In its empirical bent, its depiction of writers working collaboratively to serve the public responsibly, even in its embrace of the mechanical and commercial, this representation of the narrator's role might have come from one of Scott's prefaces. It is parodic, of course—the historical information that Scott's critics regarded as the great benefit of his work was hardly "Pickwickian knowledge"—but it nevertheless illuminates the novel's associations with editorship, and over the course of the novel, the narrator, no longer content merely to parody this version of editing, will abandon the pose entirely.

Why had Scott's representation of novel writing ceased to serve its purpose? He had attained a level of success with both critics and readers that had been previously unknown, and yet by the late 1830s the remarks of the Author of *Waverley* on the nature of novel writing had begun to seem to some critics ideologically inadequate, even disreputable. Thomas Carlyle, as influential in this way as he would prove in many others, set the terms for this reevaluation in an 1838 essay on Scott: "in this nineteenth century, our highest literary man, who immeasurably beyond all others commanded the world's ear, had, as it were, no message to deliver to the world; wished not the world to elevate itself, to amend itself, to do this or that, except simply pay him for the books he kept writing" (431). Carlyle does not exaggerate the extent to which Scott seemed to want little relationship with his audience beyond a pecuniary one—the Author of *Waverley* had frequently suggested exactly this—but for Carlyle this has become a problem. The trouble was not simply involvement with the market, but with the personality of someone who was interested in nothing more. Carlyle demands a more serious *intent*, a desire for social improvement, for spiritual elevation, for *anything* (for "this or that") beyond merely material interests: one must want to communicate some useful message to one's audience.

Scott had not, of course, dismissed the issue of his work's usefulness; his critical reputation rested on his novels' assimilation of history (which made them, in the eyes of his contemporaries, both more useful and respectable than novels of mere entertainment), and he had taken pains in his novels and their prefaces to emphasize their utility. What Scott had *not* done, and what Carlyle would later insist upon, was to claim that the character of the author himself had anything to do with the social benefits of his work. Scott had argued that it ought to make little difference to readers of novels what his motivations were, or even who he was, since the novels themselves would either please or displease the public without any reference to him. For Carlyle, however, criticism of Scott's novels blurs easily into criticism of Scott the man. "His life was worldly; his ambitions were worldly. There is nothing spiritual in him; all is economical, material, of the earth earthy" (412), Carlyle writes, hardly able to emphasize his point enough. Thus the novels themselves offer little spiritual aid: "The sick heart will find no healing here, the darkly struggling heart no guidance: the Heroic that is in all men no divine awakening voice" (455). This last phrase, drawn from Carlyle's familiar lexicon, encapsulates his whole critique of Scott. Only Heroes can awake "the Heroic that is in all men," the greatest social good is effected by society's greatest men acting as individuals, setting an example for lesser people to worship.[7] Thus the question of the worth of the *Waverley* novels ultimately rests on the chief question of Carlyle's essay, "Whether Sir Walter Scott was a great man" (402). Carlyle not only raised the stakes in asking what Scott's novels were good for (from something like historical accuracy to the communication of transcendent moral Truth), he also changed the terms of evaluation so that they were definitively linked to the life—even the soul—of the novelist: as he claims more generally, the "Man-of-Letters Hero must be regarded as our most important modern person. He, such as he may be, is the soul of all. What he teaches, the whole world will do and make."[8] Such claims might previously have been made about the work of poets, but not about *Waverley* or *The Monk* or even *Pride and Prejudice*. Novels were becoming an authored discourse, not in Foucault's simplest sense of appearing with someone's name attached to them, but in a way that made their authors (or at the very least, the sort of relationship between authors and their readers) centrally important in the assessment of value.

Carlyle's formulation of literary value was not, however, the only such argument in play in the late 1830s, nor had Scott's relatively pragmatic notion of an authoritative public altogether vanished. The tradition of "utility" on which Scott drew had given rise to the systematic philosophy of Utilitarianism, which, by that time, exerted a powerful influence both in British government and in the publishing industry. Utilitarians were notoriously skeptical of abstract claims about spiritual value, preferring instead a Benthamite calculation of the greatest good for the greatest number. In accordance with this principle, they were keenly interested in the growth of the market, and they emerged as leaders in the effort to reach a broad audience. The group that most aggressively and successfully courted the new readership was Lord Brougham's Society for the Diffusion of Useful Knowledge, whose *Penny Magazine* was designed to instruct and enlighten as many readers as possible. The content of this periodical, though, demonstrates that "utility" had become more narrowly conceived than in Scott's work. "Useful" meant practical and factual, positivist and scientific; as Richard Altick has defined it, "Useful knowledge was the good solid, employable facts of mechanics and chemistry, metallurgy and hydraulics—facts that could be applied in the workshop and on the railway line, to produce goods more cheaply and efficiently, to communicate and transport more swiftly" (131). Such an understanding of use-value placed little emphasis on authorship, and cared not at all for any arguments claiming that writers were singular, original creators with special access to spiritual truths.[9] Instead Utilitarians emphasized the usefulness of the facts themselves, facts which by their empirical nature could not have been simply imagined or created by the writer. Those who wrote for the S.D.U.K. compiled, edited, and explained facts to their readers; they did not invent.

The S.D.U.K. launched several attempts to reach large audiences: the "Library of Useful Knowledge," the "Library of Entertaining Knowledge," the *Quarterly Journal of Education*, a *British Almanac*, the *Penny Cyclopaedia*, and a prodigiously ambitious biographical dictionary, which finally broke the Society financially in the mid-forties.[10] Of their many ventures, the most successful was the eight-page, weekly *Penny Magazine*, which managed to sustain a circulation of well over a hundred thousand copies a week (and an estimated readership five times greater than the sales figures) for the first few years after it was launched in 1832. Such sales were unheard of: it outsold the major quarterly reviews, for example, by a factor in the high teens, making the *Penny Magazine* what Scott Bennett has called "the first mass-market periodical published in Great Britain" (237). Bennett's analysis of the *Magazine*'s commercial success helps to explain why this publication had reached so many readers by demonstrating that the S.D.U.K. and their publisher, Charles Knight, had crafted a plan by which they could offer new non-fiction and quality woodcuts at extraordinarily low prices by depending on huge sales rather than high profit margins to offset their costs of production. Their projected profit margin was so "razor thin," in fact, that they needed to sell 112,000 copies just to break even (240-42).

In part, then, they had reached this mass audience because they planned to, in accordance with the Society's mission of spreading useful knowledge to the greatest possible number of readers without much regard for earning more than was necessary to sustain their efforts. But they were also successful because, quite simply, they had found a type of content and format that hundreds of thousands of readers were willing to pay for. In the immediate wake of the Reform Bill, the *Penny Magazine*'s promise of self-improvement through scientific reading proved immensely popular among readers who might not otherwise have been able to spend more than a penny. The demand for the *Magazine* was so great that when rival publishers attempted to coerce booksellers to discontinue sales of the penny numbers, or even when booksellers themselves balked at the narrow profit margins, the sheer magnitude of sales overwhelmed opposition; as Bennett summarizes, "A new power was making itself felt in the trade, the power of massive numbers of readers" (244). Knight and the S.D.U.K. were particularly responsive to public demand too, and they carefully tailored their print orders to reflect recent sales of the *Magazine*. They were able to match their supply with public demand so closely that they sold, on average, about 98 percent of what they had printed, thus ensuring profitability despite the low cost per unit.

Demand for the *Penny Magazine* did fall—and quickly—as the popularity of its brand of useful knowledge waned. But the mass market it had revealed continued to grow throughout the 1830s, served by other publishers of cheap print. At first there were the predictable imitators (including two periodicals purporting to be published by "A Society for the Diffusion of Useful Knowledge,"), and borrowers (the Society for the Propagation of Christian Knowledge began publishing its widely read, religiously-inflected *Saturday Magazine* shortly after the debut of the *Penny Magazine*). In general, the *Penny Magazine* was followed by a swarm of very inexpensive periodicals in the early 1830s, most of which, according to Louis James's account, "were political or instructive, or general literary magazines containing snippets of general knowledge, dramatic criticism, and references to current affairs," and of which only a few were remunerative enough to last through 1834 (17-18). In the middle of the decade, popular taste shifted to what would later be called "sensational" subjects—histories of highwaymen, for example, and short romances about the criminal world— and to reprinted novels issued in cheap parts. By the last years of the decade, new novels were being produced directly for this penny market, and as early as 1840 fiction had begun to dominate this market, just as it had among higher-priced, solidly middle-class publishers.[11]

Into this new environment stumbled Chapman and Hall, the publishers of *Pickwick*. They had hired Dickens—still known only as the journalist and sketch-writer called "Boz"—to supply text for a projected monthly periodical that would feature humorous plates by the famous illustrator Robert Seymour. Although it had various precursors, Chapman and Hall's plan to bring out this illustrated story in twenty monthly installments priced at a shilling each was an innovative attempt to market new fiction to a large audience.[12] At a time when new novels were typically produced in print runs between 500 and 1000 copies, *Pickwick* would require a circulation of 2000 just to break even. In this way, Chapman and Hall sought to take advantage of the mass-market publishing conditions that had fallen into place during the 1830s, and they accordingly followed the lead of publishers like the S.D.U.K.'s Charles Knight in attempting to profit from large print runs at a low unit cost, and in using a serial format that would allow them to be especially responsive to fluctuations in public demand. This latter strategy proved essential to *Pickwick*'s success: beginning with a tentative printing of just 500 copies of the first number, Chapman and Hall actually reduced the number of copies after poor initial sales, but were subsequently prepared to increase production rapidly when demand unexpectedly skyrocketed to 40,000 copies a month. Such sales of a new work of fiction were altogether unprecedented; they revealed an incredible public appetite for fiction, which in turn transformed the priorities of publishers as they scrambled to profit from the new dominance of this genre.

N. N. Feltes's illuminating analysis of *Pickwick*'s commercial success describes "the moment of *Pickwick*" as signaling the transition in the literary industry "from the petty-commodity production of books to the capitalist production of texts" (*Modes* 3), and *Pickwick* itself as the first "commodity-text" (12). What distinguishes mature capitalist production of literary commodities is the form of control over the labor process, and that form of control, he argues, is series production: "Whether the commodity-text is to take the form of a series of books, a magazine serial, or a part-issue novel, series production, by allowing the bourgeois audience to be sensed and expanded, allows as well the extraction of ever greater surplus value from the very production (or 'creative') process itself" (9). This account is extraordinarily helpful in outlining the conditions under which a production like *Pickwick* could succeed so thoroughly in the relatively unexplored territory of mass-market fiction. Its cheap part-issue publication not only made it widely available, it was a mode of production that could readily respond to the desires of its audience, and effectively reinvent itself to hail a widening audience more and more compellingly.[13]

Feltes's analysis is less useful, however, in addressing the issue of authorship under these new conditions, or for explaining why it is that one of the most prominent transformations over the course of *Pickwick*'s production is the position from which this expanding audience is hailed. In part, this is because Feltes's focus lies elsewhere, though it is also a result of his adherence to a classical Marxist theory of labor value, the assumption that any surplus value must be extracted "from the very production (or 'creative') process itself" (7). Correlatively, such a perspective suggests a more or less exploitative relationship between Dickens and Chapman and Hall, one that left the writer little agency. The full commodification of the text, Feltes continues, depended on the alienation of writers from their work; their right to claim ownership of the text had to become "a commodity like any other," which left writers in the same position as "any other worker in the capitalist mode of production" (6). What Feltes fails to account for is the emerging possibility that writers could be owners of much more than just their labor-power; they could own their copyrights, too, and consequently they had a material interest in representing themselves as different from other workers, and the products of their labor as something besides commodities. It is true, as Feltes implies, that whether Dickens thought of himself as a genius, hack, or professional, Chapman and Hall had purchased his labor power for nineteen months. Yet it did not take Dickens long to realize that selling his copyright outright had been a serious error; though he

continued to serialize his texts until he died, his experience with *Pickwick*'s
sales taught him never again to sign away his rights completely.[14] Furthermore, the tight profit margins demanded by mass publication gave proven
writers enormous leverage because of their predictable drawing power,
much in the same way that today's mainstream movie industry will pay a
premium for actors who can reliably "open" a film.

The commercial takeoff of this extremely cheap periodical industry signals more than simply the formation of a lower-class market. The actual
class makeup of the newer consumers has proven difficult to pin down—
though Altick has estimated that most new readers in the first half of the
century emerged from "the amorphous stratum between the old-established
middle class [. . .] and the working class proper" (82)—and this ambiguity
supports the indication of countless contemporary anecdotes that there
was a great deal of crossover between audiences for cheap printed matter
and more expensive products. At any rate, it is certain that the entire print
market was growing significantly larger, and that across the publishing
spectrum, technological advances had made high-volume publishing less
costly and distribution quicker and cheaper, while the example of the
Penny Magazine had proved that smaller profit margins could be lucrative.
All of this tended to make the industry more profitable, but it also had
the effect of increasing publishers' reliance on fresh copy from recognized
authors to supply the growing demand for printed matter. In effect, the
enlarged market had indirectly conferred a new prominence on writers in
the relations of production, and writers used this increased bargaining
power to further their interests by bringing their case before Parliament
in the copyright reform movement of 1837-1842. The resulting debate
sparked an ideological confrontation over the nature of literary value and
the question of what, if anything, authorship had to do with it.

The writers' self-appointed spokesman was Thomas Noon Talfourd, an
M.P. who was himself a playwright and man of letters. In 1837 he introduced a bill for copyright reform that would extend authors' control of
their works as radically as he thought possible. Building on an innovation
in the 1814 Copyright Act, which had altered the limit of copyright protection from 28 years to the lifetime of the author, Talfourd proposed to
extend protection 60 years beyond the author's lifetime. Even more ambitiously, Talfourd wanted existing copyrights that had been sold outright to
publishers to revert to authors or their heirs after their existing 28-year
protection expired. This attempt to extend writers' economic power met
fierce opposition from the rest of the industry, and it reflects their growing
importance—or as Talfourd maintained, centrality—in the relations of literary production and circulation. Copyright legislation in the eighteenth
century had focused on the interests of competing booksellers or publishers, who in most cases were the owners of copyrights purchased outright
from writers. Now, for the first time, writers argued on their own behalf,

and in attempting to secure their own position, they promoted a representation of authorship to justify their claims.[15]

Talfourd's goal, simply put, was to extend the "time during which authors shall enjoy the direct pecuniary benefit immediately flowing from the
sale of their own works" (161), though he increasingly argued for a more
abstract "justice" for authors. Despite public support from prominent
writers such as Wordsworth (who worked closely with Talfourd in outlining the proposals), Ainsworth, Carlyle, Disraeli, Lockhart, and Dickens
(then a 25-year-old newcomer to the literary scene), Talfourd's campaign
stalled under pressure of considerable opposition. Foremost among the
bill's opponents, as Talfourd wrote, was an "army of publishers, booksellers, printers, and bookbinders" (166), that is, all the other members of
the book trade, whose interests would be threatened if the profitable flow
of fresh text were to be clogged by higher expenses. The bill drew further
criticism from Utilitarians and "philosophical radicals," who were concerned that longer copyrights would impede the free trade of printed matter by creating temporary monopolies that would drive up prices for the
public. The bill was ultimately adopted, but only after five years of debate,
and only after its supporters conceded a compromise term of 42 years, or
death plus seven years.[16] For the purposes of this chapter, however, the outcome of the legislative battle is less significant than the way it reveals polarizing representations of authorship in the late 1830s, and clarifies the
different interests that underlay those representations.

It would be misleading to identify too closely developments in nineteenth-century copyright law and aesthetic discourses about authorship, or
more particularly, to assume that the authorial subject of copyright law is
precisely the same kind of subject articulated by literary and aesthetic
discourses.[17] Nevertheless, in practice these distinct discourses permeated
each other, as supporters and detractors of the bill borrowed arguments
from existing representations of writing. Chris Vanden Bossche, in his
analysis of the terms in which the copyright reform debate was couched,
has shown that the arguments over the redefinition of writers' legal status
ultimately centered on a single disagreement: "The question was whether a
special privilege was to be granted to 'imaginative literature' or whether
the public's need for 'useful knowledge' should be considered primary"
(41). Both sides of the debate presented their case with reference to the usefulness of printed matter, but their different emphases resulted in strongly
opposed notions of what that use-value was. The author's party—predictably for a group that included Wordsworth and Carlyle—drew upon
familiar Romantic descriptions of imaginative literature as a force that
could cure the fragmentation of industrialized society. Authors themselves,
the argument continued, were beyond the taint of mechanization, since
their activity was not a form of labor but a organic, imaginative operation
of creation. Opponents of the bill, on the other hand, focused on the value
of spreading knowledge to the widest possible public, and they employed

the ready-made rhetoric of the S.D.U.K. to help make their point. Authors themselves make little difference, they argued, since use-value lies in the facts themselves. Laborers like any others, writers were in the business of assembling scraps of knowledge and information, and the more efficiently and cheaply they did so, the greater the social good.

None of these arguments come as much of a surprise, except perhaps insofar as they uncannily repeat points that had been made decades earlier by Wordsworth and Scott; the chief difference is that both sides of the debate were attempting to foreground the immediate social benefits of their positions more than Wordsworth or Scott had, so that the arguments more closely resemble those of Carlyle and the S.D.U.K. Still, the controversy demonstrates that at the beginning of the Victorian period, the Romantic representation of a personalized, author-centered literary value coexisted with a potent counter-argument that maintained the relative inconsequence and interchangeability of writers. Neither of these doctrines was persuasive enough to overwhelm the other without a protracted conflict, and after a period of five years (during which Talfourd himself lost his seat in Parliament), the dispute ended in compromise.

The effect of this ideological struggle on writers was, in practice, uneven. Those who sold their copyrights outright to publishers stood to gain little from Talfourd's proposed extensions of the term of protection. Such writers would include, typically, novelists who wrote for the extremely cheap press (who often did not copyright their works), or those who simply were not successful or established enough to demand their own deals with their publishers. The writers who would most benefit from the new bill would be those whose work was commercially successful enough that they could force publishers merely to rent their copyrights, which left writers in the position of being able to make new bargains for future printings or editions. This is not quite the sort of author Talfourd suggested copyright reform would serve. In his first speech on the subject (18 May 1837), he asked his listeners to imagine the writers who suffer most under the unreformed system: "Let us suppose," he begins,

> an author of true, original genius, disgusted with the inane phraseology which had usurped the place of poetry, [who has devoted] himself from youth to its service [and] who shall persevere in his high and holy course, gradually impressing thoughtful minds with the sense of truth made visible in the severest forms of beauty, until he shall create the taste by which he shall be appreciated [. . .]. As soon as his copyright becomes valuable, it is gone! (163)

Talfourd here invokes the Wordsworthian conception of the poet—in fact, a few sentences later he makes it clear that this hypothetical author is Wordsworth himself—but his reference to "poetry" is somewhat misleading. If poets in the late 1830s tended to retain their copyrights, it was only because the genre had begun to find so few readers that publishers rarely found it worthwhile to purchase them.[18] Novels were beginning to capture the most profitable share of the market, and novelists with proven abilities to sell books—at this time these included Ainsworth, Disraeli, and Dickens—had the most to gain by holding their copyrights. Such writers were beginning to realize that they had a serious material stake in treating copyright as property rather than alienated labor, along with arguing for their autonomous centrality in the production of texts and all the rest of the constellation of Romantic values that had been posited in support of authors' claims.

Talfourd's partial failure notwithstanding, his campaign helped to establish material relations of production in the book trade that, in turn, supported the rise of Romantic authorship more broadly. Talfourd had argued that literary texts constituted a special kind of product, made by a special kind of labor: copyright should be seen as a "right of property in that which the mind itself creates, and which, so far from exhausting the materials common to all men, or limiting their resources, enriches or expands them—a right of property which, by the happy peculiarity of its nature, can only be enjoyed by the proprietor in proportion as it blesses mankind" (159). The new law ultimately sustained his claim for the "happy peculiarity" of copyright, inasmuch as it treated copyright as a form of property in which authors had special rights; indeed, by establishing a special form of property that was legally defined by the originality of its production and by the duration of its creator's life, copyright law allowed for a sort of commodity that was attached to the person—if not necessarily the personality—who produced it.[19] Furthermore, in its immediate effect, the bill's success led other novelists to assert their own proprietorship of their works. John Sutherland has shown that

> The tendency of the new [1842] copyright act was further to shift the law's protection from the printer and publisher (for whom copyright legislation was originally devised) to the author, to whom it gave longer possession. Novelists, too, as a profession, had become wiser over the years and more of them followed the trade adage—never part with a copyright. (*Victorian Novelists* 95)

Instead, novelists increasingly explored alternative contracts with publishers—such as the temporary lease of copyright or division of profits[20]—with which the extensions of copyright protection could translate into a considerable increase in remuneration, even a large share of the surplus value their texts realized in publication. Since in practice the law encouraged writers to retain their copyrights, it fostered conditions under which the idea of the author as the controlling presence behind a text could become particularly visible: consider, in Dickens's case, the many editions in which he issued his work, each with a new preface by the author, or the readings he gave to encourage the sale of his texts. Furthermore, by assuming not only the creative autonomy of writers but also their preeminence in the relations of literary production, the Copyright Amendment lent itself to a market in which writers, though not actually independent of other segments of production, would be the focus of reviews and advertisements.[21] The theoretical and practical changes brought about by copyright reform supported, to a greater extent than ever before, the ideology of authors as non-alienated creators whose work was a special kind of commodity because it was a form of self-expression. And writers—particularly novelists—found in this ideology an effective way to conceptualize and justify their own relation to the forces of literary production.

There was no question in the short term, however, that Dickens increasingly wanted his readers to see him as the creative presence behind *Pickwick*'s production. He claimed more and more responsibility as the years went on for the success of the novel, gradually edging out everyone else who had been involved in planning and executing the project. His prefaces increasingly obscure his involvement in what had been a collaborative enterprise, a joint venture of writer, artists, and Chapman and Hall, who had done more than anyone to devise the new form of publication and the general outlines of its appearance. In the 1837 preface, as we have seen, Dickens recalls how "Deferring to the judgement of others at the outset of the undertaking, [the author] adopted the machinery of the club, which was suggested as that best adapted to his purpose" (41). Ten years later in the preface to the Cheap Edition, he maintains that from the start he had insisted upon following his own inclinations if he were to be involved in the project, and in this version of events, Chapman and Hall give in to his demands and allow him to begin his act of pure creation: "My views being deferred to, I thought of Mr. Pickwick, and wrote the first number" (44). This tidy revision of the direction of deference imagines Dickens in the authoritative position writers were struggling for in the late thirties. Never mind that Chapman and Hall had the prescience to restructure the production of novels, or that most of the initial ideas for a club of humorous characters had come from Seymour; what Dickens wants us to see as the genesis of the text is himself, the creative mind alone, thinking of Mr. Pickwick.

Pickwick's readers did not have to wait for the 1847 preface to hear Dickens's claims for association with the text. He had already suggested much the same thing by gradually discarding the narrator's editorial posture and refocusing the readers' attention on a newly sympathetic and familiar narrator. No longer the detached, almost scientific compiler of facts, the narrator enjoys a much more personal bond with the creatures of his imagination by the end of the novel: "It is the fate of most men who mingle with the world, and attain even the prime of life, to make many real friends, and lose them in the course of nature. It is the fate of all authors or chroniclers to create imaginary friends, and lose them in the course of art" (896). By now the narrator, an author rather than an editor, claims that his work has been a kind of creation. An emotional bond thus exists between him and his characters, a sympathy so strong as to erase the mediation of textuality earlier foregrounded by his editorial pretense; the analogy between "real friends" and "imaginary friends" hints at the depth of feeling the narrator means to express. Such friendship is crucial not only for describing the author's personal connection to his production, but also for representing his relationship to his audience: "Let us leave our old friend in one of those moments of unmixed happiness, of which, if we seek them, there are ever some, to cheer our transitory existence here. There are dark shadows on the earth, but its lights are stronger still in the contrast" (896). The editorial "we" has here been replaced by a first person plural that encompasses all of humanity (which will find happy moments "if we seek them" in "our transitory existence") as well as, more specifically, the novel's readers (the old friends of Pickwick). Mutual friendship of Pickwick, a shared sympathetic connection, unites the readers and author in a recognition of a broadly human—if rather facile—truth. And it is this sort of truth, not the facts and information of the S.D.U.K., that was valued in the Romantic rhetoric of Talfourd's copyright reform movement, this conception of literary use-value that could be mobilized to justify the claims of writers who argued that their products were uniquely theirs, and that their work was beneficial accordingly.

THE MESSENGER IS THE MESSAGE

The Pickwick Papers must be understood as a text composed over a period of two years during which the force of the mass market was growing increasingly palpable and the pressure to refine representations of authorship rose accordingly. It was under the weight of such pressures that Dickens first portrayed a system of literary values centered on a sympathetic, friendly author. By the end of *Pickwick*'s serial run, he had clearly decided to endorse an ideology of authorship like that used to support copyright reform, and Dickens chose to dedicate the completed novel to a friend who had earned his "fervent admiration" (39), Thomas Noon Talfourd.[22] But Dickens's now familiar posture emerges only fitfully and inconsistently during the text's production, though the resulting narrative gaps have traditionally been obscured by critical discussions of the novel's "unity." I have suggested already that the narrator's changing tone indicates a shift in Dickens's strategy of representing the work of writing, but this development is also evident, in a more complex way, in *Pickwick*'s thematic and symbolic gestures. Here, more than anywhere else, the text reveals the ideological gaps and ambivalences of its own production, inconsistencies that bring us nearer to understanding the stakes of rethinking authorship.

The novel's plot reflects the narrator's growing sympathy as it follows Pickwick's gradual change of affiliation from one kind of club to another. The first of these is of course the Pickwick Club, from whose "posthumous papers" the novel is initially said to be edited. It is an association dedicated to "the advancement of knowledge, and the diffusion of learning" (67), and though it may not follow the actual practices of the S.D.U.K., the influence of the Society's principles and rhetoric is unmistakable. Pickwick, motivated by what the novel's original advertisement calls a "fondness for the useful arts" (899), sets out on his travels in search of scientific knowledge to add to his "Speculations on the Source of the Hampstead Ponds, with some Observations on the Theory of Tittlebats" (67). He collects information and stories which will later be recorded and collated by the club (and by the editor of *The Pickwick Papers*) and then—presumably—diffused. The culmination of Pickwick's investigations is his discovery of the mysterious runic stone, about which he writes "ninety-six pages of very small print" offering "twenty-seven different readings of the inscription," thus getting himself "elected as an honorary member of seventeen native and foreign societies" (228). When the irate Pickwickian Mr. Blotton reveals that the inscription says nothing more than the words "BILL STUMPS, HIS MARK," he is expelled from the Pickwick Club and unanimously branded an "ignorant meddler" by the learned societies. The joke, of course, is that for all their supposed erudition, Pickwick and his pamphlet-writing associates fail to recognize ostensibly the most primal and fundamentally personal kind of text, a signature. Unlike Blotton, Pickwick has not consulted Stumps himself, and as a result, his pamphlet and those produced by members of the other societies point everywhere but to the inscription's author.

Pickwick, it must be remembered, is at first not only a writer of scientific pamphlets, but also a compulsive note-taker, a collector of folk tales and urban myths, even at one point an editor (309). In these various capacities, which resonate with many aspects of contemporary print culture,[23] Pickwick is nearly as much a figure of ridicule as the other writers in the novel. As a general rule, no one with pretensions to become a published writer, or even to be respected as a writer, escapes the novel's censure. Scientific writing is represented by the prolific learned societies and, later, by the unnamed "scientific gentleman" who writes "a voluminous treatise of great research and deep learning" on the subject of Pickwick's lantern, which he mistakes for an undiscovered atmospheric phenomenon (647). Editing is exemplified by Pott and Slurk, the factious, backbiting proprietors of the rival Eatanswill newspapers. For the more classically Romantic side of literary production, poetic pretension is represented by Mrs. Leo Hunter, with her meditative "Ode to an Expiring Frog," and by Snodgrass, who is perhaps slightly more sympathetic by virtue of never having actually written any verse. Mrs. Hunter supplies still more material for satire by hosting her "public breakfast," which is attended by journalists and literary "lions" in from London. The most highly praised writer at the breakfast, however, is Count Smorltork, the bumbling foreign observer of "all tings" English. After his two weeks in the country, the Count believes that he has collected enough information for his projected "great work on England" (284), though he continues to take even more wholly inaccurate notes during the party. In his copious note-taking, Smorltork figures as an exaggerated double of Pickwick, and the resemblance is not lost on Mrs. Hunter, who takes the opportunity to introduce these "two very clever people to each other" (283).

As a profession, writing is roundly criticized in *The Pickwick Papers*; indeed, with the possible exception of lawyers, no group is as consistently and thoroughly ridiculed. The novel subjects writers to a double critique. First, they are typically shown to misunderstand the people and events around them because their perspective of the world is impersonal and detached. Either they perceive human activity according to empirical or scientific preconceptions (by which it often cannot be recognized as human activity), or they take a more solipsistic view, imagining themselves to be somehow superior to the people around them. Thus Pott is satirically depicted at one point as having "stepped down from his pedestal, [. . .] benignly adapting his remarks to the comprehension of the herd, and seeming in outward form, if not in spirit, to be one of them" (317). The literary "lions" at the public breakfast are mocked in precisely the same terms: "here you might see 'em, walking about, like ordinary men, smiling, and talking—aye, and talking pretty considerable nonsense too, no doubt with the benign intention of rendering themselves intelligible to the common people about them" (281). Either error—the empirical or the solipsistic—results in the separation of writers from the social world, and in their consequent inability to think or behave sensibly.

At the same time, though, the novel betrays an anxiety over the possibility that these writers are too much a part of the world around them, that they are, in a word, too *public*. The narrator never ceases to remind us, for example, that Pott and Slurk are "Public Men" (809), or that they are "representatives of the public feeling of Eatanswill" (822), or that Mrs. Leo Hunter's literary gathering is a "Public Breakfast" (273). The word comes to serve as shorthand for a false or wrongheaded sort of social interaction, one which reiterates cultural and political divisions instead of bringing individuals into a sympathetic community founded on private—and generally domestic—personal attachments; the public breakfast stands in utter opposition to the festive meals at Dingley Dell. It becomes clear, moreover, that the problem with the public condition of writers is compounded by the form of their communication, the very materiality of print. The anxiety is evident in the narrator's repetition of the obvious: the "lions" are described as "authors, real authors, who had written whole books, and printed them afterwards" (281), as though publication counted as a separate offense. Similarly, when Pott and Slurk decide to substitute a textual confrontation for their physical one, the issue of its medium arises again: "When they came to think it over [. . .] it occurred to them that they could do it much better in print, so they recommended deadly hostilities without delay; and all Eatanswill rung with their boldness—on paper"

(824). The final clause here qualifies any boldness the editors might have, suggesting the insincerity of public, printed discourse; its obvious superfluity (once we have been told that the conflict will continue in print, is it necessary to emphasize the fact that it will take place on paper?) draws attention to textuality itself.

Pickwick's progress, on narrative and thematic levels, is a movement away from this kind of writing, from foregrounded textuality, and from the unhealthy forms of socialization with which it is complicit. Thus the narrator drops the editorial pretense, and with it the constant reminders of *Pickwick*'s textuality and public circulation. By the time of the Dingley Dell Christmas episode—halfway through the novel—editorship has come to mingle with something altogether more sentimental, a developing narrative attitude that chafes at the material conventions of textual transmission: "But bless our editorial heart, what a long chapter we have been betrayed into! We had quite forgotten all such petty restrictions as chapters, we solemnly declare" (480). By the novel's end, of course, the editorial detachment has vanished, replaced with a notion that Pickwick has become a friend to both narrator and readers, an immediate sympathetic relationship that effaces the distance of textual transmission: "Let us leave our old friend in one of those moments of unmixed happiness, of which, if we seek them, there are ever some, to cheer our transitory existence here" (896).

Meanwhile, Pickwick himself must cease to be a writer. As a precondition for his formation of an ideal little community, he abandons his earlier scientific detachment, replacing an impersonal epistemology with an immediate knowledge of the human—whether of human kindness, deceitfulness, or suffering. His priorities likewise change from a desire to achieve public fame as a writer to a cultivation of mutual regard with a small circle of friends. By the end of the novel, for example, his relationship with the Wellers has supplanted his previous ambitions: "He derived, at that moment, more pride and luxury of feeling from the disinterested attachment of his humble friends, than ten thousand protestations from the greatest men living could have awakened in his heart" (887). Consequently, Pickwick's activities tend to revolve less around the production of text and more around the personal supplementation or replacement of textual communication. The "mission" that draws him out of his self-imposed exile in the Fleet is not a continuation of his research, but an attempt to defend Winkle's marriage before his father: it "behoved [Pickwick], and was indeed due to his *personal* character, to acquaint the aforesaid Winkle, senior, *personally*, and by word of mouth, with the whole circumstances of the case" (759, emphasis added). Winkle's letter to his father, which Pickwick delivers and watches him read, is by itself somehow insufficient—Pickwick must himself become the medium of sympathy's communication. His new mission in the world of the novel, to establish personal bonds of understanding between other characters, is thus analogous to his emerging function as a bridge between the novel's writer and its readers.

Pickwick's repudiation of writing represents a complex negotiation between competing constructions of print culture and the writer's place
within it, and this complexity is evident not only in what the novel affirms,
but also in what it attempts to deny: an editorial framework, the alienated
condition of public writers, the circulation of supposedly useful knowledge, even the materiality of texts. We can readily appreciate the thematic
and narrative shifts in the novel as an endorsement of representations of
authorship like Thomas Noon Talfourd's, and in fact it would be impossible to explain the values that the novel rejects without recognizing them as
a code for an alternative contemporary model of print culture that Talfourd also attacked. Yet the novel cannot completely disavow its own participation in the public sphere, even as it attempts to position itself as the
non-alienated message of a friend rather than a textual product written for
a public. That is, *Pickwick* rejects a view of authorship in which widespread public diffusion is held to be more important than the private or
personal relationship of authors to their readers, but its own circulation in
the mass market has left in it traces of anxiety that point to its implication
in the very relations of production it ultimately seeks to deny. The resulting
ambivalence is thematically expressed in a number of ways. For the present
purposes it will suffice to outline two of the most telling.

We have seen already, first of all, that *Pickwick* criticizes writers to the
extent that what they do is for the public, and that writing is especially
problematized when it is published and circulated in print. But these positions must be seen in the context of the novel's more general fear of
crowds, repeatedly thematized as a fear of subjection to the public gaze. J.
Hillis Miller has identified the "nightmare" of the novel as, "at its climax,
a nightmare of eyes."[24] That is, characters in both the main plot and the in-
terpolated tales frequently find themselves at the center of a terrifying and
paralyzing public scrutiny. Pickwick himself is subject to such humiliation
on a number of occasions, from his early confrontation with the cabman to
his trial, but perhaps most memorably after he is taken to the pound for
trespassing on Captain Boldwig's property. After a picnic with his friends,
Pickwick has passed out drunk in a wheelbarrow and has subsequently
been taken to the pound, where he attracts the attention of "three-fourths
of the whole population, who had gathered round, in expectation of his
waking" (340):

> A general shout was of course the signal of his having woke up; and his
> involuntary inquiry of "What's the matter?" occasioned another, louder
> than the first, if possible.
> "Here's a game!" roared the populace.
> "Where am I?" exclaimed Mr. Pickwick.
> "In the Pound," replied the mob [. . .].
> "Let me out," cried Mr. Pickwick. "Where's my servant? Where are my
> friends?"

"You an't got no friends. Hurrah!" Then came a turnip, then a potato, and then an egg: with a few other little tokens of the playful disposition of the many-headed. (340)

Pickwick's helplessness before the collective gaze of the mob reiterates the anxiety with which the novel typically approaches the idea of the public. Here, in fact, the narrator's aversion to what he calls the "many-headed" strongly recalls his criticism of Mr. Pott, who thinks himself to be above "the herd" (317), except that the narrator is decidedly less ironic about it when a crowd is actually represented. What is true of writers specifically becomes more generally true in *Pickwick*: crowds threaten to disrupt the sanctity of close personal relationships, and the public gaze is to be avoided rather than courted. The relative ease with which Pickwick slips from an enjoyable picnic with his friends to a nightmarish mob scene—in which he is not offered food to share but bombarded with it instead—suggests something of the fragility of friendly relations in a public world. Nor, I think, is it too fanciful to hear in the crowd's taunt of Pickwick the echo of an anxiety felt by an ostensibly friendly novelist who was by then writing for the largest audience the novel had ever known: "You an't got no friends. Hurrah!"

The market has left symptoms of ambivalence in *Pickwick* because of its size—suggesting the impossibility of ever really befriending the "many-headed"—but it is also threatening because of its commercialism. Most of the impediments that the protagonists face in the novel, and all the representations of downright villainy, are directly related to greed or the pursuit of wealth (thus Jingle's mercenary marital ambitions, Dodson and Fogg's spurious lawsuits, even the dilemma of Winkle's unsympathetic father, who is, not coincidentally, a self-professed "man of business" [807]). It comes as little surprise, then, that Pickwick describes his friendly community as antithetical to the cash-nexus social relationships of the public world: announcing the dissolution of the Pickwick Club to his new friends, he explicitly opposes his new understanding of friendship to the commercial: "Nearly the whole of my previous life having been devoted to business and the pursuit of wealth, numerous scenes of which I had no previous conception have dawned on me—I hope to the enlargement of my mind, and the improvement of my understanding" (893). Of course, the narrator can barely disguise the fact that Pickwick's new society of friends has been, to a certain extent, bought and insured with the proceeds of this "previous life." The principles on which this community is founded are not in themselves sufficient safeguards against the more powerful machinations of heartless self-interest. Jingle must be bought off (209-10), and Pickwick's high-minded and just refusal to pay Dodson and Fogg after his trial lands him in debtors' prison until he concedes. "Hooroar for the principle," Sam says in support of Pickwick's resolve, but then adds more cynically, "as the money-lender said ven he vouldn't renew the bill" (577). While principle is in fact dependent on principal in *Pickwick*, there is nevertheless a general tendency to efface the importance of money, both thematically (the financially disinterested characters in the novel are its heroes) and rhetorically (in an episode that represents his vaunted charity, Pickwick gives the repentant Job Trotter not 'money,' but "something from [his] waistcoat-pocket, which chinked as it was given into Job's hand" [691]).

If there is more than a little ambivalence in the novel about the possibility of transcending or escaping commercial relations, there are also suggestions, more pointedly, that the novel is itself enmeshed in the marketplace. Take, for instance, the strikingly metatextual moment at which Sam and Pickwick set off for Bath, only to discover that the coach they have hired is emblazoned with the name shared by the protagonist and the novel: "there, sure enough, in gilt letters of goodly size, was the magic name of PICKWICK!" (582). Pickwick was in fact the name of a proprietor of coaches at the time *Pickwick* appeared, but Sam reacts violently against seeing the "magic name" displayed as an advertisement, as though it had been appropriated. By juxtaposing the start of another of Pickwick's journeys with the name of a business, the text implies a more general connection between Pickwick's picaresque adventures and commercial travel, or between *Pickwick* the novel and Pickwick the commercial enterprise. This latter, in fact, recalls Scott's coach metaphor for the relationship between narrator and readers in *Waverley*. *Pickwick*'s "editor" is implicated as well, since the coach proprietor's first name is "Moses"—the name from which the pseudonym "Boz" derives—a fact that Sam surprisingly regards as "addin' insult to injury" instead of clearing up the confusion. The connections between the editor, the novel, and the commercial transactions of the market begin to appear much more substantial when we remember that *Pickwick*'s huge sales inspired the sale of related merchandise, including "Pickwick cigars," "Weller corduroys," and—significantly—"Boz cabs."

Pickwick's trajectory towards a celebration of friendship is not as ideologically innocent as it appears. Rather, the trope of friendship represents one possible set of relations between writers, their texts, and their audience. This representation ultimately aligns Dickens with an ideology of authorship which, even as *Pickwick* was produced, his friend Talfourd was arguing before Parliament. It happens to be the position that Talfourd and other writers at the time believed was best suited to advancing the material interests and cultural capital of writers, though by pointing out Dickens's stake I do not mean to reduce *Pickwick* to an exercise in greedy self-promotion, or to suggest that it is simply "about" Dickens wanting more money or control over the relations of production. Rather, I want to emphasize that the ambiguities, anxieties, and enormous inconsistencies in this book testify both to the contingencies of the appearance of the familiar "Charles Dickens," and to its significance in an immediate historical context. *Pickwick*'s complexity is a mark of its conditions of production in a changing literary industry: it constantly rethinks its relationship to the mass market within a limited range of potential ideologies, and it is this negotiation that gives it shape.

SERIALIZATION AND THE CODE OF PRODUCTION

Up to this point I have emphasized the transformative effects of changing relations of production on the Victorian conceptualization of the work of novelists, and the ways in which developments in the environment of print culture allowed what I have called Industrial Romanticism to contend with, and to begin to eclipse, a Utilitarian valuation of writing. I want to conclude, however, by taking a closer look at the form of *Pickwick*, to examine the relationship between the novel's serial publication, which above all enabled its extremely wide circulation, and the construction of authorship mobilized to justify and valorize a writer who wrote for such an audience. In short, how did *Pickwick*'s specific mode of production influence its code of production?

Critics who study publishing history have long agreed that the form of serial publication popularized by *Pickwick* was itself largely responsible for the new intimacy between novelists and the reading public. Feltes, for instance, holds that "elements of the form of [*Pickwick*], determined as we have seen by mode of production, themselves interpellate the multitude of bourgeois readers, allowing to each his own shilling number, prolonging while measuring months of shared intimacy" (*Modes* 14). He thus elaborates in an Althusserian framework the observation made by Kathleen Tillotson more than thirty years earlier that "serial publication [. . .] induced a close relation between author and reader [. . .]. The prolonging of this intercommunication over eighteen months or more enforced the effect of contact; there was a sense of long familiar association" (33). The premise of such arguments is not only that part-issue publication substantially extended the period during which readers had contact with a novel, but that publication in progress allowed writers and readers to influence one another: writers could gauge the popularity of story lines and characters as they wrote, while readers, for their part, could influence the direction of a novel's plot, registering the degree of their approbation either collectively, through consumption, or individually, through letters to the writer.

These analyses of the formal influence of serialization make sense intuitively, and they are supported by a wealth of anecdotal evidence. But they do not constitute, ultimately, an adequate explanation for the peculiar intimacy of the Industrial-Romantic ideology of authorship. Why, after all, should the new sense of audience involvement come to focus on novelists rather than on the texts themselves, or on the communities of readers that consume them? Benedict Anderson has argued that the regular consumption of newspapers acts as a kind of "mass ceremony" by which readers imagine themselves to be part of a "community in anonymity," which re-

quires no centrally important, friendly figure to organize and channel responses (35-36). Similarly, Louis James has suggested that the "periodical
is a particularly intimate form of literature" whether it is a product of a serial novelist like "Dickens or Thackeray," or of "a community of voices,
most of whom may be anonymous" ("The Trouble with Betsey" 352). In
other words, there seems little evidence to suggest that publishing novels
serially should make novelists in particular stand out from other periodical
writers. The formal determinism implied by Feltes and Tillotson should
theoretically have had the same effect on a wide range of similarly published texts. Their argument is a helpful but not a sufficient explanation for
the advent of the personalized, friendly novelist.

To a great extent, in fact, reactions towards serial production actually
undermined the claims of novelists developing the ideology of Industrial
Romanticism. Serialization had begun to attract blanket condemnations
from reviewers. *Fraser's*, for example, said of Dickens that "We wish him
well; but talking of literature in any other light than that of a hack trade we
do not like this novel-writing by scraps against time. He can never do himself or his readers justice" (qtd. in P. Collins 90). The form itself threatens
not only the extent to which Dickens does justice to his novel but also to
himself and to his readers, since it could debase their relationship into the
pecuniary relations of a "hack trade." *Fraser's* warns that if he is to claim
that his work represents something grander or more profoundly important
than editorial work or periodical journalism, Dickens would have to
overcome the suspicious similarities in form between his novels and the
products of the press. Particularly egregious, cautions *Fraser's*, is the journalistic tendency towards wordy, fragmentary prose: "*Oliver Twist* and
Nicholas Nickleby are stuffed with 'passages that lead to nothing,' merely
to fill the necessary room. Now, in the separate monthly essays this was no
harm,—on the contrary, it was of positive good to the main objects, viz.
the sale; but when we find them collected they do not improve the sequence
of the story or advance the fame of the writer. In short, the habits of the reporter break out." A few years later, *The Prospective Review* put the case
more strongly, condemning the "serial tale" as "probably the lowest artistic form yet invented [. . .]. Nine-tenths of its readers will never think of it
as a whole. A level number, however unnecessary to the development of the
story, will be thrown aside like a flat article in a newspaper" (qtd. in P.
Collins 264). This issue of unity is not a purely aesthetic consideration, but
a yardstick to measure the distance between forms of publication and their
markets; formal fragmentation could raise a number of doubts about a
writer's motivations and cultural status.

As he finished writing *Pickwick*, Dickens was already sensitive to the
possibility that the form of its publication made it vulnerable to critical
censure, and that it could likewise inflect his audience's perception of the
nature of his work. His 1837 preface includes what would become a typical Dickensian complaint about the "detached and desultory form of pub-

lication" which circumstances had thrust upon him, but adds that he had approached the project with the ambition to produce a unified work despite serialization: "it was necessary—or it appeared so to the author—that every number should be, to a certain extent, complete in itself, and yet that the whole twenty numbers, when collected, should form one tolerably harmonious whole, each leading to the other by a gentle and not unnatural progress of adventure" (41). Not content merely to emphasize his artistic intentions, however, Dickens goes on to suggest that his success in the face of formal adversity should be taken as evidence of his merit as a novelist:

> It is obvious that in a work published with a view to such considerations, no artfully interwoven or ingeniously complicated plot can with reason be expected. The author ventures to express a hope that he has successfully surmounted the difficulties of his undertaking. And if it be objected to the Pickwick Papers, that they are a mere series of adventures, in which the scenes are ever changing, and the characters come and go like the men and women we encounter in the real world, he can only content himself with the reflection, that they claim to be nothing else, and that the same objection has been made to the works of some of the greatest novelists in the English language. (41)

Rather than defend the practice of serialization, Dickens joins with critics who suspect it to be inimical to art, even though he continued to publish novels in parts for the rest of his life. But he contends that his greater intentions and his skill allow him to transcend the limitations of his publishing mode to such an extent that he is more properly regarded as the heir of the "greatest novelists" than as a journalist or periodical sketch artist.

Dickens's attempt to align himself with his predecessors obscures the actual context of the concern over unity: if earlier novelists had been accused of writing wandering, desultory stories, it was not because they were publishing them in cheap parts for a mass audience in a way that blurred the distinction between artistry and trade. Dickens found it necessary not only to criticize the mode of production in which he engaged, but to separate himself even more from the implication of writing for hire in a mass market by revising and glossing over the story of his original relationship with Chapman and Hall. We have seen already that Dickens retrospectively positioned himself as the chief creator of the book ("My views being deferred to, I thought of Mr. Pickwick, and wrote the first number"), but it is also worth noting that the later Prefaces identify the ultimate "origin of these Pickwick Papers" as the moment when Charles Dickens became a writer:

> When I opened my door in Furnival's Inn to the managing partner who represented the firm [of Chapman and Hall], I recognized in him the person from whose hands I had bought, two or three years previously, and whom I had never seen before or since, my first copy of the Magazine in which my first effusion—dropped stealthily one evening at twilight, with fear and trembling, into a dark letter-box, in a dark office, up a dark court in Fleet Street—appeared in all the glory of print; on which occasion, by-

the-bye,—how well I recollect it!—I walked down to Westminster Hall, and turned into it for half-an-hour, because my eyes were so dimmed with joy and pride, that they could not bear the street, and were not fit to be seen there. I told my visitor of the coincidence, which we both hailed as a good omen; and so fell to business. (44)

Charged with mystical significance, Dickens's story invests his transactions with his employers with supernatural portent, and it effectively represents the origin of *Pickwick* as a mythic narrative of the creation of Dickens the author: Fleet Street is described as a gloomy underworld into which the writer anxiously descends only to reemerge, transfigured, into joyous and blinding light. It is precisely at moments like this one, where we might most certainly expect to find references to the nature of Dickens's business dealings or actual labor, that he becomes most insistently personal. "The following pages have been written from time to time, almost as the periodical occasion arose," Dickens explains in the first Preface to *Pickwick*, but if we expect him to continue by elaborating on the difficulty of reaching his monthly quotas under grueling deadline pressure, we will be disappointed by his next sentence: "Having been written for the most part in the society of a very dear young friend [Mary Hogarth] who is now no more, they are connected in the author's mind at once with the happiest period of his life, and with its saddest and most severe affliction" (41-42).

I want to suggest that Dickens's increasingly personal depiction of himself, his self-revelation as a sympathetic, sensitive human being, helped him to manage the critical concerns raised by the serial mode of production. If "writing by scraps against time" seemed to reviewers to indicate the practice of a hack trade, Dickens could assure them that he shared their concerns about serialization, and that his intentions, at any rate, were artistic rather than pecuniary. More importantly, by positioning himself as a creative artist at the very center of the productive process, he worked to convince his readers that the fragmentary product they received had originated in the unified consciousness of a sympathetic individual. Whether speaking of his aesthetic intentions, personal confidences, private emotions, or the genesis of his work, Dickens proposed an image of himself as the greater unity of his text. And though this was not sufficient to convince Dickens's less obliging critics that his work was free from the taint of hack writing, there is some proof of his success that even the Fraserians who attributed to him the habits of a greedy reporter felt it necessary to preface their criticism by stating "We wish him well." There is perhaps even greater proof in Dickens's boast in 1847 that his popular success had become sufficient to overrule the initial objections to the format of *Pickwick*: "My friends told me it was a low, cheap form of publication, by which I should ruin all my rising hopes; and how right my friends turned out to be, everybody now knows" (45). If serialization had helped consolidate the intimate relationship between early Victorian novelists and their readers, as Tillotson and Feltes have asserted, we should also recognize that at the same time, critical reactions *against* serialization prompted writers like Dickens to press further the notion of their explicitly personal presence behind their textual products, even as they disavowed the form in which they continued to publish.

The problem of *Pickwick*'s unity has persisted through twentieth-century criticism, becoming, in fact, even more prominent over the last five decades. Although today's critics no longer invoke unity, as Victorians did, as code for a form of publication that distinguished itself from cheap serialization and "hack trade" journalism, it has remained central to the evaluation of *Pickwick*'s artistic merit. Critics who have hoped to rescue this novel from the relative disfavor into which it has fallen have—almost without exception—attempted to show in one way or another that it really is what Dickens called "a tolerably harmonious whole," and that, indeed, almost every word in it can be shown to derive from some fundamental structuring principle. The question of unity always asks, what is the definitive, singular, central meaning of this text? And the most frequent answer, of which Dickens would doubtless have approved, is that the meaning lies in the author's sensibility. J. Hillis Miller, despite his formalist conviction that Dickens's consciousness is "beyond recovery," has exemplified this evaluation of *Pickwick*:

> The novel is a unity because it is the verbal expression of Dickens' mood, or sensibility, or spiritual state, at the time he wrote the novel, and we must say that this sensibility, the unique expression of a certain stage in the development of Dickens' creative genius, is not to be identified with the subjective experience of any character or characters. The consciousness of Dickens, ironically amused and detached, intervenes everywhere between the reader and the consciousness of the characters, and is the true spiritual and tonal unity of *Pickwick Papers*. (2)

A slightly more original approach to discussing the unity of *Pickwick* has more recently been proposed by Amy Sadrin, who argues that we should find in the novel's very fragmentation an expression of the inner stability of the creative mind behind it: "I would [. . .] argue that fragmentation suited [Dickens] and that serialization was more than merely circumstantial, that it corresponded to some deeper urge in him" (22-23). Sadrin excuses the novel's lack of unity, but only because it points to a consistent thematization of mutability and vicissitude across the body of Dickens's work, and because this in turn may be explained by reference to his personal life.

The quest for unity in *Pickwick* and the repeated critical performances of its discovery in Dickens himself have distracted attention from the text's clash of multiple meanings. This is not to say that its meanings are variable and irreducibly complex and elusively infinite; such endless plenitude and free play is simply the image of unity reflected in a fun-house mirror. *Pickwick*'s meanings, gaps, fissures, ironies, and inconsistencies are not random, but are determined by corresponding anxieties and ambiguities in the tumultuous print culture for which, in which, and by which it was produced. The problem is that this history of *production* and of all the factors that influenced it—serialization, aesthetic suspicions, copyright confrontations, all of which were themselves driven by the great engine of emerging mass-market conditions—has been eclipsed by a story of the book's *creation*. Dickens supplied his readers with the sacred image of the text's creation—"I thought of Mr. Pickwick, and wrote the first number"—and backed it up with a tale of his birth as a writer that is no less mystified; criticism has been complacent in letting the matter rest there, leaving Dickens as the alpha and omega of the text. In this chapter I have tried to tell another, more complicated story about *Pickwick*, which is in part the story of why Dickens framed it in this influential way. *Pickwick* is a loose, baggy monster of a novel, and it is precisely because of its rough form and its monstrous birth that it remains, for the study of authorship as well for the study of literature more broadly, a document of paramount historical importance.

* * *

In focusing on the transition between Scott and the personalized relationship of novelist and audience that Dickens exemplified, this chapter reverses the priorities usually accorded to treatments of Dickens's authorship. In the wake of theorists like Althusser and Foucault, studies of the ideological structures of the novel have focused on the ways in which novels disseminate ideology, typically by interpellating readers as subjects of a particular social structure. In the case of authorship specifically, this has meant analyzing the ideological effects that certain constructions of authorship might have had upon contemporary readers. The most familiar example is Mary Poovey's influential reading of *David Copperfield*, which argues that with this semi-autobiographical portrayal of a professional novelist, Dickens "translated the deep structural relations" of Victorian culture "into a psychological narrative of individual development, which both provided individual readers with an imaginative image of what identity was and created a subject position that reproduced this kind of identity in the individual reader" (89). As profitable as this kind of study undoubtedly is, by itself it tells only half of the story. That is, it suggests how constructions of the novelist interpellate readers as subjects, but not how readers collectively give rise to the subject position of the novelist, not how writers as individuals are bound by material and ideological systems that have always/already hailed them, not, in short, how *the public has interpellated the author*.

The mysterious critical blindspot that allows for everyone but novelists themselves to be coerced by hegemonic ideological formations has been, indirectly, one of this chapter's concerns; to ignore this second dimension of reciprocal influence is to risk recapitulating the mystifying, Romantic assumption that authors "create" their audiences. It is no more accurate to

claim without qualification that Dickens conjured up some new kind of
subjectivity in his readers than it is to cling to the notion—patently untrue
but still tenaciously held—that with the publication of *Pickwick* Dickens
"created" the mass market. I have asked, instead, how the mass market
created "Dickens."[25] Even before ideologies of authorship insinuate forms
of subjectivity that bolster hegemonic interests in a given culture, the same
interests will already have contributed to the formation of those ideologies;
thus Roland Barthes has reminded us that bourgeois social formations
have an interest in presenting the novelist as "a kind of intrinsically different being which society puts in the window so as to use to the best advantage the artificial singularity which it has granted him" (*Mythologies* 30).
To those familiar with Dickens's biography, Barthes's metaphor cannot fail
to recall a moment of the novelist's childhood, when, at the age of twelve,
he was literally placed in the window of the blacking warehouse where he
was employed as an advertisement of the diligence and industry within.[26]
The coincidence is enough to remind us that Dickens, whether as a miserable boy pasting text on jars of Warren's Blacking or as a young man producing text for a sensationally successful new novel, was in both cases
subject to the material and ideological constraints of working in an industrial society. Writers and factory boys may occupy very different social
positions, but both are subject positions nonetheless, and both have been
prepared for their occupants before they sit down to work before the
sometimes fearsome public gaze. Yet the mercurial *Pickwick*—at once a
palimpsest of early Victorian images of authorship and a map of the route
by which the paradigm of sympathetic friendship came to predominate—
remains as a testament to Dickens's imaginative agency and to his success
in adapting the available rhetoric of literary production to the emerging
world of the Victorian novelist.

CHAPTER THREE

Sympathy's Last Gasp:
The Professional Body and the Disease of Sensationalism

Count Isidor Ottavio Baldassare Fosco, one of the supreme villains of Victorian fiction, suffers a decidedly humiliating punishment. The conclusion of Wilkie Collins's *The Woman in White* (1859-60) finds Fosco's gigantic corpse stretched out naked behind the window of the Paris Morgue, "unowned, unknown; exposed to the flippant curiosity of a French mob!" (643). Fosco's ultimate anonymity is as crucial to this ignominy as his public exposure, since his great talent had been the invention of a series of flamboyant and forceful identities. According to the widowed Madame Fosco, her husband had been remarkably steadfast ("His life was one long assertion of the rights of the aristocracy" [644]), but the reader knows that his title is as much a disguise as the French artisan's costume that hangs over his body in the Morgue. Neither artisan nor aristocrat, the mercurial Fosco can be either, or anything in between. A former revolutionary and government spy, Fosco is also a cultured man of fashion, an aficionado of every art, a talented physician, and an accomplished chemist. This architect of *The Woman in White*'s criminal plot is also, tellingly, a former novelist, having written "preposterous romances on the French model for a second-rate Italian newspaper" (278). Fosco's mutability within rigid hierarchies of rank and position illustrates the ambiguous status of mid-Victorian popular novelists, and his punishment—in its paradoxical combination of the fears of total exposure and complete anonymity—perfectly crystallizes those novelists' anxieties during the moment of "sensationalism."

The late 1850s and 60s saw a dramatic clash between popular novelists and relatively unpopular periodical critics, a conflict which would produce a new construction of authorship and even reconfigure the Victorian understanding of "culture." This moment of sensationalism was, above all, a moment of discrimination, of *distinction*, a juncture during which the fantasy of a utopian, universal community of readers was ripped asunder. And the most intolerably monstrous power for a writer to wield at this time became Fosco's chameleon-like ability to please everyone, to transgress boundaries of class and taste as though they did not exist. As the ideal of sympathetic friendship weakened, even the most established novelists were scrutinized for signs of border transgression. Dickens himself experienced a downturn in his critical reputation at this time, which was attributed by an American critic to his boisterous violations of literary propriety: Dickens, this critic explained, so "surcharges his characters with vitality [. . . that] as they burst into the more decorous society delineated by other English novelists, there is a cry raised for the critical police" (qtd. in Ford 146). The new critical constabulary that answered this call took on the responsibility of sorting the proper novelists from the cultural gatecrashers, and they vigorously set about this task by changing the function of criticism itself. Taking it upon themselves to define and protect the precincts of legitimate culture, these critics asserted the public's inability to do so, with the consequence that public enthusiasm and literary merit began to part ways.

No novelist suffered the effects of this new critical scrutiny as deeply as Wilkie Collins. Having previously enjoyed nearly unanimous critical acclaim as a rising star among novelists—and having climbed in his early career to the conventional apex of praise, comparison with Shakespeare— Collins' reputation among critics tumbled rapidly in the early 1860s. As late as 1858 he had been celebrated as "a man of commanding genius, and one destined to occupy a principal place in the republic of letters" (Jeaffreson 345), but the very moment of his greatest popular success, the unparalleled circulation of *The Woman in White*, proved to be the turning point in his favor among critics, whose subsequent reviews seldom used the word "genius" (commanding or otherwise) ever again. In what was then an unusually audacious move, many critics challenged popular sentiment to savage one of the public's favorites, questioning the extent to which Collins had ever merited recognition among the great novelists. "When we have said all we can for him," a reviewer in *Dublin University Magazine* concluded, "we have said nothing that would entitle him to a higher place among English novelists, than the compiler of an average school-history would enjoy among English historians" (qtd. in Page 66). *The Saturday Review* had trivialized the popular success of *The Woman in White* even more definitively, contending that Collins's book had little to do with art: "Mr. Wilkie Collins is an admirable story-teller, though he is not a great novelist [. . .]. The fascination which he exercises over the mind of his reader consists in this—that he is [. . .] an ingenious constructor, but construction is not high art" (qtd. in Page 66). Criticisms of the novel seemed unsatisfied with merely confronting the novel itself; they often proceeded to level *ad hominem* attacks at Collins, retrospectively trivializing his entire career. Collins himself was puzzled by the wide gap in opinion between the public's embrace of the novel and the vehement objections of critics:

"Either the public is right and the press is wrong, or the press is right and the public is wrong. Time will tell. If the public turns out to be right, I shall never trust the press again" (qtd. in Lonoff 75). What modern readers perceive as a virtual inevitability—*of course* the critical elite disagrees with the mass readership—Collins disarmingly sees as a temporary anomaly, as somebody's mistake.

Collins's dilemma heralds the increasing bifurcation in Victorian culture between popular and authentically artistic literatures, and may be seen as symptomatic of the late nineteenth-century breakdown in the classical bourgeois ideology of the public sphere.[1] But rather than pursuing the significance of Collins's career in light of such a broad historical movement, this chapter will focus more narrowly on the market conditions under which the critical emphasis on distinction first arose, the terms in which it was initially perceived, and its profound effect on Victorian authorship. The new and forceful challenge to popularity as an aesthetic criterion was a blow to the ideal of a collective sensibility on which the cultural capital of novelists had depended, and we can trace in contemporary essays, reviews, and novels a struggle over the meanings and symbols of novel production. Old metaphors of sympathy and friendship, for example, began to be displaced by tropes of professionalism and by a rhetoric of disease that turned on its head the optimistic notion of universal sympathy.

"Sensationalism" was unquestionably the most significant new term in the literary discourse of the early 1860s, as important for the print industry as a whole as it was decisive in Collins's career. As a tool for distinguishing forms of types of novels, classes of readers, and categories of novelists, the charge of sensationalism was the *cordon sanitaire* of the critical police. Anthony Trollope, a much shrewder observer of this new cultural division than Collins but no more comfortable with it, remarked that sensationalism had indeed emerged as the chief critical criterion of his period:

> Among English novels of the present day, and among English novelists, a great division is made. There are sensational novels and anti-sensational, sensational novelists and anti-sensational, sensational readers and anti-sensational. The novelists who are considered to be anti-sensational are generally called realistic. I am realistic. My friend Wilkie Collins is generally supposed to be sensational. (226-27)

The great partition of novelists into these two categories, as Trollope indicates, implies a more general and fundamental schism in Victorian perceptions of print culture, suggesting not only different modes of literary production, but also of circulation and of aesthetics, whereby the great artistic doctrines of realism are easily reduced to anti-sensationalism. This deceptively simple split provided the foundation for Victorian thought about the fragmentation of the literary marketplace, the beginnings of its balkanization into the niche-driven industry we recognize today.

ROMANCING KING PUBLIC

Collins deserves his reputation as painstakingly attentive to the desires of
his readers; a novelist who so obligingly courted an audience he called
"King Public" could hardly fail to draw attention in this regard. Yet it
would be a mistake to understand his opinions as purely self-aggrandizing
or commercial, even though such motivations doubtless played some role.
Rather, Collins's unflagging interest in his popular reception indicates his
adherence to a broader ideology of authorship that held the reading public
to be centrally important to the aims and conditions of writing novels. The
comprehensiveness and depth of Collins's vision becomes more clear in his
description of the readers he served:

> They represent all nations and all ranks. Whether they praise or whether
> they blame, their opinions are equally worth having. They not only under-
> stand us, they help us. Many a good work of fiction has profited by their
> letters when they write to the author. Over and over again he has been in-
> debted to their stores of knowledge, and to their quick sympathies, for
> information of serious importance to his work which he could not other-
> wise have obtained [. . .]. In one last word, our intelligent readers are our
> truest and best friends, when we are worthy of them. Their influence has
> raised fiction to the great place that it occupies in the front of Literature.
> (qtd. in Lonoff 66)

In all of its most salient features, this statement expresses the same convic-
tions that had flourished for decades under the sway of Industrial Romanticism. In gratefully imagining the bond between novelists and a universal
public as, above all, one of friendship enabled by "quick sympathies,"
Collins rehearses the same terms Dickens had pioneered with *The Pickwick Papers*. And he continued to express the same sentiments throughout
his career: in the brief 1861 preface to *The Woman in White*, for example,
Collins ingratiatingly mentions his readers, their "kind reception," and his
"public approval" no less than ten times, and he happily concludes that the
novel's characters "have made friends for me wherever they have made
themselves known." But even though Collins had taken up the torch of Industrial Romanticism, the public that was so crucial to this conception of
authorship had changed considerably and was in the process of changing
even more quickly; with the new market came a different constellation of
literary values, along with an understanding of novelists' work that fundamentally challenged Collins's complacency.

While the success of *The Pickwick Papers* marked a watershed in the relations of production and distribution for the middle-class novels we now
consider canonical, it also proved to be a turning point in the more historically obscure world of the lower-class press. The Whig reform of the Stamp
Act in 1836 came as a devastating blow to cheaper, unlicensed newspapers,
but small publishers saw in the prodigious sales of Dickens's serial novel an
opportunity to reenter the market through the sale of serialized fiction. The

two men who would become the most prominent purveyors of cheap print to the mid-Victorian public both found their greatest early successes in direct imitations of Dickens's work: G. W. M. Reynolds, who would become the most widely read novelist in Victorian England, began his career with the serialized *Pickwick Abroad*, while *The Penny Pickwick* (written by "Bos") became the first triumph of the publisher Edward Lloyd. The career of the latter nicely demonstrates the changing complexion of the print industry over the next decades.[2] The appeal of Lloyd's *Penny Pickwick* is announced by its title, and by the end of its serial run Lloyd boasted that his sales had outstripped Dickens's shilling numbers by twenty-five percent. Following this achievement, in 1840 Lloyd launched his *Lloyd's Penny Sunday Times and People's Police Gazette*, which was largely a vehicle for inexpensive serialized romances. This paper was soon supplanted in 1843 by the relatively inexpensive *Lloyd's Weekly Newspaper*, which, buoyed early on by Lloyd's continuing sale of cheap novels, lived well into the twentieth century. But it is the *Weekly Newspaper*'s rate of growth, rather than its longevity, that best indicates the change in the reading public. Beginning with a circulation of 21,000 copies in 1843, its audience had more than doubled by the end of the decade, and had nearly reached the level of 100,000 by 1855. By 1863, the circulation figures had reached 350,000, an increase of about 265 percent in just eight years.[3] Aggressively marketing his products at low costs with a narrow profit margin, Lloyd encountered an exponentially growing demand for print among the lower classes, and he was only one of many publishers to enjoy the staggering new sales.

The combined repeals of the Stamp Act in 1855 and the Paper Duty in 1861 introduced the era of most explosive growth in the periodicals industry, particularly among cheap, widely-circulating publications (whose slim profit margins had been most threatened by these taxes), so that during these years the previously established circulation records "fell right and left." As Richard Altick has summarized, "the greatest increase in periodical-buying occurred among the lower-middle class and the working class. In the same year that the *London Journal* sold close to a half million copies an issue, *Punch*, addressed to an upper- and middle-class audience, circulated 40,000 and the *Athenaeum* only 7,200" (358). Meanwhile the old, ponderous, intellectual quarterly reviews—such as the *Edinburgh* and the *Quarterly*—had been left essentially untouched by the new market, and their circulation figures stagnated around the same level at which they had stood for fifty years. Other serious and learned journals were in a similarly unenviable position; they were not only vastly outnumbered by the burgeoning numbers of family miscellanies and cheap weekly and daily newspapers—about 170 new periodical titles were introduced during the 1860s alone (Heyck 201)—but were also individually outsold by cheaper publications by multiples between ten and fifty. The higher-priced, more exclusive periodicals were faced with the threat of failing to compete with the proliferation of cheaper products that were not only winning the support of new lower middle- and working-class buyers, but—especially through the fiction that was the mainstay of the penny press—threatened to encroach upon the readerships of more traditionally middle-class publications. To the writers and publishers of the bourgeois press, the developments in the market generally came to represent an alarming—even revolutionary—threat.

Collins's initial reaction to the new readership, characterized by an almost anthropological curiosity, was typical of middle-class responses to lower-class print culture. He set out to sketch for the readers of *Household Words* his investigations into the world of "The Unknown Public" (1858), the consumers of cheap print whose number he reckons at "three millions" (251). His aim in this essay is to exhibit the curious interests of "the lost literary tribes," the readers of "penny-novel-journals," basing his observations on a few sample issues that he examines as alien artifacts. Given Collins's patronizing assumption that a group of millions can be mysteriously "unknown," it comes as little surprise that his chief inference from the texts he peruses is that their readers are relatively ignorant. More interestingly, Collins dwells at length upon the similarities between the stories, which lead him to suspect that the public seeks "quantity rather than quality" (253), and that it perceives these texts as fundamentally interchangeable. He recreates an interview with a shopkeeper, who suggests that this is just the way in which the "pennyworths" of fiction are sold. "Some likes one, some likes another," Collins has the bookseller explain. "Sometimes I sells more of one, and sometimes I sells more of another. Take 'em all the year round, and there ain't a pin, as I knows of, to choose between 'em. There's just about as much in one as there is in another. All good pennorths" (254). Collins thus explores not only an unknown public, but also a repressed—and vaguely unnerving—conception of literary value, one founded on cost rather than merit, predictable conventionality rather than originality, and volume rather than genius.

Translating these hypotheses about the penny-journals' circulation into conclusions about their production, Collins imagines these texts as representative of a kind of unauthored discourse, a practice of writing for which the notion of a distinct, individualized writer is neither necessary nor relevant: "The first thing that struck me, after reading the separate weekly portions of all five [specimens], was their extraordinary sameness. Each portion purported to be written (and no doubt was written) by a different author, and yet all five might have been produced by the same pen" (260). Collins's equation of an anonymous audience for fiction with anonymous authorship underscores his sense of difference from this mode of production; the segment of print culture in which he worked was largely driven by the efforts of novelists to establish their reputations, with the effect that their names functioned as brands that encouraged consumer recognition and repeat sales (it was this strategy, after all, that suggested marketing *Household Words* itself as Charles Dickens's periodical, and the official medium for his fiction). But in spite of Collins's recognition of the very different principles operating in the cheaper market, he retains faith in the inevitability of new readers coming to appreciate novels in the same terms as the established middle-class press, and of their ultimately beneficial effect on the work of writing:

> the future of English fiction may rest with this Unknown Public, which is now waiting to be taught the difference between a good book and a bad [. . .]. The largest audience for periodical literature, in this age of periodicals, must obey the universal law of progress, and must, sooner or later, learn to discriminate. When that period comes, the readers who rank by the millions will be the readers who give the widest reputations, who return the richest rewards, and who will therefore command the service of the best writers of their time. A great, unparalleled prospect awaits, perhaps, the coming generation of English novelists. To the penny journals of the present time belongs the credit of having discovered a new public. When that public shall find out its need of a great writer, the great writer will have such an audience as has never yet been known. (264)

Though Collins understands that the impact of these new millions will be immense, he believes that they will conform to the existing ideological framework of print culture: the new industry would be much like the old, only larger. Existing ideologies of authorship, he believes, would also still obtain, so that novelists' "reputations" and "rewards" would alike derive from popularity, just as they had since the 1840s.

Collins's predictions about the impact of new publishing practices were to be tested almost immediately, as the spheres of literary production converged much sooner than he had anticipated. In fact, the known public and the unknown already overlapped considerably, and in practice, figures from both worlds routinely rubbed shoulders; Douglas Jerrold, to name one of many examples, was the editor of *Lloyd's Weekly Newspaper* and a friend of Dickens, Thackeray, and Collins, among other luminaries of middle-class publishing. And little time passed before the impact of the cheap periodical trade became plain in Collins's own novels. *The Woman in White*, his first novel after publishing "The Unknown Public," is a case in point. Not only is the frequent presence in the story of the periodical industry a testament to its contemporary ubiquity—Anne Catherick learns of Laura Fairlie's impending marriage from a newspaper, Count Fosco reveals that he had written romances for a cheap newspaper in Italy, Walter Hartright gives up his practice as a painting instructor to work for an illustrated newspaper, and so forth—but the very structure of the novel is indebted to the typical themes of mass-market publishing. What Collins considered most original about his narrative was his use of a revolving cast of narrators to present the tale as a series of eyewitness testimonies, an idea that was much less innovative in the penny press, for which reportage of crimes and trials, both fictional and factual, had long been a prime selling-point.[4] While it is unlikely that Collins entertained any ambitions about becoming the "great writer" for the millions whose arrival he prophesied, there can be little doubt that he had learned important lessons about emerging trends of popular taste from the success of the cheap press.

Collins had not predicted, however, that other reactions to the developments in the industry would ultimately thwart his expectations of the unknown public's smooth assimilation into existing relations of production, leaving familiar practices and ideologies essentially intact. But hostility to the rapid growth of the cheap press, couched in terms of the defense of culture, led to a concerted effort to redefine novelists' relationships with their readers, to cast aside the notions of popularity which Dickens and his early Victorian peers had established and which Collins continued to maintain. The theoretically universalizing impulse of Industrial Romanticism, which had held that a novelist could perform greater social services by reaching an ever expanding audience, could not stretch to accommodate new readers who were, in the minds of many bourgeois critics, as much qualitatively different from older audiences as they were quantitatively so. Rather than integrating seamlessly with the traditional public, the explosive growth of the cheap market opened an ideological rupture that made the demands of culture and those of the public incompatible. The backlash against popularity produced a hierarchy of novelist classes, a taxonomy that had less to do with the social strata into which writers were born than with the extent to which they prioritized the tastes of a broad public or incorporated themes and discursive forms associated with mass-market production. Collins could not have guessed that, as a consequence of this cultural revisionism, he would be portrayed in much the same way he had patronizingly described the work of the faceless penny-journal writers. Yet he too would be lumped together with other writers whose books would be either trivialized as adequately workmanlike or stridently condemned as a danger to literary culture and even to society more broadly: "A succession of sickly but exciting scenes is kept up—theft, seduction, violence, adultery, and murder, stalk through their pages as if they were the most common-place and agreeable things in the world. Contact with such literature is inevitable corruption" (qtd. in Hoggart 36). Thus wrote J. Hepworth Dixon in 1847, attacking not Collins or Mary Elizabeth Braddon, but, as part of his critique of "Literature of the Lower Orders," one of Edward Lloyd's penny novels. Yet the terms are precisely those in which Collins and other bestselling novelists were castigated throughout the 1860s. Under the social pressures of the shifting market, cultural boundaries were redrawn in such a way that even middle-class novelists writing for a predominantly middle-class readership could be considered part of a new, vastly expanded lower order. And as critics sounded alarms over the threats posed by the miscegenation of classed forms of literary production, they gave a name to their fears: "sensationalism."

THE MAKING OF AN OUTCAST GENRE

It is through the gradual consolidation of the category of sensationalism that we can most clearly perceive the pivotal crisis of mid-Victorian literary production, though the vagueness of the category has made it difficult to pin down either its precise implications or its taxonomic limits. Literary historians have been more inclined to enumerate the traits of the genre than to explain the origins of the term itself, and there have been few attempts to explain why the moment of sensationalism occurred when it did.[5] It is possible, however, to account for sensationalism's emergence with great historical specificity if we understand it as a highly mediated reaction against the same changing conditions in print culture that had sparked Collins's (qualified) optimism. The characteristics we have come to associate with sensation—from its topical criminal content to its supposedly visceral effect on its readers—were originally bound up with anxieties about the influence of a growing readership. Sensationalism thus constituted a powerful attack on the fundamentally consensualist premises of Industrial-Romantic authorship. This section will offer a relatively local explanation of sensationalism's importance by focusing on the people responsible for creating the genre, Victorian reviewers.[6]

The sudden critical construction of the category of sensation novels corresponds precisely with a movement to transform the function of periodical criticism in the late 1850s and early 1860s,[7] and it is in the context of this transition that the advent of the genre must be analyzed. From the burgeoning numbers of periodical essayists and reviewers, an influential group of writers emerged to claim a fundamentally new and more important role for literary criticism. Having been for years the enforcers of public taste, certain critics now claimed the mission of shaping and regulating taste from a position they imagined to be partly outside of—and superior to—public opinion.[8] In the same radical move, these critics withdrew from their previous role as consumer advocates (who either promoted or puffed books that readers were likely to appreciate or dismissed them from public notice) to become outspoken opponents of the literary market itself. To justify their new claims to be guardians of culture, they endorsed the notion that culture required guarding, that without their stewardship the public would inevitably err. The logic of this argument suggested that the most popular literary forms were in fact the most pernicious; novels, consequently, had to be the object of particular critical vigilance. As G. H. Lewes put it, "the vast increase in novels, mostly worthless, is a serious danger to public culture, a danger which becomes more and more imminent, and which can only be arrested by an energetic resolution on behalf of the critics to do their duty with conscientious rigor" (qtd. in Taylor 21). As the critical police set out, as Lewes puts it, to "arrest" the influence of novels by sorting the good from the vast bulk of "worthless," they likewise created divisions between novelists, appreciating their favorites in Romantic terms and condemning the rest as interchangeable cogs in the industrial marketplace. These offenders were lumped together—treated as generic—and genres were accordingly invented to contain them. As a genre, sensationalism thus appeared concomitantly with the new periodical criticism, and it was destined from its inception to be the threat against which critics defined their cultural aspirations.

The appearance of sensationalism as an important critical term occasioned more than a little confusion, but its usefulness was not substantially hampered by its ambiguity, and its use among reviewers quickly became commonplace. Braddon protested that the label was simply "an orthodox stone for flinging at any heretic author" (qtd. in W. Hughes 165), and the vagaries of critical practice did little to contradict her. "Two or three years ago," writes an *Edinburgh Review* critic in 1864, "nobody would have known what was meant by a Sensation Novel; yet now the term has already passed through the stage of jocular use [. . .] and has been adopted as the regular commercial name for a particular product of industry for which there is just now a brisk demand" (qtd. in W. Hughes 167). Attempts to characterize the genre in any more detail inevitably contradicted themselves, each other, or the evidence of literary history. Critics who defined the genre around its typical thematic elements were vulnerable to the counter-argument that no such elements were new with the sensation novel. Sheridan LeFanu, for instance, protested against the "promiscuous application of the term 'sensation'" by pointing out that these novelists were not writing about anything that had not already appeared in the Waverley Novels: "No one, it is assumed, would describe Sir Walter Scott's romances as 'sensation novels': yet, in that marvelous series there is not a single tale in which death, crime, and, in some form, mystery, have not a place" (qtd. in Brantlinger 8-9). Critics who focused on the ostensibly affective qualities of sensation also raised the question of how distinctively new these techniques were. *The Dublin University Magazine*, though it excoriated contemporary sensation novels, admitted that its technique of exciting suspense and horror could be traced back through Shakespeare to Sophocles or Apuleius's *Golden Ass*; even "our great old Chaucer," the critic concludes, "thought little of making his readers' nerves tingle now and then, and to make their flesh creep."[9] By themselves, such taxonomic principles seemed insufficient even to the Victorians. The category of sensation became useful only to the extent that it blurred together the thematic and affective qualities of sensation with a meaning that derived from its circulation. It was necessary, that is, only insofar as it offered a way of thinking about the more constant definition of the "sensation novel" suggested above by the *Edinburgh Review*: "a particular product of industry for which there is just now a brisk demand."

In practice, the normative definitions of "sensation" were never entirely distinct from definitions that had less to do with the content of the novels than with their popular reception: as *Fraser's* put it, "a novel comes out which 'makes a sensation,' and 'has a run'; that is to say, it goes through a number of editions—large and small—and serves as a fertile topic of conversation for the whole novel-reading population of Great Britain and Ireland for weeks at a time" (qtd. in Cvetkovich 14). And these novels were nothing if not sensational in this sense. Complaining of the "torrent of sensationalism by which we are just now inundated," the *Westminster Review* remarked in 1865 that novels had become more widely read than "poetry, or history, or science," and that "the Sensational" had in the same respect become "first of all novels" ("Belles Lettres" [1865] 267, 266). The widespread popularity of sensation novels became, tautologically, the most sensational thing about them. Margaret Oliphant was neither the first nor by any means the last critic to suggest that sensational reception overshadowed the sensational content of these novels when, writing of Braddon, she pointed out that the writer "never invented any circumstance so extraordinary as this public faith and loyal adherence she seems to have won" (qtd. in W. Hughes 67). Seen in this light, popularity itself, as it was expressed in sales and circulation, becomes the mystery that the critics scrutinized, the shocking circumstance it became their duty to explore, the clue they investigated to unmask a greater danger. And they took to deducing the signs of mass-market consumption with all the imaginative interpretation and ratiocinative zest of the amateur detectives they decried. The *Quarterly*, for instance, offered a charmingly Holmesian analysis of the sales of sensation fiction: "These books would certainly not be written if they did not sell; and they would not sell if they were not read; ergo, they must have readers, and numerous readers too" (Mansel 486).

The widespread sales of sensation novels ultimately became the chief anxiety of the critical police, the central cultural threat from which all the muddled objections to style or content derived their force. In their darker moments, such critics imagined themselves to be incapable of stemming the vast tide of sensationalism as it appeared to overwhelm the greater achievements of Victorian literary culture: "Sensationalism must be left to be dealt with by time, and the improvement of the public taste. But it is worth stopping to note, amidst all the boasted improvement of the nineteenth century, that whilst Miss Braddon's and Mr. Wilkie Collins' productions sell by the thousands of copies, 'Romola' with difficulty reaches a second edition" ("Belles Lettres" [1866] 127). Yet critical complaints were often even less optimistic about the improvement of "public taste", and instead diagnosed the perversion of this *taste* into sickly *cravings* or an unwholesome *appetite*. A well-known diatribe in the *Quarterly* by Henry Mansel, for example, saw in the huge sales of sensation fiction symptoms of an emerging disease, "indications of a wide-spread corruption, of which they are in part both the effect and the cause; called into existence to supply the cravings of a diseased appetite, and contributing themselves to foster the disease, and to stimulate the want of which they supply" (482-83). The *Westminster* concurred, pointing out that although sensationalism had broken out in the past, the 1860s were witnessing the effects of a much more virulent strain: "Sensation Mania in Literature burst out only in times of mental poverty, and afflict[ed] only the most poverty-stricken minds. From an epidemic, however, it has lately changed into an endemic. Its virus is spreading in all directions, from the penny journal to the shilling magazine, and from the shilling magazine to the thirty shillings volume" ("Belles Lettres" [1866] 126).

The recurring rhetoric of disease—used alternately to describe the unhealthy consumption of these novels and their seemingly contagious diffusion across the literary marketplace—provided hostile critics with their principal metaphor for the popularity of sensation fiction.[10] Still, the trope of disease was only one element of a broader rhetorical strategy to discredit sensation fiction as a form dedicated to an unhealthy or dangerous set of bodily responses, a kind of contaminating and contagious effect on readers that emerged as the dark counterpart to the universal dissemination of sympathy. Depending on the traditional hierarchy of mind and body, the distinction between aesthetic taste and physical "cravings" acquired a particularly important function during the nineteenth century as a way to police symbolically the leveling influences of mass culture (as indeed it continues to operate today). The critics' extensive use of bodily metaphors for reading sensation fiction should thus be understood not only as a response to the novels they reviewed, but also as a culturally charged objection to the enormous circulation of these novels. In fact, the latter motivation explains why the ostensibly affective qualities of sensation novels are more consistently developed in reviews of sensationalism than they are in any of the novels themselves. The critical police worked significantly harder than any novelist to portray an embodied reader.

Even though the conventional metaphors employed to challenge sensationalism can be explained by reference to the novels' sales, the precise timing of this critical intervention—the formulation of an outcast genre—cannot be adequately explained in the same terms. Neither thematic nor formal characteristics could sufficiently define the contours of this ostensibly new type of novel, and the more necessary prerequisite of popular consumption presents the same difficulty: sensational sales had also existed before sensation novels.[11] What was more importantly distinct about the moment of sensationalism in Victorian print culture was the struggle to reshape the function of literary criticism. The central project of the emerging criticism was to chart the boundaries of legitimate culture and preserve them from the impulses of the reading masses; the "business" of criticism became, as Matthew Arnold famously announced, "simply to know the best that is known and thought in the world" (270), which necessarily involved regulating the anarchic tendencies of the public, its inability to differentiate. This radical departure from the traditional claims of reviewers was spurred on not simply by anxieties about the growing size of the public, but also by the sense that it had changed in *kind*. In the context of the periodical industry, the proliferation of new, cheap texts—many of which had distinctly lower middle- or working-class pedigrees—suggested the potential demise of the more exclusive and highly priced journals. Moreover, the cheaper periodicals seemed to appeal equally to readers who might have afforded more. The problem, in sum, was the threat of a mass audience with undifferentiated tastes, tastes which did not include relatively esoteric opinion. The bogey of cultural leveling fueled and legitimated the changing priorities of reviewers associated with what Christopher Kent has called the "higher journalism."[12] The most noticeable development during these years was the sharp decline in journalistic anonymity. The use of the editorial "we"—which had previously encompassed not only a journal's writers, but to some extent its readers as well—began to give way to signed reviews by recognizable authorities.[13] This change is symptomatic of a shift in these critics' cultural role from public spokesmen to a more specialized caste whose authority would derive from professional training and superior judgment. Emerging largely from the reforming universities,[14] the rising generation of critics sparked a debate over the fundamental goals of criticism in which various professional ethics contended with ideals of disinterested amateurism. As Kelly Mays summarizes,

> While the arguments that underwrote the new orthodoxy were multiple, the overarching ideological rationale and effect was to transfer authority from the corporate text to the individual contributor and thus to understand authority as properly the outgrowth of individual personality and competence, or—as George Lewes put it—individual "sensibility and culture." [. . .] The reviewer's "competence" and authority now rested precisely upon his difference from, rather than on his similarity to, [the] "general reader," for the latter needed guidance. (168)

Since sensation novels were perceived to be—and even defined as—the most popular form of literary production in the period, they offered critics an unparalleled opportunity to elucidate and justify their own claims to a superior sense of literariness. The cultural drama such critics envisioned, featuring the heroic efforts of an enlightened elite to rescue society from cultural degradation and perverted taste, required villains as well. Constructions of taste, as Pierre Bourdieu has shown, are always arguments about *distinction* (of cultural forms, but also of consumers and producers of those forms), and any new conception of cultural legitimacy will therefore fundamentally require an elaboration of its negation:

> It is no accident that, when [tastes] have to be justified, they are asserted purely negatively, by the refusal of other tastes. In matters of taste, more than anywhere else, all determination is negation; and tastes are perhaps first and foremost distastes, disgust provoked by horror or visceral intolerance ('sick making') of the tastes of others. (56)

Because the judgments necessary in isolating the "best" cultural productions are inevitably relative, in practice these critics were just as concerned with characterizing and condemning anything that their criteria for legitimate culture found wanting. And as periodical critics developed a new role for themselves in the late 1850s and early 1860s, they developed an image of sensationalism that was both the negative definition of true culture and the threat which justified their intervention. The novels that they lumped together in the genre of sensation were particularly useful as scapegoats in this regard for two related reasons. First, because they were the best-selling novels of the time, they represented the kind of cultural productions that the public would choose without the policing of taste valued by the emerging understanding of criticism. Secondly, the very nature of the popularity these novels were believed to enjoy—a popularity that seemed promiscuously to erase boundaries between classes of readers—challenged the function of criticism as a discourse intended to demarcate strata of consumers through the naturalizing rhetoric of taste. In other words, the greatest threat to writers whose job is distinguishing the "best" of cultural productions (and hence the most enlightened group of consumers) is a form of production that seems universally embraced. As Bourdieu has suggested, "The most intolerable thing for those who regard themselves as the possessors of legitimate culture is the sacrilegious reuniting of tastes which taste dictates shall be separated" (56-57).

The crusade against sensation novels was thus a reaction not only to their popularity, but to a *kind* of popularity that seemed to question the new critical emphasis on cultural distinction. Critical salvos aimed at sensationalism frequently registered alarm over a perceived permeability of boundaries of taste, hence their recourse to metaphors of disease. But disease was only one way to represent the crisis; other metaphors presented the problem of sensationalism's popularity in more explicitly classed terms. Braddon, for example, was charged with having "succeeded in making the literature of the kitchen the literature of the Drawing Room" (qtd. in Taylor 5). This domestic image clarifies the critics' disapproval of the indiscriminate acceptance sensation fiction by revealing it to be a consequence of a failure to maintain class integrity. It also specifies the direction of influence, associating the origins of sensation fiction with the menial and the vulgar. The *Quarterly* lodges a similar complaint, pointing out that although "the craving for sensation extends to all classes of society," the source of the problem lies in "the cheap publications which supply sensation for the million in penny and halfpenny numbers":

> These tales are to the full-grown sensation novel what the bud is to the flower, what the fountain is to the river, what the typical form is to the organized body. They are the original germ, the primitive monad, to which all the varieties of sensational literature may be referred, as to their source, by a law of generation at least as worthy of the attention of the scientific student as that by which Mr. Darwin's bear may be supposed to have developed into a whale. Fortunately in this case the rudimental forms have been continued down to the epoch of the mature development.

> In them we have sensationism pure and undisguised, exhibited in its
> naked simplicity, stripped of the rich dress which conceals while it adorns
> the figure of the more ambitious varieties of the species. (Mansel 505-506)

Here the lower-class forms of sensation are not said to be identical to the
more middle-class varieties, with which Mansel assumes his readers are
more familiar, but the implication remains the same. By revealing to his
middle-class readers that the novels they have embraced are merely upstart
vulgarities disguised in the clothing of their betters, Mansel appeals directly to middle-class snobbery. The inferiority of products aimed at "the
million" (a number which was quickly becoming a gross underestimate)
goes more or less without saying; it is enough that the critic has exposed
sensation fiction "in its naked simplicity" as socially beneath the readers of
the *Quarterly*. As the criticism of sensationalism was meant to differentiate
between class-specific types of fiction, it could simultaneously distinguish
the cultural pedigrees of periodical readers. Writers like Mansel assumed
that the revelation of sensation fiction's lower-class associations could dis-
courage the *Quarterly*'s readers from reading such novels because the
Quarterly itself was priced for and targeted at a more exclusive and elite
audience. Nevertheless, the proliferation of new titles in the late 1850s and
1860s, as well as by the explosive increase in sales of cheaper publications.- threatened to overwhelm the entire market: "the craving for sensation," Mansel warned, "extends to all classes of society."

In their attempts to bolster distinctions in the market for print, these
critics attacked those segments of the industry that seemed to be indiscrim-
inately pandering to wide audiences. They therefore added newspaper
journalists to popular novelists on the list of culture's enemies. Even the
solidly middle-class *Times* was not exempt from critical hostility; Arnold
saw in it signs of a dangerous deference to a "general public":

> The *Times* tells us day after day how the general public is the organ of all
> truth, and individual genius the organ of all error; nay, we have got so far,
> it says, that the superior men of former days, if they could live again now,
> would abandon the futile business of running counter to the opinions of
> the many, of persisting in opinions of their own: they would sit at the feet
> of the general public and learn from its lips what they ought to say. (qtd.
> in Woolford 115)

To critics like Arnold, newspapers epitomized the problems of producing
print for a mass readership that was quickly growing more massive, and
the respectability of newspaper journalists dwindled in inverse proportion
to the widening circulation of their work. The size of the new readership
implied to such critics not only a homogeneity of opinion that included
both press and audience, but also—and this is the higher journalism's crucial revision—that universal opinions must necessarily be false. Whether or
not the *Times* presumptively privileged popular opinion to the extent
Arnold suggests, his critique certainly assumes the superiority of the "indi-

vidual genius" he constructs in opposition to the public. The higher journalism, in other words, marked a significant new influence on periodical
criticism by high Romanticism, the return of a suspicion about popular
tastes that had largely lain dormant during the heyday of early-Victorian
novelists. Now the elite critics began to share the assumptions that had
grounded Wordsworth's definition of the "Poet"—Arnold himself was
among the most vocal of Wordsworth's mid-Victorian champions—and
Coleridge's notion of an enlightened "clerisy";[15] such an aesthetic served as
a useful stick with which to beat the work of the most widely-read writers
in any medium, novelists and newspaper-writers alike.

The history of mid-Victorian newspapers is closely knit to the genre of
sensation fiction,[16] and even today the press is just as likely to be censured
for "sensational" appeal as are novelists. The credit for establishing this
link belongs to the anti-sensational critics who, in their general attacks
against broad circulation, suggested a market-driven complicity between
popular journalists and writers of popular novels. An essay in 1863 offered
what amounts to a sociological explanation of the parallel developments in
the two forms: "Writers have not been slow to perceive that the columns of
the daily papers were becoming formidable rivals to quiet novels; and it is
probably only as a result of the admirable organization of the literary market, that a supply of acceptable fiction has so closely followed, or has even
to some degree anticipated and created the demand" (qtd. in Taylor 4).
Though this perspective admits some uncertainty about the precise causal
mechanisms of supply and demand, its confident association of sensation
novels, newspapers, and the dictates of the market is typical. For other critics, it was enough to juxtapose the interests of newspapers and sensation
novels and attack the two with one "orthodox stone"; thus Mansel's face-
tious advice to the would-be novelist:

> Let him only keep an eye on the criminal reports of the daily newspapers,
> marking the cases which are honoured with the especial notice of a lead-
> ing article, and become a nine-days wonder in the mouths of quidnuncs
> and gossips; and he has the outline of his story not only ready-made, but
> approved beforehand as of the true sensation cast. Then, before the public
> interest has had time to cool, let him serve up the exciting viands in a
> rechauffe with a proper amount of fictitious seasoning; and there emerges
> the criminal variety of the Newspaper Novel, a class of fiction having
> about the same relation to the genuine historical novel that the police re-
> ports of the 'Times' have to the pages of Thucydides or Clarendon.[17]

Though Mansel invokes the usual bodily metaphor of eating to trivialize
sensation novels, he extends his dismissal to newspapers as well; both
somehow fail to be "genuine" for being popular and topical. In addition to
merely revealing what they saw as similarities between the works of newspaper journalists and popular novelists, the elite critics frequently remon-
strated with the former for their pernicious approval of the latter. While it

is generally true that newspapers and cheaper journals more favorably reviewed popular novels—*The Woman in White* received one of its best notices in the *Times*—the typical complaints of more elite journalists hyperbolized this partiality. In 1865, for instance, the *Westminster* derisively exaggerated Braddon's success among reviewers: "For the last three or four years, each new work of Miss Braddon's has been hailed by the press in language which would have been laudatory if applied to a new 'Hamlet.' The *Times* has lately held her up as a guide to the philosopher, and a model to the moralist" ("Belles Lettres" [1865] 267). Another article in the same journal the following year helps to clarify why these critics became so interested in denouncing newspaper reviewers; though gladly pointing out that "Of late years [. . .] a decided improvement has taken place in journalism," the reviewer contends that the acceptance of sensationalism represents an obstinately conservative tendency among newspaper journalists: "the laudations poured forth by journals of such high standing as the *Times* upon second-rate sensation novels and second-rate sensation pictures, teach us how much the ordinary newspaper critic has yet to learn" ("Belles Lettres" [1866] 129). The relatively ignorant "ordinary newspaper critic" thus serves to underscore the value of the extraordinary anti-sensational reviewer. In this way, the coupling of the most popular segments of the periodical press with popular novelists doubly legitimated the claims of higher journalists: with one hand they painted an alarming image of the effects of sensational novels while with the other they distinguished their own ability to defend culture to an extent that the mass-market press had failed to do. At the same time they suggested that both aspects of the problem were caused by a large, homogenous reading public that lacked the sense and discipline necessary to recognize literary value. The specter of a wholesale debasement of popular taste would authorize not only the cultural distinction of an elite body of upscale reviews (which peddled this distinction as part of a value-added package) but also that of the new ranks of higher journalists carving a defensible niche in the thriving periodical trade.

In elaborating a division between genuine culture and popular taste, the higher journalism split the previously dominant perception of novelists into two distinct forms. Dickens had been celebrated in terms that emphasized both his individuality and his profound unity with the public, or as Mary Poovey puts it, "the representative (literary) man was simultaneously considered unique (a 'genius') and like every other man (interchangeable) because he made his readers in his own image" (110). The juxtaposition of the novelist's individual integrity and sympathetic sameness with readers—and not a merely abstract or theoretical representativeness but an immediate and practical sense of shared values and opinions—underwrote the novel's literary value in the first decades of the Victorian period and made it possible for critical esteem and popularity to coexist harmoniously. These are precisely the elements that the higher journalism split apart. Just as Arnold complained that by making the "general public the organ of all truth" the *Times* had necessarily set itself in opposition to "individual genius," so the higher journalists more generally divided novelists into praiseworthy individuals and essentially faceless functionaries in the public's employ. The most striking aspect of the usual critique of sensationalism is not simply that popular novels were dismissed out of hand, but the extent to which critics specifically targeted the individuality of the novelists themselves, the way in which fears of a leveled-down audience evoked a leveled-down conception of writers so as to split the field of literary production into legitimate authors and interchangeable nonentities. The invention of a sensation "school" was of course already a gesture towards the interchangeability of popular novelists, but subsequent attacks on sensationalism blurred their identities even further. Mansel put it this way: "The public want novels, and novels must be made—so many yards of printed stuff, sensation-pattern, to be ready by the beginning of the season. And if the demands of the novel-reading public were to increase to the amount of a thousand per season, no difficulty would be found in producing a thousand works of the average merit" (483). Here the production of sensational novels becomes so simply a function of public demand that the market itself seems to write them; no room remains for any individual agents. Writers like Mansel did not leave the identity of these interchangeable novelists entirely mysterious, however, since the anonymity they implied was a classed anonymity. As opposed to the products of legitimate creative genius, "No divine influence can be imagined as presiding over the birth of [the sensation novelist's] work, beyond the market-law of demand and supply; no more immortality is dreamed of for it than for the fashions of the current season. A commercial atmosphere floats around works of this class, redolent of the manufactory and the shop." From the "manufactory and shop" the critics drew their common metaphors for sensation writers, typically likening them to mechanics (or machines), constructors, builders, tradesmen, or, when stressing bodily tropes of consumption, cooks. The individuality of these novelists had become unimportant, but the intimations of class anxiety had not. Ironically, Collins's own assessment of the "unknown public" had treated the authorship of the texts he examined in similar terms by suggesting that all of the samples he perused might have been written "by the same pen"; an equivalent judgment would be visited upon him.

The assault on Collins's reputation gathered force gradually with the more general repudiation of sensationalism shortly after the publication of *The Woman in White*. Margaret Oliphant's famous 1862 review, which first suggested the category of sensation novels, was not entirely unappreciative of his work: "To combine the higher requirements of art with the lower ones of a popular weekly periodical, and produce something which will be equally perfect in snatches and as a book, is an operation too difficult and delicate for even genius to accomplish without a bold adaptation of the mechanism and closest elaboration of workmanship" (qtd. in Taylor 26). Oliphant's formulation predictably aligns genius with the "higher requirements of art" and a popular mode of production with "mechanism" and "workmanship," but she implies that the combination of these elements is "difficult" rather than—as later critics would have it—impossible. Collins's harsher critics tended to elide the artistic aspects of his prose and focus instead on his "workmanship"; thus the *Saturday Review* speaks of his "mechanical talent," and even the more sympathetic Trollope qualifies his regard in the these terms: "the construction is most minute and most wonderful. But I can never lose the taste of the construction" (257). The *Westminster* opted for the culinary metaphor, writing that "Mr. Wilkie Collins informs us that he has very properly spared no pains in ensuring accuracy on all questions of Law, Medicine, and Chemistry. But we must add it is not artistic to tell this to the reader. The process of watching our dinner being cooked takes away our appetite" ("Belles Lettres" [1866] 127). Doubtless this reviewer's loss of appetite stems from the same unpleasant taste of which Trollope complained, a "taste" that ultimately has less to do with flavor than with the mandates of cultural distinction.

Though the *Westminster*'s dismissal is not unusual, this particular critique perceptively notes Collins's attention to "Law, Medicine, and Chemistry," hinting at elements of his novels (and other novels of the 1860s) that really do differ from his immediate predecessors. Dickens's introduction to *Bleak House* offers a classic example of a novelist defending the scientific plausibility of his representations (in this case the spontaneous combustion of Krook), but Collins's preoccupation with assimilating parts of these professional discourses far surpasses Dickens's awkward defense of his novel's verisimilitude. In Collins's novels, questions of law and medicine become central both to narrative coherence and boundaries of identity to a degree that later prompted Henry James to comment that they are "not so much works of art as works of science" (qtd. in W. Hughes 138). James's prejudices about the nature of "art" notwithstanding, this emerging emphasis helps to characterize Collins's own revisions of the ideologies of authorship he inherited, and point to new ways of conceptualizing the relationship of novelist and public.

REREADING THE SYMPATHETIC BODY

The lasting influence of anti-sensational criticism has long worked to banish novels like *The Woman in White* from cultural legitimacy, and to consign Collins himself to the list of unimportant second-raters. In the last two decades, however, a convergence of diverse interests (in gender history, popular culture, the mystery novel, and body criticism, to name a few) has led to serious reevaluations of *The Woman in White*'s significance. Probably the most influential line of inquiry was inaugurated by D. A. Miller's study of *The Woman in White* in *The Novel and the Police*. Miller draws attention to the bodily dimensions of sensation in a way that gives them a more nuanced relevance than had the Victorian critics' self-serving association of physical excitement and nervousness with vulgar, embodied mass consumption. Describing the genre as "one of the first instances of modern literature to address itself primarily to the sympathetic nervous system" (146), Miller argues that by making physical sensation the key to the characters' understanding of mysterious events in the story, it likewise becomes the condition of the novel's intelligibility to readers, thus encouraging a modern hermeneutics of suspicion. They begin to feel that they are being watched even as they watch others, all of which promotes the sort of supralegal self-disciplining subject theorized by Foucault: "The specificity of the sensation novel in nineteenth-century fiction is that it renders the liberal subject the subject of a *body*, whose fear and desire of violation displaces, reworks, and exceeds his constitutive fantasy of intact privacy. The themes that the liberal subject ordinarily defines himself against—by reading *about* them—are here inscribed into his reading body" (163). Miller's great contribution to the study of the sensation novel has not only been to restore attention to the bodies it describes, but also to point out that physical sensations are understood only in the context of broader discourses that prescribe their interpretation for the characters and readers alike; there is, in other words, no pure signification of the body, only historically contingent discourses that appropriate bodily signals as a part of their representational grammar. Yet, as Miller readily admits, the logic of the novel can only lead to conjecture about the specific ways in which readers themselves reacted to sensation novels or about the interpretations that somatic representations may have evoked.

On the other hand, by more carefully historicizing the bodily tropes Miller analyzes we can learn a great deal about the novel's entanglement in shifting literary ideologies and practices. Much of the representation of physical sensation in *The Woman in White* has a history in British fiction that long predates the novel itself, and in the more local context of the discursive structure to which such tropes conventionally belonged we can understand what is peculiar about Collins's novel and the historical conditions under which it was produced. Miller is only partly right when he suggests that *The Woman in White* targets the "sympathetic nervous system"; the broader discourse to which it alludes is the discourse of *sympathy*, which had become enshrined as a criterion of literariness with the influence of the Romantics and had gone on to flourish as a central tenet of early-Victorian novelists under the aegis of Industrial Romanticism. Even though the original critics of Collins's novel drew unprecedented attention to them, the bodily tropes that register sympathetic affect are really one of the least innovative things about it.

What is less traditional about the novel, in fact, is its evident dissatisfaction with sympathetic community as a solution to the problems raised in the plot; sympathy had been both the subject and justifying social medium for Collins's immediate predecessors, but in his novel it competes with an emerging emphasis on an ideology of professionalism, which is portrayed as largely incompatible with sympathy. While sympathy is often represented in terms of bodily "nervousness" and semi-somatic affect, professionalism is just as importantly portrayed in terms of composure, self-control, or self-possession, all of which figure as the suppression of the same bodily impulses involved in the discourse of sympathy. The tension in the novel between these two discourses has been obscured by the critical tradition of its interpretation grounded in the generic dictates of "sensation fiction," which overemphasizes one aspect of the narrative and renders the disunity less visible, simplifying on this level a deeply conflicted text.[18] But it is precisely in this ideological clash that *The Woman in White* reveals the historically specific forces at work on its own production. The rhetoric of sympathy, long the guarantor of an assumption of classless, utopian mutuality among readers and writers, begins to crumble in this novel as it conjures a vision of an unsympathetic and potentially hostile public. We have seen in "The Unknown Public" that Collins was no less interested in the sweeping transformation of the Victorian readership than the anti-sensational critics, and although he was not as thoroughly pessimistic, Collins expresses uncertainty about the terms in which a novelist should address the changing public. The ambiguities and contradictions in *The Woman in White* document a crucial transition towards new modes of imagining novelists' cultural status.

The rhetoric of sympathy had derived force from the language of physical affect since the eighteenth century. Adam Smith, for example, wrote that in order to understand a person sympathetically, "we enter as it were into his body, and become in some measure the same person with him, and thence form some idea of his sensations, and even feel something which, though weaker in degree, is not altogether unlike them" (qtd. in I. Armstrong 9). According to Smith's theory, the imaginary sharing of bodily sensation epitomized successful sympathetic imagination, which in turn operated as a moral sentiment and source of social stability; sympathetic sensation is thereby imagined to hover at the intersection of body, mind, and a social code of ethics. As the early-Victorian novelists took up this doctrine of sympathy as the ostensible basis of their social function, they likewise developed the melodramatically somatic components of fellow-feeling, peopling their novels with heroes who quiver at the misfortune of others, weep or grow pale in the presence of suffering, and become (literally) nervous about the welfare of their friends. These texts abound with old tropes of body-wrenching affect and feelings of the heart, and add to them specific physical responses to sympathetic friendliness or its violation. Dickens set the tone early with Pickwick's characteristically red-faced, apoplectic anger at the mistreatment of his friends, with Bill Sikes's feverish guilt and Oliver Twist's swooning compassion, and with hosts of later characters with bodily reactions to social injustices as well as villains whose antisocial tendencies are inscribed in their grotesque appearances. But these techniques were not at all limited to Dickens; one of the clearest examples of the intersection of sympathy and the body comes from Gaskell's *Mary Barton*, which dramatizes its primary moral lesson by dressing it in the language of bodily sympathy. Here the factory owner John Carson, "shaking in his agony," confronts the worker John Barton, the killer of Carson's son, thus evoking Barton's "sympathy for suffering":

> "Have I had no inward suffering to blanch these hairs? [. . .] I seemed hard and cold; and so I might be to others, but not to [my son]! Who shall ever imagine the love I bore to him? Even he never dreamed how my heart leapt up at the sound of his footsteps [. . .]."
>
> The eyes of John Barton grew dim with tears. Rich and poor, masters and men, were then brothers in the deep suffering of the heart; for was not this the very anguish he had felt for little Tom [. . .]!
>
> The mourner before him was no longer the employer; a being of another race, eternally placed in antagonistic attitude; going through the world glittering like gold, with a stony heart within, which knew no sorrow but through the accidents of Trade; no longer the enemy, the oppressor, but a very poor, and desolate old man. (365-66)

Like the narrator, Carson draws attention to the physical signs of his emotional bond with his son, and to the ways his suffering has become legible through his body. Barton is able to read and interpret the signs on this level, and he reacts physically, emotionally, and above all sympathetically to Carson's evident pain. The result, as novelist after novelist proposed, is a shared understanding of humanity that transcends the cultural barriers of rank, class, and self-interest. Gaskell's use of the naturalizing rhetoric of the body—hearts suffering or leaping in love, hair whitening in anguish, eyes dimming in sorrow—marshals old metaphors in the service of the interpretive framework of sympathetic identification, so that physical sensations are given specific meaning through the lens of social morality and stability.

Collins's frequent depiction in *The Woman in White* of physical sensitivity, nervousness, or agitation is generally consistent with the long-standing association of bodily sensation and sympathy. Like *Mary Barton*, this novel rehearses the bourgeois fantasy of a universal human understanding that ultimately maintains social divisions; if Collins's narrators are less explicit about the connection than Gaskell's or Dickens's, it may be simply because by the time the novel appeared the discursive technique was well enough established to obviate explanation. Building on this tradition, Collins tends to present powerful affect as the manifestation of a profound sympathy which not only goes without saying, but which may not even be otherwise expressible: physical sensation is thus acknowledged as the experience of "sympathies that lie too deep for words" (76). The sensations experienced by Collins's characters are ultimately read by them as indices of their spiritual unity with their intimates or their moral obligation towards others.

The sympathetic implications of the novel's rhetorical use of physical sensation are evident even in the episode that appears to be most purely about the powerful experience of nerves: Walter's description of his first encounter with Anne Catherick. "I had mechanically turned [towards London], and was strolling along the lonely high-road [. . .] when, in one moment, every drop of blood in my body was brought to a stop by the touch of a hand laid lightly and suddenly on my shoulder from behind me" (47). This famous "touch" and Walter's physical reaction to it form the basis of what Miller calls "the novel's 'primal scene,' which it obsessively repeats and remembers" (152). Physical contact snaps Walter out of his mechanical march and forcibly reminds him of his very human body. But the implications of the touch do not end with his nerves or circulatory system, and as the narrative rehearses this moment again—only a dozen short paragraphs later—Walter begins to interpret Anne's gesture in a frame of sympathy. Having feared to approach Hartright until after he had passed, Anne explains, "I was obliged to steal after you, and touch you" (49). Walter the narrator responds by repeating her words as a question in the present tense, "Steal after me and touch me?", preparing the way for further repetition and opening the question of the meaning of her gesture and his response. Anne claims that she has met with an accident and asks if she can trust him, then "touches" him again, though in a different way. "The loneliness and helplessness of the woman touched me," Walter now explains, "The natural impulse to assist her and to spare her got the better of the judgment, the caution, the worldly tact, which an older, wiser, and colder man might have summoned to help him in this strange emergency." Touching suddenly elicits a less physical but equally "natural impulse," the moral equivalent of the somatic reminder of his humanity. That Walter is as much "touched" by Anne's plight as by her hand suggests a deep relationship between physical sensation and moral compassion, that the two overlap to an extent that one becomes the pretext for the other. When Walter later experiences "a thrill of the same feeling" (86) brought on by the uncanny resemblance of Anne and Laura, he begins to sympathize with Laura, too, associating Anne's plight with Laura's future, even though there has not yet been any cause for alarm: "To associate that forlorn, friendless, lost woman, even by an accidental likeness only, with Miss Fairlie, seems like casting a shadow on the future of the bright creature who stands looking at us now" (86). The more expansive discourse of *sympathy*, in other words, inflects the signals of the sympathetic nervous system, contextualizing the body's responses in an already established, socially constructed interpretive framework: to be touched in this way immediately raises without explanation certain understood oppositions—to "judgment, caution, and worldly tact," for example—that indicate recognizable outlines of the cultural discourse of sympathy in which such responses are made legible.

Sympathy in *The Woman in White* never entertains the optimistically broad social ramifications of a *Mary Barton*, but focuses instead on a narrower, more Dickensian community of like-minded companions. Here the group in question is the trio of protagonists—Walter, Marian, and Laura—whose developing bonds of "friendly intimacy" (95) and the incipient threats to those bonds comprise the bulk of the novel's first volume. The operation of sympathy among these characters guarantees their mutual awareness of their interdependent well-being, or as Walter puts it, "Living in such intimacy as ours, no serious alteration could take place in any one of us which did not sympathetically affect the others" (91). One such alteration, of course, is the even greater intimacy that grows between Walter and Laura, those "unacknowledged sensations that we were feeling in common" (91), to which Marian feels obliged to put an end, albeit with as much compassion as possible: "Shake hands," she tells Walter,

> 'I have given you pain; I am going to give you more, but there is no help for it—shake hands with your friend, Marian Halcombe, first.'
> The sudden kindness—the warm, high-minded, fearless sympathy which met me on such mercifully equal terms, which appealed with such delicate and generous abruptness straight to my heart, my honor, and my courage, overcame me in an instant. I tried to look at her when she took my hand, but my eyes were dim. I tried to thank her, but my voice failed me. (95)

Though they seem forced, the bodily metaphors of this sympathetic exchange are doubtless meant to underscore Marian's suggestion that her motives for discouraging Walter's love derive from Laura's previous engagement rather than from his lower social position; certainly Walter is grateful for her meeting him "on such mercifully equal terms." Leaving aside for a moment the class anxiety that sympathy is used to overwrite, it seems plain enough that the novel's construction of ideal, non-alienated relationships is grounded in the notion of friendly sympathy, expressed with a familiar array of bodily idioms, gestures, and behaviors. Marian assures Walter, just as the text implicitly assures the reader, "We have understood each other, as friends should" (99).

The rhetoric of *The Woman in White* suggests that the need to read signs through the interpretive structure of sympathy extends beyond the text; it is required not only of the novel's characters but also of its readers, "the friends who read these pages." Though not necessarily a condition of the story's intelligibility, the narrative references to the "familiar sensations which we all know" (76) gesture towards an affective complicity between the text and its audience, so that the sympathies of the reader work in tandem with the storyteller's. Walter's description of Laura—"How can I describe her?"—turns out to be not a description at all, but an allusion to the readers' own experiences:

Does my poor portrait of her, my fond, patient labour of long and happy days, show me these things? Ah, how few of them are in the dim mechanical drawing, and how many in the mind with which I regard it! [. . .] Sympathies that lie too deep for words, too deep almost for thoughts, are touched, at such times, by other charms than those by which the senses feel and which the resources of expression can realise. The mystery which underlies the beauty of women is never raised above the reach of all expression until it has claimed kindred with the deeper mystery in our own souls. Then, and only then, has it passed beyond the narrow region on which light falls, in this world, from the pencil and the pen.

Think of her as you thought of the first woman who quickened the pulses within you [. . .]. Let her footstep, as she comes and goes, in these pages, be like that other footstep to whose airy fall your own heart once beat time. Take her as the visionary nursling of your own fancy, and she will grow upon you, all the more clearly, as the living woman who dwells in mine. (75-76)

What seems at first to be a curious narrative silence mimics the tacit understanding between the novel's heroes, and it conscripts readers into an imaginative extension of their community, in which the inexpressible hardly needs expressing. Belying the quasi-juridical narrative frame—by which the cast of narrators relate their own experiences as testimony—such rhetorical moves reassure readers that the most important experience is already their own, that they are the sort who understand, that their pulses beat with the rhythms of sympathetic intimacy. But this narrative strong-arm tactic is at the same time an entirely democratic assumption that the readers share—as their very birthright—the interpretive tools necessary to participate in the text's construction of meaning.

As if to emphasize the constructive personal understanding between writer and readers, the novel elaborates a theory of artistic production grounded in sympathy and personal relationships rather than in disinterested contemplation or exchange value. Thus while Walter makes his living at the outset of the novel as a drawing master, the practice of art is figured less as a form of labor than as the occasion for forging sympathetic bonds. Walter's instruction of Laura is not presented in the novel as anything but the premise of their relationship, while Laura's drawing-room piano recitals constitute her half of their unspoken courtship: "her natural enjoyment of giving me back, by the practice of her art, the pleasure which I had offered to her by the practice of mine, only wove another tie which drew us closer and closer to one another" (89). Artistic products, by the same token, are best appreciated by reference to the personal relationships that give them meaning; hence Laura's "poor, faint, valueless sketches," although financially worthless, are perceived in Walter's sympathetic economy as "treasures beyond price—the dear remembrances that I love to keep alive—the friends in past adversity that my heart will never part from, my tenderness never forget" (500). Such sentiments also underlie Walter's longest exegesis of aesthetics, in which he critiques the poetic appreciation of nature:

> Admiration of those beauties of the inanimate world, which modern poetry so largely and eloquently describes, is not, even in the best of us, one of the original instincts of our nature [. . .]. How much share have the attractions of Nature ever had in the pleasurable or painful interests and emotions of ourselves or our friends? What space do they ever occupy in the thousand little narratives of personal experience which pass every day by word of mouth from one of us to the other? (79)

Our appreciation of the natural world, Walter argues, is in fact far from natural; between nature and its admirers there exists a "want of inborn sympathy." But at the same time he promotes a reified understanding of friendship and sympathetic exchange, which represent the "human interest that the pure heart can feel." Opposing a traditional object of aesthetic regard to the "little narratives of personal experience" (a phrase that describes the narrative structure of *The Woman in White* itself), this argument uses the language of sympathy and sympathetic sensation to imply a superior and more instinctively "human" basis for artistic appreciation. The tastes of the educated, which "no uninstructed man or woman possesses," are functions of social difference rather than natural equality, and are "rarely practiced by any of us except when our minds are most indolent and most unoccupied."

This last phrase cannot fail to remind the reader of the "most indolent and most unoccupied" character in the book, the hypochondriacal Frederick Fairlie, who extravagantly represents the kind of taste the novel criticizes for its lack of human interest. Fairlie's collection of coins, watercolors, and etchings occupies him entirely, and although there is nothing wrong with his taste (Walter says that his own "taste [is] sufficiently educated" to appreciate the value of the objects Fairlie has accumulated), the novel nonetheless suggests that his pursuits are a pernicious waste of time and identifies his refined aesthetic appreciation with a condition of absolute isolation. Fairlie closes himself off from the world, and therefore from the sympathetic circulation of human interest that serves as the novel's ethical frame; sensing this immediately upon meeting Fairlie, Walter's "sympathies shut themselves up resolutely" (66). From his ominous greeting to Walter ("So glad to possess you at Limmeridge, Mr. Hartright" [66]) to his declaration that his servant is a portfolio stand rather than a man (180), Fairlie's disinterested appreciation of art, his exercise of discriminatory taste, is insistently paired with his impulse to dehumanize other characters. Objectifying those around him, he finds them wanting in comparison to the inhuman objects of art: in a particularly damning moment, he disapproves of tears "except when the refining process of Art judiciously removes from them all traces of Nature" (362). But rather paradoxically, for all Fairlie's opposition to the novel's privileged structure of sympathetic feeling, he is nevertheless its most nervously sensitive character. The same fine-tuned receptivity that guarantees the proper sympathetic sensibilities among the other characters becomes for Fairlie a justification his retreat from society and for a strongly class-inflected sense of his own distinction. Like his refined taste, Fairlie's physical hypersensitivity sets him off from others, particularly from those of lower classes. Thus while he insists upon his own nervousness, he maintains that servants are "persons born without nerves" (69), and Walter dryly observes that Fairlie's nerves are "delicate enough to detect the smell of plebeian fingers" (69). Even colder than the novel's more patently criminal characters, Glyde and Fosco, Fairlie is unmitigably villainous in his rejection of sympathy, and he is in some ways more threatening to the novel's morality; Fairlie reads the raw signification of the body through a different lens than the novel advocates, undermining and destabilizing the natural connection between instinctive sensations and the recognition of mutual human interests. Fairlie's understanding of his nerves does not lead naturally and inevitably to a universal and classless sympathy but to an affirmation of his privileged position and distinctive tastes instead: "Mr. Fairlie's selfish affectation and Mr. Fairlie's wretched nerves meant one and the same thing" (67).

If Fairlie were the only character to raise doubts about the natural basis for sympathy, we might dismiss his reading of bodily signs as an anomaly, agreeing with him when he suggests "Perhaps my own secretions being all wrong together, I am a little prejudiced on the subject" (363). But in addition to the possibility of misreading physiological cues represented by Fairlie, *The Woman in White* repeatedly implies that the ostensibly natural signs of sensation are merely rhetorical gestures without any guarantee of authenticity. The passage in which Anne first touches Walter's shoulder and then his sympathy immediately mentions yet another "touch" as Anne thanks Walter for his concern: "The first touch of womanly kindness that I had heard from her trembled in her voice as she said the words: but no tears glistened in those large, wistfully attentive eyes of hers." Now meaning something like a trace or a hint, "touch" has taken on another sense; it is both related to the two earlier forms (as her physically trembling voice reveals her "tenderness") and contradictorily unrelated (since it is accompanied by a conspicuous absence of tears). This inconsistent and even anxious repetition of the word suggests its mercurial flexibility as a sign, which undermines its "natural" appearance and reveals it to be merely a conventional metaphor. When Glyde protests Count Fosco's plans for his wife by declaring that they make his "flesh creep," Fosco replies, "Your flesh? Does flesh mean conscience in English?" (350). And in fact, "flesh" does mean conscience in English—at least in the traditional discourse of sympathy—insofar as physical reactions are figured as an important component of a moral sentiment that transcends the individual body. But at the same time, "flesh" becomes merely a hollow trope used to disguise the conventional contingency of what might otherwise seem naturally human. The visceral immediacy of sympathy becomes questionable, and sympathy itself therefore becomes suspiciously limited.

The rhetorical unreliability of sympathetic sensation is compounded at the level of the plot by the failure of the protagonists' intimacy to stave off the dissolution of their community at Limmeridge and its subsequent inability to restore what they had lost, particularly Laura's legal identity and social standing. Despite the powerfully affective responses of Marian (442) and Walter (431) as they recognize Laura, her appearance is unable to produce similar responses in anyone who does not belong to their circle of affection. Friendly sympathy, it would seem, is sufficient basis for a small, stable community—and in the novels of, say, Dickens or Thackeray, the achievement of such a community would have sufficed as a conclusion— but it is entirely insufficient for establishing a public identity, and therefore powerless to effect the broader social and legal remedies the protagonists pursue. The third volume of *The Woman in White* narrates the protagonists' search for some more authoritative means to restore Laura's identity. Thus Walter, in what might have been an affective farewell scene, purposely restrains what have become relatively useless sensations: "My voice faltered a little in spite of me. I forced myself from the room. It was no time, then, for parting with the self-control which might yet serve me before the day was out" (459). Though Walter claims still to be urged on by "sympathy and friendly feeling" (573), his new objectives demand that he discipline such feelings according to an ideology that has been associated throughout the novel with "self control" and set in opposition to affective sensation: the ideology of professionalism.[19]

The pattern of conflict between professionalism and sympathy begins early in the novel, as Walter's developing feelings for Laura are figured as a breach of professional conduct. In his professional capacity, Walter writes, "I had trained myself to leave all the sympathies natural to my age in my employer's outer hall, as coolly as I left my umbrella there before I went upstairs" (89). But ensconced in the intimate community at Limmeridge (and more particularly in the company of Laura), Walter's repressed natural "sympathies" shatter his "hardly-earned self-control." Given the happy ending that ultimately derives from Walter's failure in this regard, we might assume that the novel reckons it as a fortunate fall, yet the characters themselves are decidedly more ambivalent. Narrating long after the fact, Walter still reflects that "I should have looked into my own heart, and found this new growth springing up there, and plucked it out while it was young" (90), a belief which echoes Marian's more immediate advice about his love for Laura: "Crush it! [. . .] Tear it out; trample it underfoot like a man!" (96). There is never any clear assertion that Water's transgression is not a mistake after all, that it does not in fact expose the limits of the leveling ideology of sympathy. As a recognition of natural human bonds, sympathy (especially in an extreme form) threatens to erase the social boundaries of class and rank crucial to Victorian public identity. Walter's love for Laura thus disrupts the community at Limmeridge even before the arrival of Glyde and Fosco; it very problematically causes him to exceed the privileges of his social identity, or to forget, in other words, his place.

Laura's social "place", likewise, cannot be established on the basis of affective sympathy, since sympathy tends to blur interpersonal boundaries of position instead of confirming them. Identity in *The Woman in White* is rather the province of medicine (including those doctors who control the asylum and certify Laura's death) and law, both of which are predicated upon disinterested objectivity. It is only after his return from South America as "a changed man" at the end of the second volume that Walter has learned the self-discipline necessary to serve Laura's interests: "I had tempered my nature afresh. In the stern school of extremity and danger my will had learnt to be strong, my heart to be resolute, my mind to rely on itself" (427). What is generally praised in the novel as Walter's "resolution" is in fact his ability to subdue his "natural" sympathetic impulses and to authenticate Laura's claims in accordance with an ideology of professional discipline. Rather than appeal to the affective capacity of those who might help—or even allow himself to indulge his natural impulses—Walter endeavors to prove his case in a way that will not rely upon anyone's sentiments or compassion: "I resolved to begin by gathering together as many facts as could be collected" (456). His resolution to concern himself with factual evidence rather than instinctive feeling aligns Walter with what this novel consistently imagines as the legal method. Accordingly he enlists the aid of Mr. Kyrle, a solicitor and "self-possessed man" *par excellence*, and the terms in which Walter approvingly describes Kyrle demonstrate the extent to which the novel's early emphasis on sympathy has been overturned: Kyrle, he notes, was "not (as I judged) ready with his sympathy where strangers were concerned, and not at all easy to disturb in his professional composure. A better man for my purpose could hardly have been found" (460). Walter's purpose has become—among other things—to test the extent to which he can persuade a *public* that he now assumes to be unreachable through the more domestic medium of sympathy; an English jury, as Kyrle reminds him, is "bound to take facts as they reasonably appear" (463). The novel's link between the pursuit of factual evidence and personal composure continues through a number of scenes in which the villains' hirelings unsuccessfully attempt to provoke Walter into anger—"Never fear, Marian! I answer for my self-control" (502)—and culminates in Walter's final confrontation with Fosco, which reads as an extended duel of composure.

The tensions between sympathy and professionalism on the thematic level of the novel find a narrative counterpart in the decidedly inconsistent way the novel hails its readers: should they be addressed as kindly friends or as a dispassionate jury, as sympathetic to fine shades of the characters' feelings or as interested only in the less personal "facts" of the plot? The jarring dissonance between Collins's warm introduction (obsequiously thanking his friendly readers) and the narrator Walter's colder declaration in the preamble that the speakers themselves matter less than the presentation of "the truth" (33) nicely encapsulates the novel's move away from the more purely sympathetic rhetoric of Industrial Romanticism. What Collins took to be his novel's formal innovation, the progression of narrators as a series of witnesses who "relate their own experience" (33), is framed in the preamble in quasi-legal terms that closely correspond to the ostensible objectivity of professionalism that becomes so pronounced in the novel's third volume. At the outset the novel thus represents its readers as a kind of judge or jury, of the same sort that Kyrle later describes to Walter. Yet for the most part the testimonies of the various narrators do not restrict themselves to statements of fact; they dwell on their sensations and emotions at great length and even directly appeal at times to their readers' sympathetic understanding, suggesting that their experiences are already attuned to the readers' own. The jury described by the preamble and by Kyrle may not be quite the readership the novel imagines after all. Betraying the principles set forth in the preamble, Walter admits to a difference between what he might reveal to a jury and to his readers: at the inquest following Percival's death, he withholds his theories about Percival's motivations, later justifying his silence to the reader by claiming he could not have given his "unsupported opinion" without "producing beyond a doubt the same unsatisfactory effect on the mind of the coroner and the jury, which I had already produced on the mind of Mr. Kyrle. In these pages, however, and after the time that has now elapsed, no such cautions and restraints as are here described need fetter the free expression of my opinion" (543). It is a testament to the power of the transformative cultural forces at work on this text that it desires to be both sympathetic and professional but cannot imagine the two paradigms as anything but incompatible. Or perhaps more accurately, given that Count Fosco serves as the only example of their synthesis, the novel relegates this combination to monstrosity.

"I combine in myself," Fosco boasts, "the opposite characteristics of a Man of Sentiment and a Man of Business" (627), affirming this opposition even as he paradoxically undermines it. But this is only the most resonant of the many contradictions that structure his character. Fosco is capable of becoming all things to all people, of marketing himself to the most disparate tastes of multiple audiences; his stories, Marian says, "all flowed in succession so easily and so gaily from his lips, and all addressed our various curiosities and various interests so directly and so delicately, that Laura and I listened with as much attention and, inconsistent as it may seem, with as much admiration also, as Madame Fosco herself" (278). Fosco's skill in pleasing multiple audiences, "inconsistent as it may seem," nicely expresses the fantasy of the novelist in the ideologically fragmenting literary market of the 1860s, and indeed, Fosco is the novelist's most identifiable surrogate in this text. Still, the protagonists ultimately find him just as revolting as engaging, and the final image of him dead and naked in the Paris Morgue reveals that the cost of such imposture is the humiliating public loss of all identity. The only legacy of the novel's most original character is his confident relativism, his unchallenged belief that truth is fragmentary, local, and entirely subject to perspective. And after a few more years of critical abuse, Collins put the same ideas in the mouth of another of his fascinating villains, Captain Wragge in the suggestively titled *No Name*, who more clearly expresses the relevance of the fragmented market on understandings of authorship: "Narrow minded mediocrity, envious of my success in my profession, calls me a Swindler. What of that? The same low tone of mind assails men in other professions in a similar manner—calls great writers scribblers—great generals, butchers—and so on. It entirely depends on the point of view" (169).

***

Given the unusual incongruities of Collins's reception, it is not surprising that he was among the first Victorian novelists to explore points of view as a theme and as a narrative technique. The same concern with perspective would loom large in literature from the 1860s on, in diverse forms that ranged from Browning's *The Ring and the Book* (1869) to the vessels of consciousness in Henry James's fiction. I have tried to suggest here that responses to the mid-Victorian mass market played a decisive role in these innovations in theme and technique, and that they profoundly challenged existing ideologies of authorship. Without the assurance of speaking to and for an audience who could be assumed to share his opinions, Collins turned away from the rhetoric of sympathy in favor of a juridical model of professionalism. The moment of sensationalism was in many ways a crisis of narrative authority in the novel,[20] but its impact was not limited to sensation novelists; George Eliot, for example, also experimented with legal metaphors, as in a well-known passage from *Adam Bede*: "I aspire to give no more than a faithful account of men and things as they have mirrored themselves in my mind. [. . .] I feel as much bound to tell you, as precisely as I can, what the reflection is, as if I were in the witness-box narrating my experience on oath."[21] Collective sympathy remained an important ideal to both Collins and Eliot, but just as for Collins its efficacy had become suspect, for Eliot it had become a complex psychological and philosophical problem rather than a human instinct on which writers could complacently rely.

The critical movement that had revealed the menace of sensationalism in order to preserve cultural distinction against the threat of a leveling mass market continued to exercise great influence over the succeeding decades. As the gap these critics had introduced between cultural legitimacy and popular appeal widened, the writers whose work they valued were likewise disassociated from society and, increasingly, from social influence. For Arnold, only disinterested "aliens" could hope to preserve culture from factionalism and anarchic class struggle, and he, like Lewes, worked to promote the value of individual genius over public opinion. For Walter Pater, not long after, separation from quotidian social life became something of a precondition of artistry, and the goal of art became individual appreciation rather than widespread sympathy. This train of logic would finally arrive at the conclusions Oscar Wilde suggested in "The Soul of Man under Socialism" (1891), an essay less concerned with using literature to make social harmony possible than with reforming society to make literature possible:

> A work of art is the unique result of a unique temperament. Its beauty comes from the fact that the author is what he is. It has nothing to do with the fact that other people want what they want. Indeed, the moment that an artist takes notice of what other people want, he ceases to be an artist and becomes a dull or amusing craftsman, an honest or dishonest tradesman. He has no further claim to be considered as an artist. (17)

Wilde's comments bear marks of their descent from the anti-sensational screeds of three decades earlier, notably in their denigration of writers who seek public approval as craftsmen or tradesmen. The degree of artistic autonomy Wilde calls for, however, goes well beyond what the mid-Victorian critics had desired; it is a consequence of the late Victorian debate over the art of the novel and the artistry of the novelist.

CHAPTER FOUR

The Death of the Victorian Author:
Mastery and Mystery in James's *The Princess Casamassima*

Oscar Wilde's posture of flagrant indifference to public opinion appears to bring us, full circle, back to the Wordsworthian representation of authorship with which we began. Wordsworth, after all, had been one of the first British writers to champion the privilege of a separate sphere for writers by challenging the aesthetic criterion of popularity as it was expressed in the market for print. In the 1860s and 1870s, moreover, Wordsworth enjoyed something of a revival in the criticism of Matthew Arnold and Walter Pater, so that his prestige by the end of the century far outstripped the recognition he had achieved while he wrote. Yet we should not mistake the Wordsworthian echoes in late-Victorian aesthetics for a return to unadulterated Romanticism, or—worse still—for a confirmation of Wordsworth's assurance that his genius would inevitably prevail. The critical rediscovery of Wordsworth was effected only through a series of strategic misreadings that remind us of the extent to which ideologies of authorship had changed.[1]

Despite Wordsworth's evident distaste for immediate popularity, he had maintained a moral conviction that his work would eventually—in whatever vague and attenuated fashion—help to redeem society from the malaise of industrialism. Literature, once properly appreciated by the public, would address the most comprehensive social problems. By contrast, writers of the late nineteenth century despaired of even a hypothetically universal appeal, and for them the goals of literature stopped short at individual appreciation. Where Wordsworth stressed the importance of autonomous genius as a means to counter the debilitating effects of self-interest and the specialization of labor—so that writers were unusual largely because of their special access to what was most broadly human—Wilde and others of his generation celebrated the "unique temperament" of artists as its own end. Wordsworth's authoritative prophet of spiritual integrity had given way to a fetish of artistic individualism. The bonds of social sympathy, which theoretically limited the individuality of writers and justified the work of the Romantics and their novelist inheritors, would be severed at the century's end. As Wilde provocatively put it, "An artist has no ethical sympathies. All ethical sympathy in an artist is an unpardonable manner of style" (*Dorian Gray* 3).

Along with these revisions of writers' social responsibilities came a fundamentally new basis for expressing literary authority. Writers near the end of the century discarded the roles of soul-baring Romantic poet or friendly mid-Victorian novelist in favor of a rhetoric of artistry designed to keep the artist's personality mysteriously enshrouded. Wilde was not alone in arguing that "to reveal art and conceal the artist is art's aim" (*Dorian Gray* 3). Given Wilde's relentless effort to create a highly visible public persona, his call for authorial self-effacement may seem paradoxical, but only until we recognize that concealment can attract a great deal of attention, too. The conspicuous absence of authors from their texts further mystified the work of writing, and led ultimately, in the work of modernists, to the subtlest and boldest constructions of literary authority ever claimed by writers of fiction. After the "personality of the artist [. . .] refines itself out of existence," Joyce's Stephen Dedalus would explain in *A Portrait of the Artist*, "the mystery of the esthetic like that of material creation is accomplished. The artist, like the God of the creation, remains within or behind or beyond or above his handiwork, invisible, refined out of existence, indifferent, paring his fingernails" (233). Joyce's equation of authorial invisibility and divine mystery is the culmination of practical and ideological developments that had begun decades earlier; as we shall see, in fact, the same point had been made by one of the most aesthetically influential late-Victorian novelists, Henry James. More vehemently than any other writer of his day, James strove to dignify novelists as impersonal artists, even as he worked to establish his own authority as a "Master" of the form. Shaped by a complex web of tensions between potential audiences, publishing strategies, and cultural institutions, James's career spans the demise of the familiar Victorian novelist and the advent of a newly mystified literary authority that continues to sway criticism today.

Mark Seltzer has remarked that "Criticism of James has always been Jamesian," and if this observation seems more forcefully true or important than, say, calling Dickens criticism Dickensian, it is because "criticism of the novel," as Seltzer points out, "has proceeded along the lines that James has so clearly drawn" (14). James's powerful attraction for critics may not have been surprising through the years of formalism's ascendance, in which authorial effacement itself helped to ratify James's mastery, but it appears more perverse during the more recent turn to historicist and political criticism. James's mastery remains seductive, and the fundamental ambiguities around which his authority is constructed have allowed critics to accommodate James to new theoretical schemes while perpetuating his cultural prestige. He remains, like a deity, infinitely mercurial, endlessly interpretable, and always already authoritative.[2] Thus David McWhirter, despite noticing the contiguities between James's mastery and modern techniques of power, "would like [. . .] to keep open the possibility that [James's] New York Edition enacts a more genuinely subversive conceptualization of literary authority, as well as a related, potentially liberating revision of the self" (13). Critics may now prize subversion over style, but James remains the genuine article; the terms of approbation have changed, in other words, but James's mastery has not. More striking is John Carlos Rowe's reading of *The Princess Casamassima*, in which he implies an intellectual resemblance between an unexpectedly prescient James and contemporary theorists such as Foucault, Derrida, and (especially) Fredric Jameson. Rowe argues that James, who has "profoundly radical depths in his own political thinking," recognizes a complicity between the institutions of the ruling class and anarchism in that both rely on theatrical representations of their authority and power. In addition, James "subversively" demonstrates that the ruling order invites radical movements such as those in the novel because they authorize its surveillance and infiltration: "As soon as 'the Princess' is permitted entrance into any radical group, then the *resistant force of that group must be put into question*" (187). This chapter questions instead the resistant force of theories of subversion that embrace Henry James. Seen in the context of late-Victorian literary production, which had practical sociopolitical consequences of its own, James's arguments for artistic dignity begin to look less like a manifesto for liberated selfhood than an exclusive and socially vitiating valorization of rarefied artistry.

The Princess Casamassima (1886) represents a turning point in James's career as well as a crucial manifestation of the particular pressures brought to bear on the late-Victorian novelist. The story of a young bookbinder's ambivalent involvement with a secret society of anarchists, the novel simultaneously alludes to a wildly popular group of contemporary novels about clandestine revolutionaries and to a more Arnoldian sense of anarchism, in which such broadly popular books would seem culturally menacing. But Naturalism had shown that studies of the lower classes might open a space in fiction for serious aesthetic innovation, and James's hopes to achieve some degree of popularity had not yet vanished behind the dense syntactical thicket of his later novels. As political revolution comes to serve as a metaphor in the novel for the democratization of culture, we begin to see James's anxieties about publishing in the mass market not as subversive, but as an extension of the concerns of the repressive critical police who censured sensation fiction in the 1860s: artistry would have to be defined against vulgarity, and the ideal of universal *sympathy* would give way to a sharply limited relationship of *appreciation* by which both novelists and their readers could demonstrate their cultural distinction. By recognizing James's subtle mastery, readers could confirm their own sophistication.

James's early efforts to construct a new model of dignified authorship, legible in the themes and form of *The Princess Casamassima* as well as in his participation in the debate over the art of fiction in the middle of the decade, reveal the difficulties of rethinking distinction in the context of late-Victorian consumer culture. Faced on the one had by vulgar consumers whose dreams were shaped by the shoddy luxuries of the new department stores, and on the other by aesthetes whose tastes James portrayed as an equally suspect version of conspicuous consumption, he worked to establish an economy of cultural capital that could insulate his own meticulous productions from the cheapening visibility of gaudily displayed commodities. His self-representation, at once authoritative and obscure, would be underwritten by the fantasy of an elite audience who could perceive the delicate operation of his exquisite sensibility and on whom his intricate ironies would not be lost.

ANARCHY AND ARTISANS

When describing the work of writing, the canonical novelists of the late nineteenth century shared a common tone of anxiety, loss, and estrangement. The divisive, alienating menace of industrial capitalism, against which Wordsworth had long since warned writers and readers, had caught up with novelists. Of course, Wordsworth had considered novels themselves among the chief symptoms of literary decay, though this irony was lost amid the novelists' hand-wringing over the inhospitable marketplace. Proponents of the "serious novel" rehearsed a narrative of degradation and decline, as though consensus about the novel's artistic legitimacy was older than the genre's association with commerce. George Gissing has earned a place as the great spokesman of this misleading nostalgia; his *New Grub Street* (1891)—that memorable clash between Jasper Milvain, the bureaucratic "literary man of 1882," and Edwin Reardon, "the old type of unpractical artist" who "can't supply the market"—is certainly the gloomiest representation of authorship that the Victorians ever produced. Milvain, insensible to all that has ostensibly been lost, pragmatically explains the source of Gissing's pessimism: "Literature nowadays is a trade. Putting aside men of genius, who may succeed by mere cosmic force, your successful man of letters is your skillful tradesman. He thinks first and foremost of the markets; when one kind of goods begins to go off slackly, he is ready with something new and appetising" (38). Though the fear of cheap and shoddy literature is an old one, the binary terms of Gissing's apprehension mark its direct descent from the rhetoric of the "higher criticism" of the 1860s, which supported the artistic distinction of fiction by emphasizing its vulgar, commercial Other. The particular concern is not simply inferior production or a financial motive, but an entirely reconfigured system of writer-reader relations spurred by the mass market. The taste of the burgeoning audience (typically figured in this line of argument

as a gross, collective appetite) threatens to overwhelm the traditional distinctive properties of taste itself, and thus to level the cultural status of elite
artistic writers whose cultural capital depends on it. They would cease to
be artists by thinking "first and foremost of the markets," and become instead mere tradesmen. When another of Gissing's writers wonders whether
she might soon be replaced by a "Literary Machine" (138), her anxiety has
ultimately less to do with the old opposition of mechanical and organic
composition than with the staggering influence of industrial production
and mass consumption.

Gissing's pessimism corresponds to actual changes in the late Victorian
literary industry. Though the causes for the continuing expansion of the
reading public were not particularly new ones—Richard Altick attributes it
to the existing trends of declining production costs and generally increasing leisure time, literacy, and real income (306)—the public's growing diversity led to a heightened sense that readers could no longer be imagined
as a collective totality. Novels and periodicals alike sought to target increasingly specific groups of readers from a broad spectrum of interests, attitudes, and economic backgrounds, which resulted, as Peter Keating
writes, in "the relentless fragmentation and categorization of fiction in the
last two decades of the nineteenth century" (340). Conventional critical
wisdom tells us that the balkanization of both production and consumption took a profound toll on earlier constructions of novelistic authorship,
particularly on the close relationship of writers and readers. As Daniel H.
Borus summarizes,

> The size and growing complexity of the readership in the late nineteenth
> century rendered unworkable the intimate narrator, whose confidences
> had their social basis in the assurance that in interests and position the au-
> dience and narrator were much alike. [. . .] Both the potential and actual
> audiences [. . .] were fragmented and impersonal, separated from them-
> selves and the authors by diverse interests, desires, and abilities. Where
> earlier writers had counted upon a language of shared assumptions, real-
> ists could not.[3]

This explanation of late nineteenth-century changes in writer-reader relations is quite compelling—in the previous chapter I argued that the process
began decades earlier than is commonly supposed—but it requires significant qualification. We must also account for distinct and competing ideological reactions to these structural changes; not everyone perceived
audience fragmentation with Gissing's cynicism, nor indeed did everyone
believe that the novel's old function of promoting social harmony had become "unworkable." If the 1880s and 1890s were a period of intensified
fragmentation, they were also the age in which the literary industry became
particularly aware of the sort of book that seemed magisterially to overwhelm the divisions of particularized tastes; such books became known as
best-sellers.[4] Cultural fragmentation may have been a pressing concern for

the late Victorians, but serious novelists were equally anxious about the prospect of an undifferentiated mass of readers without taste.

The decreasing intimacy of writer-reader relations and the emerging impersonal authorial style were neither universal nor inevitable. Rather, impersonality was just one of a range of aesthetic responses to changing conditions, while the novelists most drawn to it and most concerned with the artistic integrity of their genre were precisely those who were least inclined to act as spokesmen for a collective culture. Thus Gissing's Edwin Reardon equates writing for a broader audience with "endeavoring to adapt himself to an inferior public" (240). It is no coincidence, as John Goode has observed, that "the division between 'the serious novel' and 'the best-seller' which became so acute after 1884 [. . .] is coeval with the development of a sense of the high artistic integrity necessary to the novelist" (245).

James shared Gissing's misgivings about the late nineteenth-century literary market and a good deal of his nostalgia as well. Near the end of his life, James worried that the thrill of a genuine literary event had become almost unimaginable: "Is anything like that thrill possible to-day—for a submerged and blinded and deafened generation, a generation so smothered in quantity and number that discrimination, under the gasp, has neither air to breathe nor room to turn round?" (*Notes* 66). But James was less constrained by backward-looking laments, and rather than ignore the mass market for fiction, he looked for ways to keep discrimination alive and to enhance his position both within and against the literary industry.[5] He found in the fragmenting readership new opportunities to redraw the traditional contract between novelist and audience: "The public we somewhat loosely talk of as for literature or for anything else is really as subdivided as a chess-board, with each little square confessing only to its own *kind* of accessibility." It would be precisely these divisions that would allow the best writers to find a niche in the market without deferring to the great vulgar mass, and to insulate "individual genius" from "the grossness of any view, any taste or tone, in danger of becoming so extravagantly general as to efface the really interesting thing, the traceability of the individual."[6]

In the service of this individualism, James repeatedly countered existing notions of symbolic exchange with what he called an "economy of interest." In "The Lesson of Balzac," for example, James describes the general decline of the novel's dignity in economic terms:

> [The novel's] misfortune, its discredit, what I have called its bankrupt state among us, is the not unnatural consequence of its having ceased, for the most part, to be artistically interesting. It has become an object of easy manufacture, showing on every side the stamp of the machine; it has become the article of commerce, produced in quantity, and as we so see it we inevitably turn from it, under the rare visitations of the critical impulse, to compare it with those more precious products of the same general nature that we used to think of as belonging to the class of the hand-made. (134)

The same wide sales that had helped to establish the novel as one of the most reliably lucrative genres has, in James's shadow economy of cultural capital, brought it to the brink of bankruptcy. James imagines the degradation of the novel's artistic interest as a shift in phases of capitalist development—from a petty commodity mode of production to a fully industrialized and alienated mode[7]—which allows him to contrast two very different models of the work of writing, the mechanical and the artisanal. Of course, the image of the "hand-made" novel is no less an ideological fiction than that of the novel-writing machine, but it offers James a way to conceptualize a different system of production and circulation, one which creates "more precious products" because they bear the marks of unique production—"the traceability of the individual"—and imply a more limited audience. James had likewise turned to a metaphor of the artisan in one of his earliest efforts to develop a theory of novelistic production that could restore the genre's symbolic capital, *The Princess Casamassima.*

The story of Hyacinth Robinson, the "little bastard bookbinder" (478) whose psychological turmoil results largely from the incompatibility he perceives between social responsibility and artistic sensibility, readily lends itself as an illustrative analogue of James's own opinions and anxieties, and critics have found in this novel a rare opportunity to rethink the image of James as an artist removed from and indifferent to the social implications of artistic practice. Given Hyacinth's involvement in a nebulous revolutionary movement, the issue for such critics typically becomes the extent to which the novel suggests that the aesthetic and the political may be reconciled, though their lack of consensus underscores the ambiguous reticence in the novel's approach to matters of politics.[8] For a story about revolutionaries, *The Princess Casamassima* pays surprisingly little attention to specific political questions; we do not find Hyacinth agonizing over the fine points of revolutionary ideology, the particulars of reform, or the shape of an ideal government. From Hyacinth's perspective, in fact, the social crises of the day have more to do with aesthetic vulgarity than poverty, more with artistic representation than political representation. This is not to say that he naively separates the circulation of wealth or power from the production or consumption of art—quite the contrary. But he considers the former only in terms of the latter, so that social structures become a grid onto which he maps the artistic concerns that increasingly preoccupy him. Hyacinth pities the disinherited not for their lack of food or economic opportunity but for their want of discrimination, "their brutal insensibility, a grossness impervious to the taste of better things or to any desire for them" (477). His understanding of the wretchedness of poverty as a matter of taste rather than as a simple matter of material privation is not his alone. As Hyacinth observes of the Princess, "it was plainly her theory that the right way to acquaint one's self with the sensations of the wretched was to suffer the anguish of exasperated taste" (421). In such ways, the novel repeatedly gestures towards abstractly political questions only to be drawn back to its preoccupation with artistic distinction. Categories of class are typically invoked as shorthand for degrees of cultural refinement, and revolution figures primarily as a radical redistribution of the opportunity for aesthetic appreciation, as in the utopian fantasy of a post-revolutionary society as an enormous café in which "the human family" sits together drinking coffee and "listening to the music of the spheres" (116), or Hyacinth's fear that the anarchist movement wants to carve works of art into small, equivalent pieces (396-97). It thus appears rather misleading to describe the novel's central tension as an opposition between the aesthetic and the political, or, at least, it would be more accurate to specify that the bulk of this tension lies between taste and socioeconomic factors of artistic production and reception.

This is not to say *The Princess Casamassima* is not topical, or that it has nothing to teach us as a response to broad shifts in the late Victorian political landscape. Rather, I want to emphasize that the cultural contexts that most clearly shaped the novel were of a much more immediate concern to contemporary novelists. *The Princess Casamassima* is deeply embedded in the questions of literary production and consumption that aroused immense controversy in the last decades of the nineteenth century, a debate to which James most famously contributed with "The Art of Fiction" (1884). The struggle of economic capital and cultural capital can more usefully inform our reading of Hyacinth's anxieties over social engagement than reference to contemporary political debates. Though masked by a superficial opposition of the political to the aesthetic, these anxieties might be understood as tensions within a single domain of the socioeconomic uncertainties of late-Victorian artistic production. That is, Hyacinth's inability to reconcile social engagement with his pursuit of beauty points not to an insurmountable division between social reform and aesthetic appreciation, but to ideological gaps between different possible configurations of art, the artist, and the public. The terms of contemporary debates over the cultural status of the novel structure the pattern of conflicts in Hyacinth's career, just as many of the novel's characters typify potential audiences—as James saw them—in the late-Victorian literary market. Hyacinth's frustrated desire to define an appropriate connection to "the people" is likewise analogous to James's need to reconcile his aesthetic ambitions with an equally strong desire to be read and appreciated. Like James, Hyacinth seeks to negotiate some form of social engagement that would be neither a submission to an undifferentiated vulgarity nor a personally vitiating and ethically suspect isolation.

In analyzing the basis of Hyacinth's impasse, it is instructive to begin with a character who suffers no such perplexity. Eustache Poupin, the talented artisan who secures Hyacinth's position at Crookenden's bookbindery and who plays mentor to Hyacinth's "disciple" (120), represents in many ways the equilibrium that Hyacinth feels incapable of achieving. A passionate socialist who never sacrifices his commitment to his artistic production, Poupin never considers that his taste is at odds with his sympathy for "the people." He combines, as we are told shortly after his introduction,

> a red-hot impatience for the general rectification, with an extraordinary decency of life and a worship of proper work. The Frenchman spoke, habitually, as if the great swindle practised upon the people were too impudent to be endured a moment longer, and yet he found patience for the most exquisite 'tooling,' and took a book in hand with the deliberation of one who should believe that everything was immutably constituted [. . .]. He delighted in the use of his hands and his tools and the exercise of his taste, which was faultless. (124-25)

Poupin is not alienated from his labor—his skill and taste make it a personal delight and a satisfying form of self-expression—nor is he estranged from the masses. Unlike Hyacinth, he unproblematically identifies himself with "the people," so that despite the fact that these classes are probably unable to purchase his work, he never considers his art to be incompatible with their interests: it is never a sacrifice or a betrayal. His revolutionary social engagement and his faultless taste are expressions of the same undivided identity, and both are motivated by a commitment to the diffusion of beauty.

As an artisan, Poupin's ability to synthesize taste, aesthetic production, and devotion to "the people" closely echoes familiar doctrines of William Morris, whom James himself met on arriving in London in the 1870s. As a socialist and leader of the arts and crafts movement, Morris hoped to combat the drudgery and alienation of industrialized existence by restoring what he saw as a lost sense of commitment to beauty in the production of commodities. In "The Lesser Arts" (1882), Morris proposes that artisans such as Poupin and Hyacinth are precisely the sort of people who are most capable of reconciling artistic quality with social engagement. The problem, as he frames it in this essay, is that the bulk of the population, "the public in general," has lost its sense of taste. They are "set on having things cheap, being so ignorant that they do not know when they get them nasty also" (250). The truly excellent, at the same time, has become "isolated and exclusive" in the hands of those who can afford it. But artisans enjoy a unique potential to combine taste and popular production: "I say all classes are to blame in this matter, but also I say that that the remedy lies with the handicraftsmen, who are not ignorant of these things like the public, and who have no call to be greedy and isolated like the manufacturers or middlemen; the duty and honour of educating the public lies with them" (250). As laborers and wage-earners rather than capitalists, the artisans' position in relation to the public is one of identification rather than "greedy and isolated" predation. And as members of this public, artisans can spread the aesthetic values to a society crucially devoid of them:

but now only let the arts which we are talking of beautify our labour, and
be widely spread, intelligent, well understood both by the maker and the
user, let them grow in one word *popular*, and there will be pretty much an
end of dull work and its wearing slavery [. . .]. I believe there is nothing
that will aid the world's progress so much as the attainment of this; I
protest there is nothing in the world I desire so much as this, wrapped up,
as I am sure it is, with changes political and social, that in one way or another we all desire. (235-36)

Like Poupin, Morris suggests that artistic production makes for non-alienated
labor, and that the diffusion of aesthetic values, in turn, will transform the
world in such a way as to make it more hospitable for beauty. Here the two
horns of the alienation dilemma are confronted with a single solution.

But if Poupin can understand the relationship of art and the public as
mutually beneficial, why is Hyacinth unable to share this optimism? Why
is he incapable of sustaining the level of satisfaction in his work that
Poupin maintains and that Morris suggests as the inevitable consequence
of combining art with labor? Why does he imagine the repercussions of a
revolutionary popularization of art as destructive rather than productive?
One explanation the novel repeatedly offers is the purely personal conflict
of Hyacinth's ambivalent heritage, his descent from the violent union of an
aristocratic father and a plebian mother. Hyacinth's belief that his taste derives from his ostensibly aristocratic blood prevents him from allowing for
the possibility of locating aesthetic taste among what Morris calls the
"public in general." His failure to reach Poupin's equilibrium would thus
be a matter of "his mixed, divided nature, his conflicting sympathies, his
eternal habit of swinging from one view to another" (478). Viewed in this
way, Hyacinth's dilemma, a result of his "nature," "feelings," and "habit,"
ceases to have much bearing on the broader social debate over the cultural
status of art and the artist. It becomes naturalized, reified as an individual
and unique problem rather than appearing as a structural problem dictated
by temporally specific, historically contingent developments in the production and consumption of art. The quirks of Hyacinth's heritage, however,
are only part of the problem; equally important is the novel's logic of taste,
discrimination, and popularity.

The key to Morris's solution is, "in one word," for art to become "*popular.*" But for Hyacinth, the idea of a popular form that meets his aesthetic
standards never enters the realm of the possible. Hyacinth, like everyone
else in the novel, never imagines any form of art except that associated
with privilege, leisure, and scarcity; "culture," in this novel, can mean only
high-culture. Popular art (by Hyacinth's very definitions) can never be
good art, and taste itself depends on discrimination and even outright class
antagonism: "The great monuments and treasures of art, the great palaces
and properties, the conquests of learning and taste," as he writes the
Princess, are based upon "the despotisms, the cruelties, [and] the exclu-
sions [. . .] of the past" (396). The idea, then, that a new, popular audience

could take control represents to Hyacinth the threat of a despotism of vulgarity that would oppress taste, and a new basis for exclusion which could very well banish his own art: "In spite of the example Eustache Poupin gave him of the reconcilement of disparities, he was afraid the democracy wouldn't care for perfect bindings or for the finest sort of conversation" (478). Of course, this is precisely what Hyacinth should not learn form Poupin, a figure who demonstrates—almost to absurdity—the possibility of political commitment coexisting with aesthetic appreciation. But it is not so much that Hyacinth fears that "democracy"—as a social system—will disdain high-culture; we have already seen how Poupin is a Democrat with "faultless" taste. He fears, more specifically, that the "public in general" would begin to have an influence over artistic production, to have the power to dictate how books are bound (if at all) as well as, presumably, control over the extent to which conversations are of "the finest sort." In short, he lacks Poupin's faith that, given the opportunity, "the people" would like to drink coffee and listen to the music of the spheres, or Morris's sense that a popular art could be predicated on intelligence and taste, that it could be "well understood both by the maker and the user." In direct contrast to Poupin's utopian image of a collected "human family," Hyacinth's "happier vision" of a potential future is "the vision of societies in which, in splendid rooms, with smiles and soft voices, distinguished men, with women who were both proud and gentle, talked about art, literature, and history" (145). Even Hyacinth's fantasies require a divided society in which men are "distinguished" and women "proud." The nightmarish counterpart to his dream is the anxiety of a triumphantly homogeneous vulgarity, for which there could be no cure but obliteration:

> There were nights when everyone he met appeared to reek with gin and filth, and he found himself elbowed by figures as foul as lepers. Some of the women and girls, in particular, were appalling—saturated with alcohol and vice, brutal, bedraggled, obscene. 'What remedy but another deluge, what alchemy but annihilation?' he asked himself, as he went his way; and he wondered what fate there could be in the great scheme of things, for a planet overgrown with such vermin, what redemption but to be hurled against a ball of consuming fire. (481)

The general public in *The Princess Casamassima* is the subject of more extended scrutiny in the person of Millicent Henning, whom both Hyacinth and the narrator treat as a representative of its taste, a synecdoche for the masses. As "the genius of urban civilization, the muse of cockneyism" (93), Millicent may laugh "with the laugh of the people" (160), but she also represents their vulgarity:

> for our hero she was magnificently plebeian [. . .]. She summed up the sociable, humorous, ignorant chatter of the masses, their capacity for offensive and defensive passion, their instinctive perception of their strength on the day they should really exercise it; and as much as any of this, their

ideal of something smug and prosperous, where washed hands, and plates
in rows on dressers, and stuffed birds under glass, and family photographs, would symbolise success. She was none the less plucky for being
at bottom a shameless Philistine, ambitious of a front-garden with rock-
work; and she presented the plebeian character in none the less plastic a
form. (161)

In representing both the masses' incipient power and their want of discrimination, Millicent is a distressing allegorical figure for Hyacinth, particularly because of her opinions about his own artistic pretensions. In an early
conversation with Hyacinth's guardian, Miss Pynsent, Millicent learns that
he has gone to work for Mr. Crookenden:

> "A bookbindery? Laws!" said Miss Henning. [. . .] Then she added, "But I
> didn't think he would ever follow a trade."
> "A trade?" cried Miss Pynsent. "You should hear Mr. Robinson speak
> of it. He considers it one of the fine arts."
> Millicent smiled, as if she knew how people often considered things,
> and remarked that very likely it was a tidy, comfortable work, but she
> couldn't believe there was much to be seen in it. (97)

Since Millicent stands for Hyacinth's estimate of popular taste more generally, we can understand why he doubts—as Morris does not—that there
could be a mutual basis of understanding between producers of art and a
popular audience. When Millicent later asks Hyacinth if she may see samples of his work, he declines, saying "You wouldn't know how good they
are" (111).

Hyacinth fails to imagine a productive symbiosis between his art and
the audience represented by Millicent, but he is similarly displeased by the
prospect of becoming entirely estranged from "the people." Such aesthetic
detachment is represented as the other extreme in the novel by Captain
Sholto, a "particular specimen" of a "man of fashion" (229-30), in whose
cold calculations, not unlike those of Wilkie Collins's Frederick Fairlie,
both works of art and human beings become commodities to be collected.
Sholto is completely divorced from the world of labor and production, and
it becomes clear that this separation is the cause of his depravity: "He was
a cumberer of the earth, and purely selfish, in spite of his devoted, disinterested airs. [. . .] whatever feeling poor Sholto might have, four-fifths of it
were purely theatrical. He was not in the least a natural human being, but
had a hundred affectations and attitudes, the result of never having to put
his hand to anything; having no serious tastes and yet being born to a little
'position'" (352-53). In his indolence, his artificiality, and his callousness,
Sholto closely resembles contemporary stereotypes of aesthetes, of whose
reputed separation of art from human sympathy James was sharply critical;[9] that there is also "something sinister in him" is typical of the usual
logic of James's critique. Greedy and isolated (like Morris's capitalists),
Sholto stands for an alternative possible audience, but one which is just as

unsatisfactory in its effete posturing as a popular audience is in its ignorance: "That, at bottom, was all he represented—idle, trifling, luxurious, yet at the same time pretentious leisure, the sort of thing that led people to invent false, humbugging duties, because they had no real ones" (352). The "pretentious" Captain is so disengaged from a sense of human importance, a feeling of actual duty, that he becomes a collection of affectations without any "serious tastes." Sholto collects for reasons of fashion and personal gain, which is to say that his motivation is linked to his own status rather than the status of art; the actual quality of art, its beauty, becomes unimportant. The "bindings of his books," as Hyacinth pointedly observes, "were not very good" (232).

Sholto demonstrates to Hyacinth what might happen if he gives up on the public altogether—a social detachment that would debilitate his taste—while Millicent shows that the vulgar mass is likely to be unreceptive. The problems they represent to Hyacinth become more pronounced when we recognize that they are the novel's two greatest consumers. Millicent is a devotee of vulgar fashion, and despite spending her working days in a department store surrounded by "the freshest products of modern industry," she is nonetheless "addicted" to "looking into the windows of shops, before which, in long contemplative halts, she picked out freely the articles she wouldn't mind calling her own" (162). Sholto, at the other end of the social scale, keeps his rooms "filled with the spoils of travel. There was not a country in the world he did not appear to have ransacked" (230). Understood as two sides of the same dilemma of audience reception, the convergence of Millicent and Sholto to exclude Hyacinth in the last scene before his suicide becomes particularly suggestive. The collapsing together of wealth and vulgarity into an undifferentiated and insidious consumerism is Hyacinth's nightmare.

SYMPATHY AND APPRECIATION

As a self-proclaimed artist himself, Hyacinth suffers a paralyzing fear of his work's reception. After binding a volume of Tennyson as a gift for the Princess, he finds that he is afraid to give it up to anyone but her. Offered the chance to have his package forwarded to her at the address of her aristocratic friends, Hyacinth experiences "a sudden indisposition to launch his humble tribute into the vast, the possibly cold unknown of a ducal circle. He decided to retain his little package for the present; he would give it to her when he should see her again, and he turned away without parting with it" (254). As I have suggested, though, it is not simply ducal circles that scare Hyacinth, but public audiences more generally. To launch his art into a void, to hand it over to some unknown public, to allow it to become an alienated commodity, is an act that frightens both Hyacinth and James. The latter describes his failures in terms very like the ones Hyacinth uses here. As James wrote to William Dean Howells in 1886, "I have lately published 2 long-winded serials [*The Bostonians* and *The Princess Casamas-sima*], lasting between them far more than 2 years—of which, in all that time no audible echo or reverberation of any kind, either in America or here, has come back to me. If I had not my bread and butter to earn I should lay down my pen tomorrow" (qtd. in Anesko 101). The "vast [. . .] unknown" of the ducal circle and the grim silence of the marketplace both represent public audiences, from the artist's point of view, as a great void into which art must be sacrificed, an abyss at the edge of which the artist stands alone, alienated both from the work and from the public, hoping in vain for some indication of its effect.

Despite the setback in presenting the Princess with his work, Hyacinth's connection to her represents his closest and most important relationship, and through it the novel implies a new alternative of artistic exchange, an aesthetic of the personal that could obviate dependence on a possibly un-grateful public. When he works on the volume of Tennyson for the Princess, he feels none of the drudgery that he often associates with his work at Crookenden's. Taking his materials out of the workshop and working only at home, he binds the book "with passion, with religion, and produce[s] a masterpiece of firmness and finish." Refusing to give it up to anyone but her, Hyacinth finds that the book "seemed to create a sort of material link between the Princess and himself [and] turned into a kind of proof and gage, as if a ghost, in vanishing from sight, had left a palpable relic" (254). By creating the book outside of his workplace, and by keeping it out of public circulation, Hyacinth prevents it from becoming a com-modity disassociated from his labor and out of his control. Indeed, rather than making him feel alienated, this "masterpiece" allows him to feel un-usually attached. He makes of the Princess an ideal audience of one, and consciously separates their relationship from the world of the marketplace, just as he later decides to refuse her offer of wages for the work he does for her. The affinity that makes their connection possible is based on similari-ties in taste and background—both have a mixed heritage and a somewhat ambiguous class position—but also on a more profound ability to under-stand and appreciate one another. The Princess, for example, is uniquely capable of recognizing the crux of Hyacinth's dilemma:

> she broke into an exclamation which touched him almost more than any-thing she had ever done, giving him the highest opinion of her delicacy and sympathy and putting him before himself as if the words were a little portrait. "Fancy the strange, the bitter fate: to be constituted as you are constituted, to feel the capacity that you must feel, and yet to look at things only through the glass of the pastry cook's window!" (337)

The predicament that the Princess recognizes here is precisely the same as that which James, in his preface for the New York edition, emphasized as the very germ from which the character Hyacinth Robinson grew.[10] Her ability to read Hyacinth so insightfully indicates the interpretive power of her "delicacy and sympathy," while the "little portrait" she thus figuratively gives him suggests the reciprocity of their aesthetic union.

The relationship between the Princess and Hyacinth is fleeting, but its suggestion of a possible appreciative affinity between artist and audience recurs frequently in James's fiction. What seems striking about James's formulation is how infrequently such an understanding may be reached, and how tenuous it will be. James's artists are often so hard to appreciate that their ideal audience is likely to be limited to a few bright individuals, and sometimes only to one.[11] Herein lies the substance of James's new argument for the novel's potential artistic dignity. Rather than invest the value of fiction in its potential to reach and influence great numbers of readers, James's model emphasizes appreciation as a kind of precious rarity, which could serve as a proof of distinction for the limited group of readers who could get the most from it. The Victorian keyword "sympathy" thus undergoes a crucial redefinition, becoming a tool of cultural discrimination rather than a means of imagining universal cohesion. The Princess's sympathetic understanding of Hyacinth, for example, marks her difference from Millicent, "whose sympathy couldn't have the fineness he was looking for, since her curiosity was vulgar" (110); she comes closer instead to that "disinterested sympathy which, under favouring circumstances, establishes itself between the artist and the connoisseur" (115). The most crucial of those "favouring circumstances" is exactly the selective application of sympathy that distinguishes both the artist and the connoisseur.

The historical significance of James's revision of the notion of sympathy can hardly be overemphasized, for it is at the very core of his contribution to the contemporary debate over the cultural value of fiction and the status of novelists. For Walter Besant, James's chief adversary in this debate, sympathy was in fact the basis of the novel's claim to artistic preeminence, although his use of the term could not be more different from James's. Fiction, Besant argues,

> not only requires of its followers, but also creates in readers, that sentiment which is destined to be a most mighty engine in deepening and widening the civilisation of the world. We call it Sympathy [. . .]. The modern Sympathy includes not only the power to pity the sufferings of others, but also that of understanding their very souls; it is the reverence for man, the respect for his personality, the recognition of his individuality, and the enormous value of one man, the perception of one man's relation to another, his duties and responsibilities. Through the strength of the newly born faculty, and aided by the guidance of a great artist, we are enabled to discern the real indestructible man beneath the rags and filth of a common castaway, and the possibilities of the meanest gutter-child that steals in the streets for its daily bread. Surely that is a wonderful Art which endows the people—all the people—with this power of vision and feeling. (25-27)

For Besant, sympathy derives its force from its ability to *erase* distinctions; theoretically, at least, it embraces popularity and tends to counteract taste. In practice, Besant, like Wilkie Collins before him, supplemented the novelist's function as a sympathetic guide with a rhetoric of professional specialization that sits uneasily with this egalitarian ideal. Yet Besant's reiteration of the old Victorian model of sympathy reminds us that the distinctions and divisions of the late Victorian readership were neither welcomed nor pursued by all novelists. Like Morris, Besant believed that the future of civilization depended on popular art. James, on the other hand, was more inclined to protect art from the populace. While James's "The Art of Fiction" is as preoccupied with reception as Besant's argument, it is, as John Goode has observed, "less concerned with the effect of the novel on the public than with the effect of the public on the novel" (251).

Though James's "Art of Fiction" was in many ways a reaction against the professional and ethical rules laid out by Besant—James wrote to Robert Louis Stevenson that his rejoinder was "simply a plea for liberty" (qtd. in Goode 259)—his theory of the novelist's art suggested new rules of its own, particularly new criteria for judging the artistry of novelists. Against Besant's argument that the novel's value depended on its ability to reach and reform a wide audience, James offered a more individual model: "A novel is in its broadest definition a personal, a direct impression of life: that, to begin with, constitutes its value, which is greater or less according to the intensity of the impression" (50). While Besant clings to the notion of a common humanity that novelists may reveal and reinforce, James privileges the personal over the collective, and individual impressions over shared assumptions. He thereby grants novelists a great deal more importance, since literary value will depend not on any effect novels might have, but on the quality and intensity of authors' impressions. The elaborate advice that Besant offers aspiring novelists thus gives way in James's theory to one fundamental injunction: "Try to be one of the people on whom nothing is lost!" (53).

The logic by which James's system of literary value emphasizes the distinctive sensitivity and intensity of the novelist's perspective leads in his work to a narrative focus on the impressions of a central consciousness, which likewise privileges individual interpretation. In *The Princess Casamassima*, Hyacinth must, like a novelist, become a "youth on whom nothing was lost" (164). Otherwise, as the novel's preface suggests, the economy of interest would be upset: "We care, our sympathy and curiosity care, comparatively little for what happens to the stupid, the course, and the blind" (35). Indeed, the understanding between writers and readers depends upon a complicity between them and a mediating protagonist, all of whom come to resemble one another:

> the person capable of feeling in the given case more than another of what
> is to be felt for it, and so serving in the highest degree to *record* it dramat-

ically and objectively, is the only sort of person on whom we can count
not to betray, to cheapen or, as we say, give away, the value and beauty of
the thing. By so much as the affair matters *for* some such individual, by so
much do we get the best there is of it, and by so much as it falls within the
scope of a denser and duller, a more vulgar and more shallow capacity, do
we get a picture dim and meagre. (39-40)

The person qualified to "*record*" feelings must of course be the author as
well as the protagonist, while the person capable of feeling such experiences in a way that will not cheapen them must also be an appreciative and
discriminating reader, since the readers will find the utmost value in a
novel only insofar as they are capable of understanding the protagonist's
feelings as the author presents them. This ideal convergence of writer, character, and reader thus serves to confirm a mutually high degree of sensibility and to prove the difference between their perspective and something
"more vulgar." In this way, a protagonist like Hyacinth comes to stand in
relation to James and his potential readers as the tastefully bound edition
of Tennyson stands between Hyacinth and the Princess; the central character, and the novel constructed around him, links the distinction of artist
and reader.

Hyacinth is the first in a long line of Jamesian protagonists whose interpretation of events stands between the reader and any objective certainties,
thus drawing attention to the reader's own interpretive activity. A number
of critics in recent years have approvingly cited James's narrative innovations not only as an aesthetic breakthrough, but as a morally admirable,
anti-authoritative epistemology. Sarah Chapman, for example, has called
this method the basis of a "new humanism": "the writer will recognise the
essential, collaborative role of the reader, for, having limited his portrayal
of reality to that experienced by one or a few characters only, that is, having abandoned omniscience, the writer will require the reader to interpret
the experience of the fiction for himself" (5). I will examine in the next section whether giving up narrative omniscience necessarily entails sacrificing
authority, but for now I want to suggest an important limit to the ethics of
James's new methods. As far as collaborations go, the sort that James offers is hardly an equal partnership. James does not celebrate the capacity of
readers to create interpretations of their own, but their potential to recognize on their own the genius of the author, who becomes the end of all interpretations. We should read, as "The Art of Fiction" explains, so that
"we can enjoy one of the most charming of pleasures, we can estimate
quality, we can apply the test of execution. The execution belongs to the
author alone; it is what is most personal to him, and we measure him by
that" (50). Readers are free to exercise their own taste, in other words, but
the issue before them is the ability of the writer. At the same moment that
Besant was arguing—however naively—for the recognition of fiction as a
means to force the Victorians to recognize their common humanity, James
concentrated on valorizing the novelist's superior intellect as an end in it-

self: "the deepest quality of a work of art will always be the quality of the mind of the producer. In proportion as that intelligence is fine will the novel, the picture, the statue partake of the substance of beauty and truth. To be constituted of such elements is, to my vision, to have purpose enough" (64). The theoretical egalitarianism of invitations to readers to interpret his work should be measured against James's historical context, in which his representations of superfine artistic sensibilities and discriminating readers appear ambitiously elitist.

THE SUICIDE OF THE AUTHOR

Walter Besant may be the chief adversary named by James's "Art of Fiction," but Anthony Trollope emerges in the essay as another significant villain. James casts Trollope as one of those novelists who "have a habit of giving themselves away which must often bring tears to the eyes of people who take their fiction seriously." Trollope's threat to the novel's dignity lies in the double implication of "giving themselves away." On one hand, Trollope appears to cheapen the symbolic exchange value of novels by pandering directly to his readers, thus undercutting James's delicate economy of cultural capital. On the other hand, he manages to demystify the illusion of artistic performance, in much the same way we might speak of magicians "giving away" their secrets: "In a digression, a parenthesis or an aside, he concedes to the reader that he and this trusting friend are only 'making believe.' He admits that the events he narrates have not really happened, and that he can give his narrative any turn the reader may like best. Such a betrayal of a sacred office seems to me, I confess, a terrible crime" (46). For James these two complaints are closely entwined. Demystifying the creative presence behind the text is much the same as admitting that the novelist writes in the service of no higher power than market demand. Such a performance was, as James had complained about Trollope in an earlier review, "deliberately inartistic": "He took a suicidal satisfaction in reminding the reader that the story he was telling was only, after all, a make believe" ("Anthony Trollope" 1343).

James's concern about the exposure of the novelist within the text corresponded to similar misgivings about would-be professionals such as Besant, who publicly argued that authorship was something decidedly more quotidian than a "sacred office." As James wrote privately to Edmund Gosse,

> authorship is guilty of a great mistake, a gross want of tact, in formulating and publishing its claim to be a 'profession.' Let other trades call it so— and let it take no notice. That's enough. It ought to have of the professions only a professional thoroughness. But never to have that, and to cry over the housetops instead that it *is* the grocer and the shoemaker is to bring on itself a ridicule of which it will simply die. (qtd. in Anesko viii)

James's recurring metaphor of death underscores his pessimistic sense of the dignity of authorship, but it also provides a link between the "suicidal satisfaction" of Trollope's too visible narrators and the equally self-destructive advertisement of professionalism. Pressed on all sides by novelists with a reckless death wish, James turned in *The Princess Casamassima* to a different kind of suicide, one which represents less a resignation to those forces which threaten to shred artistic dignity than a form of liberation from them.

Hyacinth's suicide at the conclusion of the novel has been read as an affirmation of his integrity in the face of the equally intolerable deaths (at the hands of the revolutionaries or the police) to which any other action would lead. In this respect, his suicide may be understood to thematize the emerging novelistic emphasis on preserving individual wholeness amid cultural fragmentation. Indeed, Hyacinth's fate begins to seem rather typical in context with works by other late-Victorian writers of "serious" fiction; consider, for example, the suicide of Harold Biffen, the misunderstood Naturalist in *New Grub Street,* or the final self-annihilating impulses of Thomas Hardy's Michael Henchard and Jude Fawley. In the case of *The Princess Casamassima*, suicide offers Hyacinth the radical proof of autonomy analogous to that which James sought for novelists. But Hyacinth's mysterious death—he vanishes from the story before his corpse appears in the final scene as "something black, something ambiguous, something outstretched" (590)—points to the more important narrative corollary to James's thematic interest in suicide. It is in the narrator's refusal to document the moment of Hyacinth's death, in his deliberate ambiguities, and in his reticence in describing anything beyond Hyacinth's direct experience that we really find the death of the Victorian novelist. Rather than writing with Trollope's suicidal visibility, James's narrator withdraws into a strangely conspicuous absence at the plot's most crucial turning points. His self-effacement recalls what Fredric Jameson, in reference to the "radical depersonalization" of Gissing's prose, suggestively describes as a sort of "preventative suicide" (204).

In drawing attention to the similarities between what James saw as Trollope's suicide and what we might read as James's own, I do not mean to suggest that the two are functionally equivalent. Instead, we should read James's narrative self-effacement and wonted ambiguity as a reaction against the representations of authorship he viewed as inimical, and even against forms of publicity with which the novels of many of his contemporaries were advertised.[12] We should not be inclined, then, to understand James's absence from his narratives as a sign of his political neutrality, or as a token of his novels' autonomy from contemporary market forces. Self-effacement works instead as a paradoxical kind of authority. If James's narrative absence is a form of death, it does not so much imply his inconsequence as it does his empowered transcendence. James's well-known praise for Flaubert's impersonal style may thus be read as a program for his own authorial performance: "The Artist must be present in his work like God in Creation, invisible and almighty, everywhere felt but nowhere seen."

James's portrayals of the suggestive force of what remains unsaid or unseen are so pervasive, especially in his later stories and novels, that such absences have come to be the clearest hallmarks of his work. In "The Turn of the Screw" alone there are, despite its brevity, "approximately six hundred long dashes"[13] indicating half-finished sentences, inexpressible surmises, and unspeakable anxieties. But *The Princess Casamassima*, which represents a critical stage in James's development of the center of consciousness technique and of his own invisibility, offers James's most thorough exploration of obscurity as a technique of social power. The anarchist movement that provides the backdrop for Hyacinth's career is consistently described with a logic that echoes James's admiration of Flaubert. "It is more strange than I can say," Hyacinth tells the Princess, "Nothing of it appears above the surface [. . .]. The invisible, impalpable wires are everywhere, passing through everything, attaching themselves to objects in which one would never think of looking for them" (330). And as the novel repeatedly explains, the anarchists' elusiveness—rather than, say, their political principles or popular support—is the source of their power:

> the forces secretly arrayed against the present social order were pervasive and universal, in the air one breathed, in the ground one trod, in the hand of an acquaintance that one might touch or the eye of a stranger that might rest a moment on one's own. They were above, below, within, without, in every contact and combination of life; and it was no disproof of them to say it was too odd they should lurk in a particular improbable form. To lurk in improbable forms was precisely their strength.

In the novel's only reference to the anarchists' doing anything besides lurking menacingly at the fringes of perception, a vague "attempt" made in the sixties, it is once again their obscurity that constitutes their greatest success: the "very fact of the impunity, the invisibility of the persons concerned in it had given the predatory classes, had given all of Europe, a shudder that had not yet subsided" (288). The leader of the abortive coup had been the enigmatic Diedrich Hoffendahl, still the mastermind of the anarchist movement to which Hyacinth pledges himself and the most strikingly absent figure in the novel. The omission of the scene in which Hyacinth meets Hoffendahl and commits his life to the revolution, like the exclusion of Hyacinth's suicide, constitutes a silence so blatant that our attention is drawn to the narrator's reticence . It is the same mystery that establishes Hoffendahl as the movement's "holy of holies" (330), its unrepresentable "genuine article" (295). "The Master," as Hyacinth imagines him, is also an artist figure,[14] a "great musician" and "composer" who treats "all things, persons, institutions, ideas, as so many notes in his great symphonic revolt" (333).

Hoffendahl, like James, is no less authoritative for being invisible. In light of this similarity, it is instructive to recall the conclusion to the novel's New York Edition preface, in which James considers his initial concern over writing a novel about a revolutionary world of which he knew so little. Instead of allowing his lack of direct knowledge hinder him, he made a virtue of his limited experience: "if you haven't, for fiction, the root of the matter in you, haven't the sense of life and the penetrating imagination, you are a fool in the very presence of the revealed and the assured; but [. . .] if you are so armed you are not really helpless, not without your resource, even before mysteries abysmal" (48). James thus stands in relation to political radicalism in much the same way that readers stand in relation to James, and the resemblance helps us to understand how authorial obscurity helps to enhance the prestige of readers as well as writers. Such mysteries open an interpretive space in which readers with a "penetrating imagination" can distinguish themselves. In this way, James's narrative method seems made to order for the emerging critical tradition that found its *raison d'être* in the idea that the general public was incapable of truly appreciating great literature without skilled help. As this tradition gave rise to the academic study of literature, James became the prototypical "Master" of his genre.

The extent to which either Hoffendahl or James can be construed as subversive is open to debate, and in both cases the question is held open by the mystery each cultivates. The dynamic that allows characters in *The Princess Casamassima* to envision Hoffendahl as "the genuine article" is uncannily similar to that which allows McWhirter to call James's New York Edition "genuinely subversive." But even though any novel can be shown to be internally divided, unstable, and multivalent—and hence potentially subversive of any ideology it espouses—we can judge with some confidence its implications for the practices of reading and writing in which it was produced. In this context, we can see the tendency of James's representation of authorship to consecrate fiction as a field of individual appreciation rather than collective action, and to exploit the fragmentation of the public as an opportunity to enforce a hierarchy of tastes and sensibilities. James's influence in this regard, in fact, is still noticeable in Rowe's desire to discover new ways to appreciate the novelist himself, or as Rowe puts it, "to read the theoretical potential of Henry James" (xiii). This continuing impulse to treat an author as the goal of criticism rather than as a starting point for larger cultural questions is a legacy of James's generation, and the mysterious death of the intimate novelist has left behind an authoritative ghost that haunts criticism still.

CHAPTER FIVE

Veiled Women in the Marketplace of Culture:
Authorships and Domesticities in Gaskell and Eliot

"Currer Bell," "Mrs. Gaskell," "George Eliot": the very names under which the work of the most canonical Victorian women novelists circulated immediately suggest unexamined complications in the narrative of authorship I have proposed. If, after all, the advent of the properly Victorian novelist may be symbolized by the transformation of the impersonal and ironic "Boz" into the intimate and sympathetic "Dickens," then the persistence of pseudonymity and even anonymity among women writers must mean that they were improper indeed. The prospect of making friends with authors, even if only in the most fanciful ways, is considerably troubled when those authors conceal themselves behind pen names or—as in the case in Gaskell's early career—refuse to identify themselves at all. The problems suggested by these names indicate much more serious difficulties in failing to account for gender differences in Victorian authorship; in a society that so starkly divided economic privileges, legal rights, and educational opportunities between the sexes, the practical experiences of writing and publishing were inevitably uneven for men and women. And if women writers cannot be smoothly integrated into a unified tradition with men, neither can they be simply understood in relation to one another. These same three names imply a diversity of genders—the evasively androgynous, the conventionally feminine, the confidently masculine—that reveals a complex array of strategies for self-representation that can hardly be reduced to a stable and coherent women's tradition. On the other hand, attempts to transcend the individual differences in women writers' experience by analyzing, more abstractly, the gendered implications of fictional discourse in the period pose an altogether contrary problem: from this perspective, it becomes difficult to describe the place of women writers in the history of Victorian authorship not because they are too different from men, but because they are too similar.

Modern accounts of Victorian fictional discourse hold that novels, regardless of the sex of their producers, were effectively gendered feminine. The central preoccupations of the genre with family life and marriage plots, its valuation of intimacy and sympathy over competition and commerce, and, above all, its ideal of the fundamental moral integrity of domesticity: all of these are virtues Victorians routinely associated with women. And thus, as Nancy Armstrong has argued, the "authority" of novelists was "not a matter of biological gender, for any use of language was considered essentially female if sufficiently detached from the contentious ways of the marketplace and rooted instead in the values of the heart and home" (41). By these criteria, the most feminine of novelists, the great champion of domesticity, is not Brontë or Gaskell or Eliot, but Dickens. No other writer had so relentlessly or successfully positioned himself at the center of the Victorian home; the titles he devised for two of his journals, *The Cricket on the Hearth* and *Household Words*, are only the most conspicuous tokens of an ideology maintained throughout his career. As Mary Poovey has observed, "Dickens constructed and appropriated a representation of work that rested on and derived its terms form the ideological separation of spheres and from the representation of women's domestic labor as nonalienated labor" (125). Here we begin to see the reasons why a woman writer might feel discouraged from representing herself as the visible and intimate nucleus of cultural sympathy in the same spectacular way that Dickens did, and why anonymity and pseudonymity remained so attractive: the cultural logic with which Dickens validated his work also dictated that women had duties other than writing. As Poovey continues,

> if the feminization of authorship derived its authority from an idealized representation of woman and the domestic sphere, then for a woman to depart from that idealization by engaging in commercial business was to collapse the boundary between the spheres of alienated and nonalienated labor. A woman who wrote for publication threatened to collapse the ideal from which her authority was derived and to which her fidelity was necessary for so many other social institutions to work. (125)

Poovey implies the rather paradoxical problem that women writers threatened Victorian fiction's domestic values precisely because they were associated with domesticity, or, to put it another way, women writers could not be as effectively feminine as men could be. This counterintuitive clash between (public) ideology and (private) experience produced women's subordination and effacement, and it continues to present a pitfall for the feminist study of the novel's history even now, since the feminization of the genre as a whole eclipses the particular representational strategies women writers explored.

If there is one generalization we can make with confidence about women writers in the nineteenth century, it is that they felt the tensions between private and public life even more acutely than their male counterparts. And discussions of authorship, the ideology poised between the private work of writing and the public circulation of texts, makes these tensions especially evident. Gaskell's biography of Charlotte Brontë, for instance, notes that authorship divides her subject into two different lives: "Henceforward Charlotte Brontë's existence becomes divided into two parallel currents—her life as Currer Bell, the author; her life as Charlotte Brontë, the woman. There were separate duties belonging to each character—not opposing each other; not impossible, but difficult to be reconciled" (*Life* 271). Torn between such "separate duties," women writers learned that domestic realism is not quite the same as domestic reality, and that, while male writers could benefit from images of authorship that imaginatively minimized differences between public and private identities, their own authorship could silence their identities as women.

Despite the perplexing fissure between the gendered expectations of individual experience and those of novelistic discourse, it remains possible to recover some sense of the particular interventions of women writers in the transformations of Victorian authorship. But first this separation itself must be scrutinized; as Gaskell reminds us, the discordant imperatives that structured the experiences of women writers may be "difficult to be reconciled," but the task is "not impossible." I propose that the key to such a reconciliation lies in the construction of *domesticity*, a term that shaped *both* the specific concerns of women writers and the distinctive aesthetic of Victorian realism. But rather than treating domesticity as the consoling representation of a fantasy of purified private life, I will read it as an ideological field in which the very division between public and private is painstakingly interrogated. This perspective challenges the claims of a number of eminently influential critics, such as Nancy Armstrong, Mary Poovey, and Catherine Gallagher, all of whom have concluded that the cultural legitimacy of the Victorian novel depended on imagining the domestic space as a tranquil haven, safe from the self-interested predations of a competitive market and the vexations of political unrest.[1] This hypothesis rehearses what more recent feminist scholarship has called "the conventional critical notion of separate spheres" (Eger, et al. 3), the misleading tendency to uphold and even to reify those boundaries between public and private that seem so quintessentially Victorian. While Armstrong, Poovey, and Gallagher are well aware of the constructedness of the gendered division of culture, and while none of them approve of it, their arguments about fiction's social role are reluctant to acknowledge the ways in which novels defied and breached this barricade. Not all of the Victorians—and certainly not all Victorian women—were entirely persuaded by the ideal of the household as a place where social problems are effortlessly resolved, and where politics recede into invisibility. In fact, it takes only a slight shift in emphasis to perceive the extent to which Victorian novels show us the reverse: the domestic, *par excellence*, is the realm of anxiety, constantly menaced and frequently torn asunder by economic pressures, class antagonism, adultery, illegitimacy, greed, crime, marriage and property laws, and by every other public and political problem the most fevered Victorian mind could imagine. Instead of claiming that such novels represented domesticity as a retreat from public problems, we might more accurately generalize that they employ it as the primary lens through which such problems are perceived and expressed. Indeed, the plots of Victorian novels are generated precisely by the *absence* of an idealized, harmonious domesticity, which we find elusively retreating to the very horizon of narratability, where it briefly glimmers as a tentative conclusion to storytelling, as the unrepresentable future of a strife-wracked present. In this troubled field, women novelists could address issues that pertained directly to concerns about gender and about the publicity of their work.

Once we recognize domesticity as a sphere of anxious contention rather than as a static ideal of placid isolation, we can more clearly perceive that it has a history. This chapter focuses on novels by two writers, Elizabeth Gaskell and George Eliot, to demonstrate how two strongly contrasting representations of domesticity—neither one of which bears much resemblance to the harmonious, apolitical territory of the domestic ideal—contributed to the ongoing revisions of Victorian authorship. In Gaskell's *Mary Barton*, the home is never independent of political and economic crises, and in representing a constant movement across the domestic threshold, she advances an image of authorship not subject to strictures of contemporary femininity. In *Middlemarch*, on the other hand, Eliot launches a withering assault on domestic ideals in order to underscore her own novel's superior realism and to bolster her own cultural authority. In keeping with the general methods of this study and with the narrative framework outlined in my previous chapters, I will emphasize the ways in which both of these writers, in their divergent constructions of authorship and of domesticity, responded to changes in the reading public. Thus I do not only ask how women novelists differently address an emerging mass market, but also how the changing pressures of the market produced different domesticities and different authorships.

DOMESTICITY AND DEMAGOGUERY

First published anonymously in October 1848, *Mary Barton* was an immediate popular success. Its immense circulation may be partially attributed to the continuing shrewdness of Chapman and Hall, the pioneering publishers of *Pickwick*, who brought out Gaskell's book in two volumes for eighteen shillings, a substantially lower cost than the thirty-one shillings of the triple decker and cheaper even than the twenty shillings of a monthly serial. But the text itself could hardly have been more perfectly calculated to ensure immediate and widespread attention. Appearing against the backdrop of the Chartist unrest at home, mass starvation across the Irish Sea, and, most emphatically, the lingering specter of the great European revolutions of that year, the Carlylean "condition of England" question to which the novel speaks had never been more ominously pressing. The spirit with which *Mary Barton* addresses such fears, moreover, was familiar and optimistically reassuring. Conforming to the rhetoric of sympathetic harmony popularized by Dickens—the paradigm that I have called Industrial Romanticism—the novel contends that contemporary social crises need not demand a radical restructuring of wealth or privilege but only a relatively intuitive, natural, and indeed Christian adjustment of feelings.

Asked by Chapman and Hall to provide a preface to her novel, Gaskell responded with a thoroughly conventional statement of her purpose. In what had become by 1848 an almost ritualized performance of authorial intimacy and sympathy, the author explains that

> I had always felt a deep sympathy with the care-worn men, who looked as if doomed to struggle through their lives in strange alternations between work and want; tossed to and fro by circumstances, apparently in even greater degree than other men. A little manifestation of this sympathy, and a little attention to the expression of feelings on the part of some of the work-people with whom I was acquainted, had laid open to me the hearts of one or two of the more thoughtful among them [. . .]. (3)

Sympathy, according to the preface, is both the genesis of this narrative and its medium, so that the author—no less than the story's characters—must model the requisite manifestations of sympathy through which the threat of class conflict may be defused. Expressing her own feelings as well as those of the Manchester laborers she describes, this author figure can enlist the reader in a grand social recognition of common feelings, a sentimental foundation for the ameliorative political and economic ideology of "common interests" (3). Such logic, it is worth reiterating, is not new; the same implicit claims for the value of novels and the influence of novelists may be found in the works of Dickens, of Collins, or of any of a dozen other writers of the period. The only customary element missing in this preface, in fact, is an explicit reference to friendship.[2] This absence might be explained in part by the author's anonymity, or by the fact that *Mary Barton* was her first novel, and it had not had a serialized novel's opportunity to develop familiarity with readers. Gaskell was not yet acquainted, as it were, with the public, though friendship would later become and important component of her representation of authorship. In one of the passages of her *Life of Charlotte Brontë* that tells us as much about Gaskell's views as her subject's, she quotes a letter she received from Brontë that that equates actual intimacy, private correspondence, and the circulation of her fiction: "thank you for your letter; it was as pleasant as a quiet chat, as welcome as spring showers, as receiving a friend's visit; in short, it was very like a page of 'Cranford'" (436). But at the time of *Mary Barton*, the absence of more visible representations of friendship, coupled with the book's anonymity, implies a significant variation on Dickensian authorship, one that begins to explain very real differences in Gaskell's self-representation as an author. Her tendency towards self-abnegation rather than self-display, the relative unobtrusiveness of her narrator, and her apparent lack of ease with or command over her readers and the materials of her own fiction all distinguish Gaskell's authorship from Dickens's, and have all contributed to the long critical marginalization of the demure "Mrs. Gaskell." In returning to the moment of *Mary Barton*'s anonymous publication, I will argue that the distinctive qualities of Gaskell's authorship are neither accidental nor indicative of artistic incompetence. Instead, they are determined obliquely by her experiences as a woman writer and explicitly by her understanding of the novel's relationship with the reading public. Both of these related causes are legible in the novel's revisionist representation of domesticity.

Dickens was quick to recognize Gaskell's talent and her compatibility with his own sense of the novelist's mission, and she became one of the major contributors to *Household Words*, where her *Cranford* (1851-1853) and *North and South* (1854-1855) were serialized. Yet in a journal where Dickens's name appears on every page, Gaskell's work continued to appear anonymously.[3] This satisfaction with anonymous publication in her early career, much like the conventionally decorous "Mrs. Gaskell" by which she would later be known, would seem to indicate a significantly gendered departure from Dickensian authorship, proof of a restrictive double standard that prevented female novelists from representing authorship as an unmediated expression of their personality and individuality. And indeed, Gaskell's private letters are filled with demonstrations of the tensions she experienced between domestic responsibilities, those "daily small Lilliputian arrows of peddling cares" and her literary ambitions: "One thing is pretty clear, *Women*, must give up living an artist's life, if home duties are to be paramount."[4] Comments like this support the notion that Gaskell's career was fissured by an understanding of domesticity that demanded a choice between private and public life and that kept her from fully realizing an authorship of her own. As Elsie B. Michie has explained, "Elizabeth Gaskell confronted a definition of femininity as split between a proper, private realm, the home, and an improperly public one, the 'streets,'" and therefore "Gaskell was unable to participate fully in professional literary life because her activities as a professional author might make her seem an 'improper' woman in the eyes of the Victorian public" (Michie 5). Such a reading would tend to confirm Poovey's argument that women could not write even domestic fiction without threatening to collapse the boundary between separate spheres, or Armstrong's correlative claim that Victorian fiction imagines politics and domesticity only in opposition. Of *Mary Barton*, Armstrong writes that "Although Mrs. Gaskell includes political material in its most topical form, history virtually disappears from the novel as class conflict comes to be represented as a matter of sexual misconduct and a family scandal" (178). In the same vein, Catherine Gallagher charges

Gaskell with the "suppression" of the story's tragic political narrative and with "retreating into the domestic reality of her heroine"; "the book seems to divide into not merely separate but mutually exclusive stories" (67). The leading critical tradition of the last two decades thus reads *Mary Barton* as an affirmation of the Victorian separation of spheres, so that its domestic dimensions can be regarded only as a retreat from or evasion of public problems.[5]

But while private life may represent an obstacle to public discourse in Gaskell's letters, *Mary Barton* constructs a domesticity that becomes, in effect, simply a different mode of engagement with the social. Gaskell's domesticity insistently undermines the division of privacy and publicity, so that the household becomes an emphatically public space while women work in both worlds without rebuke. Some recent criticism has begun to reveal, in fact, how thoroughly the domestic and the political overlap in the novel. Robin Colby, for example, argues that the novel draws attention to Mary's assertiveness and work both "within and outside the home" as part of its "case for integrating women within the public sphere" (37). Similarly, Susan Zlotnick strongly qualifies the critical myth that Gaskell used sentimentalized domestic values to condemn industrialization; on the contrary, as she points out, Gaskell welcomes the new possibilities for women's activity presented by the tumultuous growth of the factory system and focuses her concern primarily on the narrower issue of unemployment, whether of factory workers or of women (80). Such interpretations allow us to begin to take more seriously Gaskell's rhetoric of reconciliation between public and private, and not only in *Mary Barton*. Gaskell's *Life of Charlotte Brontë*, long chided for taming its subject by depicting her as a proper Victorian angel, is now beginning to be read as a skillfully calculated attempt to establish Brontë's genius as an effect of her domestic life; as Linda Hughes and Michael Lund have argued, the biography "dissolves the boundaries" between "the home [and] the public world" (136), and thus "brilliantly established a continuum between professionalism and domestic propriety" (148). And even in *Cranford*, regarded as the most thoroughly feminine and domestic of Gaskell's novels, the bankrupted Miss Matty solves her difficulties by turning her home into a place of business: "The small dining-parlour was to be converted into a shop, without any of its degrading characteristics" (197).

The permeability of household walls is the central political fact of *Mary Barton*'s Manchester, and the exposure of domestic space is articulated in many different forms, both troubling and liberating. In the darkest, most literal manifestation of this theme, we encounter the dwelling of the impoverished Davenport family, a dank cellar whose walls are moist and muddy from leakage of the slop and sewage from the streets and pigsties outside; John Barton finds there "three or four little children rolling on the damp, nay wet brick floor, through which the stagnant, filthy moisture of the street oozed up" (60). Albeit less dramatically and more figuratively, the homes of all the working-class characters are also radically open to the harsh conditions of the industrial city. Rather than sanctuaries free from the conditions of the market, these spaces bear the signs of the city's economic fluctuations, so that the details of the Bartons' home do not merely denote novel's domestic realism, but also serve as a barometer of the financial health of the mills: their furniture, for example, appears and vanishes with tides of the business cycle (15). But it is not only the homes of the working poor that are vulnerable to Manchester's economic instability, since Gaskell inexorably returns to domestic images to represent both sides of the city's class antagonism. In times of prosperity, the employer's wealth is demonstrated by "removing from house to house, each one grander than the last" (23), while in harder times, "Large houses are still occupied, while spinners' and weavers' cottages stand empty, because the families that once filled them are obliged to live in rooms or cellars" (24). We might expect that those large houses of the masters, relatively insulated from the vicissitudes of the market, might serve also as a retreat from political turmoil. And after production is halted by a fire at his mill, the employer John Carson finds time to pursue "domestic enjoyments" with his family, appreciating his daughters' expensive musical accomplishments and lingering with them over leisurely meals. Yet this gesture towards the wholesome, rejuvenating separation of domestic leisure and public industry is immediately undermined:

> There is another side to this picture. There were homes over which Carson's fire threw a deep, terrible gloom; the homes of those who would fain work, and no man gave unto them—the homes of those to whom leisure was a curse. There, the family music was hungry wails, when week after week passed by, and there was no work to be had, and consequently no wages to pay for the bread the children cried aloud for in their young impatience of suffering. [. . .] The evil and good of our nature came out strongly then. There were desperate fathers; there were bitter-tongued mothers (O God! what wonder!); there were reckless children; the very closest bonds of our nature were snapt in that time of trial and distress. (58)

"Carson's fire" is not only the conflagration of his factory, but also the fire at his hearth, illuminating the poverty outside the family walls. In the narrator's subversive commentary, the idealized domestic space conjures, as "another side" of the same picture, the shadows of privation and despair against which the ideal is defined. Economic suffering is portrayed in terms of a very different domestic experience, where time at home is time away from life-sustaining labor, and where even the "natural" relationships of family cannot be preserved. The imagined separation of the middle-class home from public crisis is achieved only at the price of a dangerous ignorance, and it cannot last. Just as *Bleak House*'s wealthy Londoners fall victim to an epidemic born out of the slum into which they have herded the poor, so too will *Mary Barton*'s factory owners find that their comfortable houses are not proof against the resentment produced by their isolation. The repressed public world of economics and class anxiety will reassert it-self at the very center of the middle-class private space, and Carson will first encounter his murdered son's corpse laid out on the family dinner table (208).

In a world where public anxieties do not halt at the domestic threshold, women's duties cannot be confined to the house. Like many other social problem novels, *Mary Barton* expresses fears about a repugnant intermingling of women and commerce with the figure of the prostitute[6]—in this case, Mary's aunt Esther, whose story looms as a grim portent of Mary's own ambitions—but Gaskell's images of public women are not restricted to this conventional bogey, and here we begin to see important differences from Dickens's women. No shame attaches to Margaret, for example, when she makes her début as a public singer, thus transforming the quintessential domestic accomplishment of middle-class girls into economic self-sufficiency. On the contrary, Margaret proudly displays the "bright golden sovereign" she has earned singing at the Mechanics' Institute, delighted that her incipient blindness will no longer make her "a burden to any one" (94-95). The kind encouragement Margaret receives as a public performer symbolizes an acceptance of women's work and even a recognition of its considerable potential to benefit society: "what a pity there isn't more o' that way, and less scolding and rating i' th' world! It would go a vast deal further" (96).

The novel's most crucial scene of a woman's public action, though, is Mary's testimony at the murder trial of her lover, Jem Wilson. In the witness box before a "sea of faces, misty and swimming before her eyes" (323), Mary confronts not only a crowd's eager curiosity, but also an expectation of feminine behavior that commands her silence. Her response to the insolent barrister's question about her affections is explicitly framed as a triumphant transcendence of gender conventions and of the ostensibly private sphere:

> And who was he, the questioner, that he should dare so lightly to ask of her heart's secrets? That he should dare to ask her to tell, before the multitude assembled there, what woman usually whispers with blushes and tears, and many hesitations, to one ear alone?
> So, for an instant, a look of indignation contracted Mary's brow, as she steadily met the eyes of the impertinent counselor. But, in that instant, she saw the hands removed from a face beyond, behind; and a countenance revealed of such intense love and woe,—such a deprecating dread of her answer; and suddenly her resolution was taken. [. . .] Now, when the beloved stood thus, abhorred of men, there would be no feminine shame to stand between her and her avowal. (324-25)

What the novel portrays as Mary's heroism derives precisely from making very public her most private feelings despite the dictates of "feminine shame." It is true that Gaskell qualifies this audacity: Mary will pay for her assertiveness by developing a case of brain fever, and her agency diminishes in the chapters that follow. Moreover, while Mary's testimony lends Jem a new "self-respect in his attitude, and a look of determination on his face" (327), it accomplishes very little, in strictly legal terms, to assist in his defense. But this is not to say that this scene of love on trial is a merely an intrusion of an incongruous romance plot upon the novel's political concerns. To read Mary's public appearance in that way is to repeat the error of Jem's accusers, who misinterpret the murder as an apolitical case of jealousy and courtship gone horribly awry.[7] The effect of Mary's testimony is to prove them wrong: her two suitors, she explains, did not know of one another, and thus the attempt to deflect political transgression onto a private love story is just as perniciously misguided as the bourgeois dream of homes as inviolable havens. Mary's declarations, furthermore, are hardly incompatible with the novel's broader political message. Gaskell has argued from the outset that masters and workers need to understand each another in economic terms and, even more importantly, through a mutual recognition of intense feelings. The unfeminine publicity of Mary's disclosure of disinterested love conforms exactly to this agenda. Domestic dilemmas arise during the trial, as they do throughout the book, in a conspicuously public manner, but never as an *alternative* to public crises.

In this inextricable relationship between private and public we find the distinguishing characteristics of Gaskell's representation of domesticity. Returning to the example of Dickens, we see that both writers portray romantic or familial relationships that are constantly ravaged by impersonal social forces driven by an ideology of competition and self-interest, and both counter this menace by invoking the values associated with the home. Yet Gaskell goes much further, in practical terms, to suggest that the solution to such threats is a fusion of civic responsibilities and domestic sympathies. John Barton and John Carson begin to understand one another when they perceive their mutual grief as fathers who have lost sons, thus becoming "brothers in the deep suffering of the heart" (366). But Carson's sympathy transcends these familial terms to become social policy. He comes to believe

> that a perfect understanding, and complete confidence and love, might exist between masters and men; that the truth must be recognized that the interests of one were the interests of all, and [. . .] hence it was most desirable to have educated workers, capable of judging, not mere machines of ignorant men; and to have them bound to their employers by ties of respect and affection, not mere money bargains alone; in short, to acknowledge the Spirit of Christ as the regulating law between both bodies.
>
> Many of the improvements now in practice in the system of employment in Manchester, owe their origin to short, earnest sentences spoken by Mr Carson. (388)

This representation of the practical, social consequences of Carson's change of heart is flimsy and vague—hardly amounting to more than a passing reference to education—while the proposal of sentiment as one more way in which workers could be "bound to their employers" is a bit chilling. But Gaskell's logic of sympathy is crucially extended beyond the Dickensian model. Where his characters would turn from implacably destructive social institutions to a small domestic community, Gaskell's integrate a wisdom of the heart with conservative economic doctrine ("the interests of one were the interests of all") and a vision of social reform. Private understanding becomes public policy, which in turn reinforces private "respect and affection."

Mary Barton, of course, positions itself as the axis of this of this spiral of benevolence, bearing its gospel of domestic sympathy before a sizable readership. And in its own relationship with the public, the novel is particularly direct in imagining its own wide circulation. In the story itself, we see not only that private lives have social consequences, but also that they become the explicit subject of public discourse. After Jem's trial, Mary's neighbor Sally informs her that she has become famous, and that events of her story are "all in print": "There's no use shunning talking it over. Why! it was in the *Guardian*,—and the *Courier*,—and some one told Jane Hodgson it was even copied into a London paper. You've set up heroine on your own account, Mary Barton" (358). Still distraught over her father's guilt, Mary is less inclined to see herself as a national hero, but the novel's preface supports Sally's enthusiasm for publicity rather than Mary's reticence. Gaskell alerts readers to the immediate political relevance of her story's illustrations of emotional unrest in the working class: "To myself the idea which I have formed of the state of feeling among too many of the factory-people in Manchester, and which I endeavored to represent in this tale (completed over a year ago) has received some confirmation from the events which have so recently occurred among a similar class on the Continent" (4). As Hilary Schor has argued, Gaskell's comments promote "an hysteric response: readers who might fear what 'recently occurred among a similar class on the Continent,' ought to read *this* book, *now*" (27). And Gaskell's correspondence with Chapman and Hall reveals her desire to hurry production of *Mary Barton* so that it could capitalize on recent events and ensure a large circulation.[8] Rather than hindering her novel's engagement with the concerns of her readers, Gaskell's particular conception of domesticity as a means of clarifying and addressing pressing social problems is calculated to generate a large audience and to wield enormous influence. The domesticity of *Mary Barton*, in short, is aggressively topical.[9] This topicality ultimately qualifies what might otherwise be read as evasiveness at the novel's conclusion, Mary and Jem's emigration. Mary's life in Canada, described in terms of her marriage and maternity, suggests that, under more placid circumstances, something like the traditional woman's role might be preferable. But circumstances being what they are in *Mary Barton*'s Manchester, she has acted heroically. And these same circumstances, the preface points out, are the conditions of contemporary Britain.

The distinctive character of Gaskell's construction of authorship—implied by her anonymity, her preface, and her use of narrative perspective—must be approached at the nexus of these related imperatives: a domesticity which is never purely private, a positive engagement with a large readership, and a self-conscious topicality. Yet her significant revisions of the typical mid-Victorian representation of *authorship* have long been obscured by the vexed issue of Gaskell's *authority*. Gaskell's reputation has suffered from a condescending marginalization because of a perception of her conventional femininity; thus the longstanding perpetuation of her characterization as "Mrs. Gaskell," the model Victorian housewife who wrote novels in her spare time. She is, in this view, amateurish and irresolute, weaknesses suggested by such comments in *Mary Barton* as her famous disavowal of economic credentials: "I know nothing of Political Economy, or the theories of trade. I have tried to write truthfully; and if my accounts agree or clash with any system, the agreement or disagreement is unintentional" (4). More recently, however, critics have tried to salvage her reputation by arguing that Gaskell does in fact speak with authority, a particular kind of authority founded on domestic—or more specifically, feminine—principles.[10] From this perspective, her claim not to know of "Political Economy" is not so much an instance of self-abnegation as a subversive rejection of masculine discourse. While I find this argument a welcome corrective to Gaskell's traditional trivialization, it introduces problems of its own, not the least of which is a concession of economic knowledge to masculinity that would have pleased the most misogynistic Victorian patriarch. Such separate spheres, in *Mary Barton*, are never really separate: as we have seen, the novel never questions the fundamental legitimacy of the social order (or of "Political Economy") by attempting to demolish it with a set of idealized domestic values; instead, the relationship between the public and the domestic is always a negotiation, through which the happy household and the productive factory are shown to be mutually constitutive. And it is not Mary Barton but a male character, the working-class naturalist Job Legh, who serves most clearly as the narrator's spokesman by the end of the novel, even to the point that he echoes the preface's claim: "I'm not given to political economy," he says, "but I can use my eyes"(384). In light of such complications, we need to reconsider how feminine—and how authoritative—the author of *Mary Barton* really is.

The assumption that, as a woman, Gaskell would naturally construct a feminine persona and would of course be perceived as a woman by her readers is misleading. In fact, the gender of *Mary Barton*'s anonymous writer occasioned some controversial speculation at the time of its publication (Lund and Hughes 36), and it seems unlikely that Gaskell herself considered her narrative to be obviously feminine: she had decided at the last minute to publish under a male pseudonym, "Stephen Berwick," and was prevented only because the novel had already gone to press.[11] The blurring together of domestic and public spheres in the novel has undeniable feminist implications—and certainly Mary's brave assertiveness in the courthouse suggests a parallel with Gaskell's own courage—but the empowerment of women is only one aspect of an even larger project. That the novel's dream of sympathetic understanding between classes is ultimately illustrated by two men, John Barton and John Carson, demonstrates that sympathy is not only a feminine virtue. Indeed, if it were so gendered, much of Gaskell's argument about the integration of domesticity and politics would be undermined. In this way, Gaskell's androgynous anonymity, her refusal to fix her authorship in one sphere, is entirely appropriate for a novel calculated to achieve the maximum possible applicability. The narrator's refusal to judge matters only in terms of political economy is a correlative rejection of specialized discourse, which would limit the novel's reach and popular impact in much the same way that it would be limited if it confined itself to a narrowly-defined, segregated domesticity. Instead, Gaskell appeals to ostensibly universal truths and to common sense. This is not just feminism; it is demagoguery.

In the same way that the gender of the author of *Mary Barton* becomes unsettled—and for the same reason—Gaskell's authority, as it is expressed in the novel, appears equivocal. This is not to say, with Gaskell's detractors, that her ambiguous authority is a sign of aesthetic weakness; it is simply to suggest, as I have in earlier chapters, that not all forms of authorship are predicated on an individual writer's Wordsworthian will to power.[12] And after all, the degree of Gaskell's self-effacement is unusual for a mid-Victorian novelist.[13] The author of *Mary Barton* is not the sage of Carlyle or Eliot, nor does she indulge in the sometimes bullying friendship of Dickens. Rather, Gaskell presents a narrator who withholds opinions at key moments and invites readers to form their own. "It is not for me to judge," says the preface about the justice of working-class bitterness (3), and this gesture of abnegation is repeated soon after: "How far [John Barton's] strong exaggerated feelings had any foundation in truth, it is for you to judge" (26). One implication of this withheld judgement, certainly, is to insulate Gaskell from the charge of radicalism, of a perverted sympathy that threatens the divisions of class instead of preserving them. But its equally significant effect is to cede to readers the authority to pass judgment, to propose a collective authority constituted by the novel's audience. That the novel challenges readers actively to judge for themselves becomes particularly apparent at the crucial moment when Mary takes the stand at Jem's trial, when the narrator surprisingly withdraws from the posture of omniscience:

> Many who were looking for mere flesh and blood beauty, mere colouring, were disappointed; for her face was deadly white, and almost set in its expression, while a mournful bewildered soul looked out of the depths of those soft, deep, grey eyes. But others recognized a higher and a stranger kind of beauty; one that would keep its hold on the memory for years.
>   I was not there myself [. . .]. (324)

The narrator's disappearance from the scene presents a puzzling contradiction since the trial scene is related in as much detail as any other in the book. The narrator continues to represent the unspoken opinions of all the characters present—as in these lines, which explain not only what the crowd at the trial felt at the time, but also what they felt years afterwards—so in what sense is the narrator "not there"? According to the conventions of verisimilitude the narrator's absence is paradoxical, but the gesture makes sense as an expression of Gaskell's overriding concern with audiences. Its effect is to draw readers' attention to the collective reaction of the spectators at the courthouse rather than to the narrator's individual opinions. At this critical juncture, it is this public audience that will model for *Mary Barton*'s readers the perception of social truth through the performance of sympathy. And while not everyone at the trial fully appreciates Mary (particularly "disappointed" are those whose notion of feminine beauty prizes "flesh and blood" over emotional expressiveness), this scene is remarkably optimistic compared with similar scenes in other Victorian novels. In *Pickwick*, for instance, the trial scene becomes an occasion for Dickens to ridicule the arbitrary authority of the law and the hopeless befuddlement of jurors. But more generally, the Victorian novel's representation of crowds tends to be, at best, ambivalent; crowds are almost always invested with the menacing potential to devolve into mobs. By contrast, *Mary Barton*, like its heroine, is relatively unafraid. It expresses its hope in a jury inclined to err on the side of mercy, and in that still larger jury of public opinion.

Such optimism lends credibility to the extension of Gaskell's argument from collective judgement to collective responsibility, and this the reader shares with the narrator: "you and I, and almost everyone, I think, may send up our individual cry of self-reproach what we have not done all that we could for the stray and wandering ones of our brethren" (269). Just as John Barton's tragedy would become meaningless (and infinitely repeatable) without John Carson's effort to translate sympathetic growth into practical reform, so too would the novel's purpose be blunted without an analogous transformation of its readers. It is in the text's circulation, therefore, that Gaskell's work finds its final justification, as the quotation from Carlyle that serves as the novel's epigraph makes clear:

> "'How knowest thou,' may the distressed Novel-wright exclaim, 'that I, here where I sit, am the Foolishest of existing mortals; that this my Longear of a fictitious Biography shall not find one and the other, into whose

still longer ears it may be the means, under Providence, of instilling somewhat?' We answer, 'None knows, none can certainly know: therefore,
write on worthy Brother, even as thou canst, even as it is given thee'" (1).

Even the "Foolishest" of novelists, in other words, will be justified in his
work's reception, so the individual genius or power of the author is less a
concern than the audience's response. In this way, we might say that
Gaskell's version of authorship is less *authoritative* than it is *authorized*.
This distinction does not detract from the cultural value of her novel, but it
does limit the necessity of her personal exposure.

Ultimately, Gaskell's refinements of Industrial-Romantic authorship are
overdetermined: to her experiences as a woman writer we may ascribe her
reluctance to perform under her own name the Dickensian spectacle of
public intimacy, while the limitations of women's control over their own
work in the contemporary publishing industry confirmed and perpetuated
her anonymity for years. But just as surely, her perspective on the division
of the public and private spheres helped her to imagine the transcendence
of that boundary, particularly through positive representations of women's
activity in the most public arenas. To existing models of authorship, meanwhile, she owed her sympathetic ideal, which provided both the narrative
conditions of her story and the rhetoric of her narrator's engagement with
readers. Gaskell's extension of this logic, her emphasis on a domesticity
that embraces the public sphere and is in turn shaped by it, shifted authority to the public in a way that managed Gaskell's anxieties about the gender of authorship even as it increased the urgent relevance and force of her
claims. But all of these innovations are enabled and justified by Gaskell's
conception of the mid-Victorian reading audience, her deliberate courtship
of the widest possible readership and her faith—real or assumed—in its
fundamental sympathy and collective power.

AUTHORSHIP IN THE PARROT-HOUSE

While *Mary Barton* is one of the most self-consciously topical Victorian
novels, *Middlemarch* (1871-1872) is one of the least. In the arguments
over sensationalism during the 1860s, we have already seen an obvious explanation for Eliot's distaste for topical fiction: the sensation novelists were
censured in part for drawing the on controversial current issues and popular themes of the most widely circulating texts as the basis for what were
sometimes called "newspaper novels." Far from topicality of a turbulent
present, *Middlemarch*, like most of Eliot's novels, is set prudently and nos-
talgically behind the conciliatory sweep of history. This historical turn necessarily introduces different pressures on the representation of authorship,
not only because it requires a different formulation of the novel's relationship to the reading public, but also because it raises the specters of authorship's own history, particularly the venerable tradition of representing the

novelist as historian. The celebrated opening of *Middlemarch*'s fifteenth chapter underscores Eliot's self-consciousness in this regard:

> A great historian, as he insisted on calling himself, who had the happiness to be dead a hundred and twenty years ago, and so to take his place among the colossi whose huge legs our living pettiness is observed to walk under, glories in his copious remarks and digressions as the least imitable part of his work, and especially in those initial chapters to the successive books of his history, where he seems to bring his arm-chair to the proscenium and chat with us in all the lusty ease of his fine English. But Fielding lived when the days were longer (for time, like money, is measured by our needs), when summer afternoons were spacious, and the clock ticked slowly in the winter evenings. We belated historians must not linger after his example; and even if we did so, it is probable that our chat would be thin and eager, as if delivered from a camp-stool in a parrot-house. (141)

The sly irony of this passage—a digression about the inadvisability of digressions—does not entirely mask concerns that resonate with the novel's persistent anxieties, which are also those of novelists more generally in those post-sensational days. Is it still possible to maintain Fielding's informal, friendly, and relaxed relationship with his audience, or has that posture gone the way of pre-industrial consciousness? For industrialism has not only shortened the day, it has transformed the public. Where once novelists could assume a relationship that easily combined the private and the public, the arm-chair and the proscenium stage, the comfortable and the stately space of privileged leisure, they now face the relatively degrading and cheapening prospect of the parrot-house: the cacophonous and chaotic zoo of the contemporary literary marketplace.

For a Victorian writer, the issue of the novel's historicism cannot fail to conjure other ghosts besides Fielding's. The most obvious is Walter Scott's, who effectively literalized the trope of novelist as historian and, in doing so, helped to consolidate the cultural legitimacy of the genre by incorporating "real" history into fiction and, as Ina Ferris has argued, by opening the novel to history's more masculine discourse. But *Middlemarch*'s engagement with Scott, and with the template of realistic historical fiction he established, is profoundly vexed. While Scott's heroes rub elbows with princes and kings and participate directly in the military clashes and political uprisings recorded in traditional histories, Eliot's characters, thoroughly entangled in the quotidian, are emphatically prevented from becoming actors in the kind of narratives Scott popularized. The narrative of *Middlemarch*, in fact, seems to repudiate Scott's formula in a flagrantly provocative way: published in the wake of the second Reform Bill and taking as its setting the period of the first, the novel invites readers to expect a historical fiction with immediate contemporary relevance. Instead, the desperate political confrontations of the Reform Bill, save for one particularly anxious scene, recede into the text's unnarratable margins, while the narrator, in one of the few comments on the social transformations of the 1830s, compares them not to the 1870s, but to the world described by Herodotus (95-96). We are left with a text that amounts to a contradiction in terms, or, as Terry Eagleton has put it, "a historical novel in form with little substantive historical content" (*Criticism and Ideology* 120). *Middlemarch* represents an ambitious departure from Scott, whose influence remained so strong in the decades following his death that nearly all of the major Victorian novelists had tried their hands at the historical novel. Eliot's text, by contrast, is what we might call (borrowing a term from her conclusion) an "unhistorical" novel: the "reality" of *Middlemarch* is not the verifiable actuality of historical events but a realism defined by the improbability of individual agents rising above obscurity to effect narratable social change. Scott's masculine historicism becomes a foil for the "unhistorical acts" of Eliot's heroes (838), whose stories are inscribed only in the secret history of privacy, femininity, and domesticity.

The domestic underpinnings of *Middlemarch*'s realism, however, are not those defined by the domestic ideal. To perceive the distinction, we need to consider Eliot's relationship with one last novelist brought up in the novel, Miguel de Cervantes. *Middlemarch* explicitly alludes to *Don Quixote* with the quotation from Cervantes that serves as the epigraph to the second chapter, which implies the quixotism of Dorothea's regard for Casaubon, but Dorothea's more general connection to *Don Quixote* is implied by her name, an echo of "Dorotea," Cervantes's pious ingénue. As had a number of British novels before it, *Middlemarch* invokes *Don Quixote* to announce its own innovative realism: Charlotte Lennox's *The Female Quixote* had heralded the triumph of the novel over the romance in 1752; Scott's *Waverley* confronted its hero's reading of romance with his involvement in real historical events; *Pickwick* ridiculed the bumbling scientism of "useful knowledge" to teach its protagonist the more meaningful epistemology of sentiment. If each of these novels self-consciously positions itself as a turning point in literary history by introducing an original principle of narrative realism, what is the principle that drives the new realism of *Middlemarch*?

The answer is suggested by the prelude's opening anecdote about the young Saint Theresa, who set out, "wide-eyed and helpless looking," with her younger brother on a crusade, "until domestic reality met them in the shape of uncles, and turned them back from their great resolve" (3). While not necessarily manifested in the shape of uncles, this domestic reality is precisely the force which derails the quixotism of Eliot's heroes, whether it take the form of spirit-crushing marriages, the vengeful return of forgotten familial cruelties, or even, more happily, the achievement of stable personal relationships in which more modest desires become coterminous with reasonable duties. More intriguingly, the quixotism of the two major protagonists, Dorothea and Lydgate, is also expressed in domestic terms. Dorothea's plot, that of "a mind struggling towards an ideal life" (45), leads her to mistake marriage to Casaubon for her path to a worthy destiny, just as surely as Don Quixote mistakes a brass basin for the helmet of Mambrino. But her particular choice of Casaubon is not the whole of her error, which lies more generally in "notions of marriage [that] took their colour entirely from an exalted enthusiasm about the ends of life" (28). Dorothea's blunder, in other words, is to believe in the ideal of domesticity, which likewise enthusiastically exalts marriage as exactly the means through which women exerted a beneficent influence on their nation. And her mistake is compounded when, even after Casaubon's deficiencies are exposed, she cleaves to the conventional ideal of wifely submission: "Neither the law nor the world's opinion compelled her to this—only her husband's nature and her own compassion, only the ideal and not the real yoke of marriage" (481). Lydgate's professional crusade, meanwhile, illustrates the same problematic quixotism from a masculine angle. He brings to Middlemarch the customary perception of marriage as a refreshing refuge from professional toil, a "paradise with sweet laughs for bird-notes, and blue eyes for a heaven" (95), and it is this vulgar assumption, the most destructive of his "spots of commonness" (150), that pairs him, ruinously, with the stereotypical flower of femininity, Rosamond Vincy. Both Lydgate and Dorothea conceive of marriage according to the terms of the domestic ideal, and Eliot distinguishes her novel's more realistic aesthetic by revealing them to be quixotically deluded.

Middlemarch's realism depends on a revision of domesticity, but this necessarily entails a new attitude toward the public. Indeed, Eliot's realism, like her politics, often takes the form of a reaction against the idealization of the two quintessentially disempowered groups of Victorian England, women and the working class. In "Silly Novels by Lady Novelists" (1856), for instance, she attacks the "mere left-handed imbecility" of many women writers (320), along with the critics who grant them "exceptional indulgence" out of a delusive chivalry (319). Among the novels she protests, the first is notable for its own idealization of women, particularly in granting its heroine "a great facility in learning languages": "Of course! Greek and Hebrew are mere play to a heroine; Sanscrit is no more than *a b c* to her; and she can talk with perfect correctness in any language except English" (299). Given that Dorothea hopes to learn Latin, Greek, and Hebrew herself (*Middlemarch* 64), we can understand her frustrated ambition as a means with which Eliot defines her novel against a kind of fiction she understands to be characteristically feminine. And the same resistance to the literary idealization of female characters typifies Eliot's views about women's political status: as she laments in her essay on "Margaret Fuller and Mary Wollstonecraft" (1855), "unfortunately, many over-zealous champions of women assert their actual equality with men—nay, even their moral superiority to men—as a ground for their release from oppressive laws and restrictions. They lose strength immensely by this false position" (185). Eliot's feminism, in short, depends on revealing the privations of actual circumstances rather than celebrating illusory possibilities or beguiling ideals. Her objection to the claim of women's "moral superiority," in particular, is a blow to one of the fundamental premises of domestic dogma. But given that most of the practical advances of feminism in Victorian England depended on the strategic manipulation of the terms with which women were allowed "superiority," Eliot's tendency to measure women's reality in almost purely negative terms, in attacks on idealization, begins to seem a particularly crippling prognosis of the possibility of women's participation in public progress. Thus, while Dorothea, purged of the quixotic notion of domesticity expressed in her marriage to Casaubon, settles into the more realistic domestic arrangements of her marriage to Ladislaw, the two situations are, from the point of view of women's activity, nearly indistinguishable: in both cases she is reduced to offering "wifely help," since there is nothing else "in her power she ought rather to have done" (836). The novel's revision of domesticity, its greater domestic reality, is thus largely a matter of enforcing women's confinement to the home.

But it is also a matter of rethinking the relationship of domestic virtues to the problems of class; Eliot, like Dorothea, will give up the project of designing model homes for the poor, since her approach to class antagonism depends on challenging idealistic representations of the working class. In her article on the responsibilities of the voters enfranchised by the second Reform Bill, the "Address to Working Men, by Felix Holt" (1868), she begins by giving her fictional working-class speaker an unflattering truth to convey: "as a body we are not wise or virtuous" (338). The same deflation of the working classes underlies her realistic aesthetic as well. Her celebrated demand for greater psychological insight in "The Natural History of German Life" (1856) centers on a rejection of the artistic idealization of "'the people,' 'the masses,' 'the proletariat,' 'the peasantry'" (261). Artistic truthfulness, she argues, may be advanced only when writers abandon the conventional flattery of workers:

> This perversion is not the less fatal because the misrepresentation which gives rise to it has what the artist considers a moral end. The thing for mankind to know is, not what are the motives and influences which the moralist thinks *ought* to act on the labourer or the artisan, but what are the motives and influences which *do* act on him. We want to be taught to feel, not for the heroic artisan or the sentimental peasant, but for the peasant in all his coarse apathy, and the artisan in all his suspicious selfishness. (264)

The logic of Eliot's realism makes a subtle but crucial leap in this passage: beginning with a claim about verisimilitude (artists must deal with the actual rather than the ideal), she moves to an ideologically-charged definition of actuality (the truth is that peasants are apathetic and artisans selfish). Artistic truthfulness, defined in opposition to sentimental and idealized stereotypes, can be demonstrated only through representing the most intractably negative characteristics of the working poor. And insofar as *Mid-*

dlemarch presents working-class characters at all, it is in precisely these
bleak terms.

The novel's most extended commentary of the question of the Middlemarch peasantry's place in the organic social whole centers on Mr.
Brooke's encounter with his tenants, the Dagleys, whose son has been
caught poaching. Brooke is not entirely unsympathetic with the boy's
delinquency, and he is prepared to regard the offense as something "rather
comic," partly because of its traditional treatment in novels: "Fielding
might have made something of it," Brooke points out, "or Scott, now—
Scott might have worked it up" (393). Eliot's realism, however, demands
her to "work up" the episode into something quite different from the
comic impulse of Fielding or Scott, or of the sentimental comedian whom
Brooke cannot yet name, Dickens.[14] As Brooke approaches the Dagleys'
home, the narrator reminds us again of the misleading ways in which other
artists might paint this scene of rustic domesticity:

> an observer, under the softening influence of the fine arts which makes
> other people's hardships picturesque, might have been delighted with this
> homestead called Freeman's End: the old house had dormer-windows in
> the dark-red roof, two of the chimneys were choked with ivy, the large
> porch was blocked up with bundles of sticks, and half the windows were
> closed with grey worm-eaten shutters about which the jasmine-boughs
> grew in wild luxuriance [. . .]. Mr. Dagley himself made a figure in the
> landscape, carrying a pitchfork and wearing his milking-hat [. . .]. (393-94)

Eliot's realistic approach, the repudiation of this sentimental perspective,
must rid the scene entirely of charm, and reveal, with grim resolution, Dagley himself to be drunk, belligerent, and benighted. *Middlemarch*'s rejection of artistic convention continues, more subtly, by challenging the
notion of friendship as a means of alerting different classes to their common interests, so that Brooke's sympathetic greeting is met with a hostile
rebuff: "'Dagley, my good fellow,' began Mr. Brooke, conscious that he
was going to be very friendly about the boy. 'Oh, ay, I'm a good feller, am
I? Thank ye, sir, thank ye,' said Dagley, with a loud snarling irony which
made Fag the sheepdog stir from his seat and prick up his ears" (395). In
ridiculing the prospect of friendship between these men, *Middlemarch* declares its secession from the dominant assumptions of Victorian fiction,
which stretch back to the warm mutual friendship of Pickwick and Weller,
and thus radically undermines typical ideals of sympathy as well. Eliot's
claim that such realism teaches us "to feel for" Dagley—much less feel
with him—seems hollow. It is true that the novel explains Dagley's brutish-
ness in terms of his social conditions ("nothing could be easier in those
days for an hereditary farmer of his grade to be ignorant" [397]), but we
are nowhere invited to identify with him as the narrator so frequently asks
us to do with other characters; the more explicit relationship is drawn between Dagley and his dog. Having countered an insistently positive repre-

sentation of the poor with an equally insistent negative one, the novel never requires us to muster a more charitable opinion that that pronounced by Caleb Garth on the menacing peasants Fred Vincy is obliged to horsewhip: "The poor fools don't know any better" (559).

Eliot's representations of working-class ignorance, largely colored by her reaction against Victorian literary convention, also reveal the particular anxieties of a novelist writing in the post-sensational literary market of the 1870s. The anti-sensational critics had raised fears of a lower-class readership that could overwhelm distinctive middle-class standards, "making the literature of the kitchen the literature of the Drawing Room" (qtd. in Taylor 5), and therefore cast doubt on the potentially leveling ideal of wide circulation suggested by sympathetic friendship or a deliberate, audience-courting topicality. In this context, we can read *Middlemarch*'s preference for unhistorical, ordinary, private lives as a significant withdrawal from the broad public platform from which novels were previously imagined to speak, and from the universally pressing issues that, as in Gaskell's work, they had tried to address. *Middlemarch*'s most public scene in this sense, and the one in which it most directly imagines the actual history of reform politics, Mr. Brooke's campaign speech, is an anxious depiction of mass disorder and humiliation. Once again, Brooke's good intentions and chatty friendliness ("and no candidate could look more amiable than Mr. Brooke" [503]), do not protect him, and the anarchic crowd pelts him with eggs: "There was a stream of new men pushing among the crowd; whistles, yells bellowings, and fifes made all the greater hubbub because there was shouting and struggling to put them down. No voice would have had wing enough to rise above the uproar, and Mr. Brooke, disagreeably anointed, stood his ground no longer" (506). Brooke has disastrously underestimated the potential hostility of his audience, repeating his assumption that he could approach Dagley in friendly terms, but also exacerbating his mistake by addressing the crowd in his usual confidential manner, characterized by rambling digressions and personal asides: "Pray pity him: so many English gentlemen make themselves miserable by speechifying on entirely private grounds!" (503). He has failed, in other words, for precisely the reasons to which the novel earlier attributed the success of Henry Fielding, whose comfort before his audience was clearly demonstrated by his "copious remarks and digressions" (141). In *Middlemarch*'s solitary scene of historical political action, which is specifically concerned with the politics of widening enfranchisement and the popular unrest symbolized by machine-breaking, we learn the lesson of the contemporary novelist's distance from Fielding: in addressing the new audience, the comfortably domestic and the theatrically public cannot be reconciled. And in yet another reminder of the narrator's remarks on Fielding, an invisible heckler in the crowd maliciously mimics Brooke with "the note of the cuckoo, a parrotlike, Punch-voiced echo of his words" (504). Brooke, like the contemporary novelist, is lost in the parrot-house.

A writer who strives to advance fiction's artistry by deflating the idealization of women and of the lower classes inevitably challenges the prevailing notions of sympathy as well, since it was understood to belong to the list of feminine virtues, and was measured primarily (as in Gaskell's or Dickens's work) by its ability to ameliorate class anxieties. Sympathy remains a keyword in Eliot's rhetoric, and her references to it are almost incessant, more common and explicit, in fact, than those of any other novelist this book has considered. But the visibility of the term indicates how complicated it had become; rather than merely assuming the fundamental value of the sympathy articulated by her predecessors, Eliot constantly interrogates it, qualifies it, measures it. In *Middlemarch*, the question of Dorothea's sympathy serves as the test of her heroism, but the novel depicts her achievement as the result of a hard-fought emotional and philosophical struggle rather than as a viscerally immediate reaction to suffering. And the conditions of her victory are not predicated, as in *Mary Barton*, on a sympathy between classes; Ladislaw dismisses Dorothea's early concern for the poor, figured as her inability to enjoy exclusively expensive works of art, as a "fanaticism of sympathy" (219). Indeed, what is strikingly different about Eliot's use of the term is how sharply circumscribed it is. The novel's project is not simply to remind its readers, through the medium of sympathy, of the extent to which their lives are intricately interwoven with everyone else's, but also to consider such connections as both a narrative and a cultural problem; thus the narrator, while offering the memorable metaphor of the social "web," explains that the novel "has much to do in *unravelling* certain human lots" (141, emphasis added). Such an effort to disentangle individuals from the collective entirely reverses the imperative of previous novelists to narrate their connections; in *Middlemarch* those connections are already all too obvious and, as often as not, troublesome. Lydgate, for instance, will ultimately be trapped in this web, pulled down by "the hampering threadlike pressure of small social conditions" (180). What was once a solution, in short, has become part of the problem.

Dorothea's great crisis, her reaction to what appears to be a violation of the Lydgates' marriage by her own beloved Ladislaw, epitomizes the novel's ambivalent curtailment of sympathy. At first, her resolution to save the marriage takes a relatively conventional form:

> All the active thought with which she had before been representing to herself the trials of Lydgate's lot, and this young marriage union which, like her own, seemed to have its hidden as well as evident troubles—all this vivid sympathetic experience returned to her now as a power: it asserted itself as acquired knowledge asserts itself and will not let us see as we saw in the day of our ignorance. She said to her own irremediable grief, that it should make her more helpful, instead of driving her back from effort. (788)

Other than its representation of sympathy's power as that of an "acquired knowledge" rather than that of bodily affect, as a matter of the will instead of the heart, this passage resembles the logic of Eliot's predecessors. And like those earlier novels, *Middlemarch* seems in the next moment to widen Dorothea's particular insight into a more encompassing vision of sympathy's transformative scope:

> She opened her curtains, and looked out towards the bit of road that lay in view, with fields beyond, outside the entrance-gates. On the road there was a man with a bundle on his back and a woman carrying her baby; in the field she could see figures moving—perhaps the shepherd with his dog. Far off in the bending sky was the pearly light; and she felt the largeness of the world and the manifold wakings of men to labour and endurance. She was a part of that involuntary, palpitating life, and could neither look out on it from her luxurious shelter as a mere spectator, nor hide her eyes in selfish complaining. (788)

But the novel has already warned us against such an idealistically picturesque "view," which treats the poor as hazy and indistinct icons of "labour and endurance"; viewed more closely, that "shepherd and his dog" might turn out to be Dagley and "Fag the sheepdog." But Dorothea will turn back from her window and leave these potentially threatening figures in the landscape alone. Such a sublime feeling for "the largeness of the world" is mercifully unsustainable, as the narrator has earlier explained: "If we had a keen vision and feeling of all ordinary human life, it would be like hearing the grass grow and the squirrel's heart beat, and we should die of that roar which lies on the other side of silence" (194). Dorothea's more limited resolution will send her back to the middle-class household in an "attempt to see and save Rosamond" (790). This turn to domesticity, however, is no simple affirmation of private and feminine virtues. The home is not the idealized haven from which sympathy naturally springs, but the place in which Eliot's more narrowly-defined version of the ideal will be tested; the domestic is the proving-ground of sympathy, not its guarantee.

There are reasons to doubt, moreover, whether sympathy can be relied upon even in this circumscribed frame. Dorothea's rescue of Rosamond (which, given Ladislaw's disinterest in her, was never really necessary to begin with) implies that the bonds of understanding forged by sympathy may be illusory after all, an individual misperception of real differences. Dorothea opens the floodgates of her own sorrow, and receives from Rosamond in return what seems to be—but only seems to be—a reciprocal gesture of fellow-feeling: "Her immediate consciousness was one of immense sympathy without check; she cared for Rosamond without struggle now [. . .]. With her usual tendency to over-estimate the good in others, she felt a great outgoing of her heart towards Rosamond for the generous effort which had redeemed her from suffering, not counting that the effort was a reflex of her own energy" (798). What seems to be Rosamond's generous effort—explaining that Ladislaw is guiltless—is merely an effect of Dorothea's own generosity. The two share an emotional exchange, and even reciprocal gratitude and fellow-feeling, but not the profound mutual understanding of sympathy. And in this context, we might note how little, in practical terms, Dorothea's heroic intervention has really accomplished: it seems to have helped the Lydgates resign themselves a little more fully to their miserable marriage. Dorothea, on the other hand, learns enough to make her reunion with Ladislaw possible, but this happy outcome is far more limited than we might have expected from her realization that she should try to be helpful to others, and even to "save" them. The episode suggests that the benefits of sympathy are actually to be measured in individual terms, just as the operation of sympathy may exist only in the individual consciousness, rather than in the true convergence of multiple consciousnesses.[15]

Middlemarch's narrowing perimeters of sympathetic action, like its anxious treatment of the lower classes, cannot be wholly attributed to its philosophical complexity or to its aesthetic innovations; both of these are bound up with its more fundamental challenge to the traditional relationship of the novel to its audience. We find the same ambivalent conjunction of old rhetorical forms and original interpretations of them in the narrator's addresses to readers. Constantly asking us to consider the characters' foibles and failings in light of our own, the narrator demands our sympathy even more forcefully than Gaskell had. In the opening chapters alone, we are asked to identify with Casaubon ("if he was liable to think that others were providentially made for him [. . .] this trait is not quite alien to us, and, like the other mendicant hopes of mortals, claims some of our pity" [85]), with Mrs. Cadwallader ("Let any lady who is inclined to be hard on Mrs. Cadwallader inquire into the comprehensiveness of her own beautiful views, and be quite sure that they afford accommodation for all the lives which have the honor to coexist with hers" [60]), and, of course, with Dorothea ("Has anyone ever pinched into its pilulous smallness the cobweb of pre-matrimonial acquaintanceship?" [22]). The narrator, characters, and readers are brought together in the typically Industrial-Romantic form of address, but here the emphasis is on the darker traits they are now assumed to share: ignorance, hypocrisy, arrogance. Eliot's contemporary readers, as Suzanne Graver has shown, were disturbed by the novel's combination of sympathy and a creeping, corrosive mistrust of the society she depicts: they wrote of their "dismay at the 'biting power' of the 'acid criticism' in *Middlemarch*," and "were disconcerted by the 'blending of the author's bitterness with her profound tenderness'" (270). And this mistrust, by Eliot's own logic, extends to her audience as well; the ubiquitous narrative asides instructing readers on the finer points of sympathy often shade into chiding reminders that they share the characters' blindnesses rather than the author's more comprehensive sympathetic vision; little wonder then that some of Eliot's first reviewers found the book offensive.[16] Such doubts about her readers, and about the public more generally, lie at the very heart of Eliot's authorship, and they are the necessary justification for her own distinctively pronounced narrative authority.

Eliot's authority practically goes without saying: of the Victorian novelists, her reputation most closely approaches the Carlylean "sage," though in her case such commanding wisdom was further mystified and feminized by critics' tendency to call her a "Sybil."[17] I have emphasized how this construction of authorship diverges from its predecessors largely over the question of audience. Just as Gaskell's self-abnegation relied upon a performance of faith in her society and in her readers more specifically, Eliot's relative mastery arises from her ambivalent concerns about her own relationship to the intimidating "parrot-house" in which novelists were compelled to work. The crucial differences between these two authorships are proof of the wide range of strategies by which women writers might engage the public, but they also suggest the ways in which perceptions of that public exerted pressure on their assumptions; their divergent representations of domesticity and domestic values, in particular, demonstrate how readily the treatment of private life responded to changing perceptions of the public. In this way, both Gaskell and Eliot are very much of their respective times: Gaskell writes in the heyday of Industrial Romanticism's pursuit of wide readerships, Eliot at the moment of its transition to new forms after the "higher journalism" had raised fears about lower class readers' pernicious influence.

Eliot's authorship, in fact, bears signs of the recrudescence of Wordsworthian ideals that would contribute to Arnold's redefinition of culture. Like Wordsworth, she begins to chart a course for authorial dignity that will not rely on immediate public enthusiasm:

> Fame is but another word for the sympathy of mankind with individual genius, and the great poet or the great composer is sure that that sympathy will be given some day, though his Paradise Lost will fetch only five pounds, and his symphony is received with contemptuous laughter, so he can transport himself from the present and live by anticipation in that future time when he will be thrilling men's minds and ravishing their ears. ("Liszt" 83-84)

To claim that "the sympathy of mankind" can be indefinitely deferred in this way is to reiterate Wordsworth's argument that genius must create the taste by which it will be appreciated, so that its immediate, pragmatic effect becomes relatively inconsequential. And to conceptualize sympathy this way—as a matter of recognizing the "individual genius" rather than the social whole—is of course radically to alter what Dickens or Gaskell meant by the term. As we have seen, *Middlemarch* also occasionally suggests that sympathy derives from an individual capacity rather than a broadly human birthright, and that it therefore might serve as a tool of distinction instead of proof of moral community: "Only those who know the supremacy of the intellectual life—the life which has a seed of ennobling thought and purpose within it—can understand the grief of one who falls from that serene activity into the absorbing, soul-wasting struggle with worldly annoyances" (*Middlemarch* 737). *Middlemarch* stands at an ideological crossroads, and the sentiment expressed in this comment is not unequivocally maintained in the novel. But such a limited view of readers' understanding does foreshadow the logic of Henry James's proto-modernist description of authorial appreciation, and it begins to sketch the epitaph of those ideologies of authorship that we think of as particularly Victorian.

Conclusion

I have argued that the emergence of a mass market for print—and its attendant economic and ideological pressures—structured the profound transformations in Victorian constructions of authorship. I cannot claim, however, that the impulse to assess the mediating function of authorship in the context of material practices of publishing and circulation is entirely innovative. Indeed, this perspective might be more suggestively considered as a return to the pre-Victorian sense that writers—and especially novelists—were fully enmeshed in what Scott called "the ordinary business of the world." It was precisely this understanding of social engagement that began to dwindle as authorship came to eclipse other traditional criteria of literary value. Wordsworth's strategic hostility to the tastes of the growing public reinforced his sense that poets should be valorized in terms of their special access to a separate sphere of timeless human verities, and that the question of a writer's practical influence, like the question of his popularity, could be indefinitely deferred. As the early Victorian novelists grew more powerful in the relations of literary production, they drew on Romantic models of the glorified poet to justify their claims for intellectual property and cultural capital. Even as they accepted Carlyle's vision of a socially-engaged, heroically influential writer, the practical terms of literary criticism began to reflect the increasing importance of authors: novels were to be judged not only by their effects on readers, but also by the sincerity, friendliness, and sympathy of their writers. When concerns about a massive influx of new audiences began uncomfortably to dilate the circle of friendly readers, writers turned uneasily to discourses of professionalism or artistry to supplement or replace the imperatives of Industrial Romanticism. By the last years of the century, a critical fetishization of authors had almost entirely effaced the issue of their novels' social impact, supporting instead the ideal of individual appreciation of—or even imaginary communion with—the artistic sensibility of the writer. James's portrayal of novel-

ists as serenely aloof from quotidian demands of the market was the culmination of a century-long ideological attenuation of writers' engagement
with the reading public, even though it recapitulates the same market
forces that were leading to the accelerating fragmentation of audiences and
the increasing specialization of intellectual labor. The ordinary business of
the world exerted a powerful influence on all of these metamorphoses,
even though the effect of the changes was increasingly to obscure its continuing importance.

We should nevertheless take care not to assign economic and juridical
developments too determining a role in the shifting meanings of Victorian
authorship. The ideological experience of material crises—expressed in an
elaborate system of metaphors, gestures, and stock images—can rarely be
shown to correspond strictly and predictably to specific historical moments or particular socioeconomic causes. The trope of sympathy, for example, endured across the century's many cultural upheavals, though its
precise implications and its centrality in imagining writers' relationships
with their readers varied considerably. The metaphor of sensation, on the
other hand, appeared with such startling rapidity that few novelists knew
what to make of it. The combination of emergent and traditional terms
such as these—along with creativity and mechanization, diffusion and disease, professionalism and artistry, utility and appreciation, friendship and
divinity—formed the vocabulary with which Victorians discussed the cultural status of novelists. The material practices of producing and circulating novels, meanwhile, provided a grammar through which this vocabulary
received its various inflections and emphases. Neither of these two dimensions of representing authorship could make sense without the other.

We may find further proof of the relative autonomy of ideology and material practice in the persistence of Victorian metaphors of authorship long
after the controversies of the nineteenth-century marketplace have faded
away. Consider, for instance, John Fowles's interestingly vexed attempt in
1969 to represent himself as a novelist who has grown beyond the philosophy of his Victorian predecessors:

> The novelist is still a god, since he creates (and not even the most aleatory
> avant-garde novel has managed to extirpate its author completely); what
> has changed is that we are no longer the gods of the Victorian image, om-
> niscient and decreeing; but in the new theological image, with freedom
> our first principle, not authority. (97)

Fowles's attitude illustrates the tenacious appeal of the same metaphors of
divinity and freedom that attracted James's generation, though he indicates
that those ideals have taken on slightly different implications. Yet while
Fowles is quick to note the differences between his understanding of novelists and the Victorians', he fails to recognize the differences between the
Victorians themselves, implying instead a monolithic "Victorian image" of
both authorship and authority. The late nineteenth-century notion of a

godlike novelist was in fact a relatively radical departure from previous ideals; one cannot help but to imagine Scott greeting such theological rhetoric with ridicule, Gaskell with moral apprehension, or Collins with bewilderment. Nor should we assume a consistent mode of novelistic authority that can be judged simply by narrative technique. James, ostensibly the most authoritatively godlike of the writers I have discussed, was also the least "omniscient and decreeing."

While there are certainly identifiable trends in nineteenth-century representations of novelists, what most characterizes authorship in the period as a whole is its instability. The images of a disenchanted Edward Waverley poised uneasily at the crossroads of history and romance, of Pickwick impounded before the jeers and taunts of an unsympathetic crowd, of Mary Barton insolently challenged to overcome feminine reticence in a crowded courtroom, of the body of Count Fosco, that consummate performer, lying naked and anonymous in the Paris Morgue, of the mocking echoes that punish Brooke of Tipton for his attempt to address a political mob as though he were merely engaging in a friendly chat, of Hyacinth's corpse locked in the dingy apartment where he finally achieved his Pyrrhic resolution to the personal and social dilemmas that tormented and isolated him: all of these, I have argued, are dark reflections of nineteenth-century novelists. All of them point, on one level, to a paralyzing difficulty of reconciling the conflicting demands of an expanding audience or to a claustrophobic impotence in the face of hostile cultural expectations. At the same time, the very pessimism of these images reveals how anxiously uncertain, how threateningly tenuous, the construction of authorship had become. The Victorian novelist was made and remade, by writers, critics, publishers, booksellers, and readers, out of a century of continual debate. The only unbroken intellectual tradition in this history is the unflagging desire to confront fundamental assumptions about the meaning of culture, the limits of community, and the responsibilities of the writer. It is a struggle worth remembering in all of its complexity.

Notes

NOTES TO CHAPTER ONE

¹ Even materialist critics have granted Wordsworth undue power in inaugurating an unchallenged ideology of authorship. See, for instance, Catherine Belsey, who finds Wordsworth's conception of authorship at the genesis of the literary paradigm of expressive realism, the theory that lurks behind today's "common sense" understanding of literature and consumerist criticism, where the author "still reigns as the source and explanation of the nature of the text" (134). Belsey tracks this notion from the Romantics through John Ruskin, then through F. R. Leavis and into the popular imagination. Terry Eagleton suggests a slightly different route through the work of Matthew Arnold before reaching Leavis, and finally declares that "English students in England today are 'Leavisites' whether they know it or not" (31). Wordsworth's "Essay Supplementary" in particular has been singled out as a locus classicus in the formulation of Romantic authorship; Raymond Williams, for instance, draws upon it extensively in his classic discussion of the Romantic artist (*Culture and Society* 30-48), and more recently, Martha Woodmansee has claimed that "We owe our modern idea of an author to the radical reconceptualization of writing which came to fruition in [Wordsworth's] essay of 1815" ("Introduction" 16).

² Hartley Coleridge, for example, could not resist the temptation to read Wordsworth's rejection of popularity as a knee-jerk reaction to his own lack of a large audience, and he memorably captures this opinion in his parody of Wordsworth's "She Dwelt among the Untrodden Ways":

> There lived among the untrodden ways
> To Rydal Lake doth lead;
> A bard whom there were none to praise
> And very few to read.
> [. . . . .]
> Unread his works – his "Milk-white Doe"
> With dust is dark and dim;
> It's still in Longman's shop, and O,
> The difference to him!

³ For an overview of transforming perceptions of the public sphere in early nineteenth-century print culture, see Klancher 76-97.

⁴ Patrick Parrinder has summarized the gap between Wordsworth's argument and prevailing notions of authorship in the eighteenth century in terms of Wordsworth's internalization of aesthetic criteria: "It is notable what a solitary and internalized picture [Wordsworth] gives of poetic creation. The key determinants – the author's mental endowments, his experiences of observation and habits of meditation, and finally the inspiration itself – are all held within the self. Thus the poet is not, as Johnson had said, a "general challenger" who 'offers his merit to publick judgment'. There is no challenge or submission or reward, only the eventual recognition of his intrinsic and inalienable merits" (44).

⁵ Riede 93. For an extended analysis of the contradictions in Wordsworth's authoritative claims, see Riede 92-164.

⁶ M. H. Abrams has shown how this tendency is the definitive preoccupation of Romanticism more generally: "The major lyric innovation of the Romantic period, for example, the extended poems of description and meditation, are in fact fragments of reshaped autobiography" (123).

⁷ Millgate x. Millgate's important study is one of few that attempts to consider Scott as both a poet and a novelist, but as her title suggests, she reads Scott's earlier work through the lens of the novels he would eventually write, thus emphasizing a continuity between these aspects of his career instead of the rift I am suggesting here.

⁸ His "Essay on Minstrelsy," which accompanied the *Minstrelsy of the Scottish Borders*, explained the social circumstances in which, Scott believed, these ancient poems had been composed. As John Sutherland puts it, for Scott "these ballads were originally the single creation of bards or minstrels in the employ of a king or chief. They were, in origin, acts of duty and homage to their lord by peculiarly gifted followers" (*Life* 75). In his first major poem, the *Lay of the Last Minstrel*, Scott would metaphorically assume the mantle of the ancient bard for himself: in the poem's introduction the eponymous minstrel, a thinly disguised figure for Scott ("The last of all the bards was he, / Who sung of Border chivalry") is patronized by Anne Scott, first Duchess of Buccleuch and ancestor of the Buccleuchs who would be Scott's primary political patrons and who, as Scott's distant relatives, he would consider the "chiefs" of his clan. When the minstrel is commanded by the Duchess to sing of the history of the Scott family, Scott's metaphor is complete: he invites a comparison between his poetic production and that of the minstrel who sings for the leader of his clan, in return for which he is granted support and praise. Lest the reader miss the point, the poem is dedicated to Charles, the Earl of Dalkieth and heir to the dukedom, just as the *Minstrelsy* had been dedicated to Henry, the current Duke of Buccleuch. The fact that Scott was writing for a public that would buy 15,000 copies of the *Lay* in the next five years never enters into his representation of poetic production. Scott would continue to experiment with the patronage model – his next poem, *Marmion* (1808), is framed with a series of epistles to Tory friends, a device based on Dryden's verses to his political patrons – but he did not abandon it until he turned to *Waverley*.

⁹ Ina Ferris, for instance, treats Scott's sudden anonymity as a non-problem, claiming – a bit too easily – that "Scott's anonymity was never an obstacle to his first reviewers" (10). Ferris's otherwise remarkable study finds it necessary to gloss over Scott's anonymity because her argument partly depends on proving that one of

the reasons the *Waverley* novels were so acclaimed was that Scott, a respected male writer, was known to be the author. Other critics have offered half-hearted explanations for Scott's decision, usually restating what Scott had offered as his own motivations, before moving on to a different question. John Sutherland's biography of Scott, though it acknowledges that he was "morbidly careful" about protecting his secret, has only this to say about Scott's anonymity: "He gave a number of reasons at different times, most of which boil down to Shylock's surly 'it was my humour'. A number of explanations have been forward on his behalf, none of which is absolutely convincing. (1) Scott hated criticism, and [Francis] Jeffrey's criticism of *Marmion* had particularly stung him. (2) His father would have disapproved of his writing novels, and even as a forty-three-year-old he could not shake off this sense of filial guilt. (3) A sheriff like himself needed to observe 'some solemnity of walk and conduct'. (4) Anonymity was a useful sales gimmick. 'Humour' serves as well as anything" (*Life* 294).

[10] Scott's fears in this regard were not entirely unfounded. His friend, Henry Cockburn expressed something of the shock with which the news of Scott's business associations had been greeted: "Ballantyne and Constable were merchants, and their fall, had it reached no further, might have been lamented merely as the casualty of commerce. But Sir Walter! The idea that his practical sense had so far left him as to have permitted him to dabble in *trade*, had never crossed our imagination" (qtd. in J. Sutherland, *Life* 294).

[11] As Sutherland points out, "[H]e inserts the successful author into the production process under two heads: in general terms, as the employer or master-manufacturer who has put into circulation for profit a certain capital sum; and more specifically, as the workman whose creative effort is one stage in the book's manufacture, the value of which will be added to the end-product in the same way as the labour of the printer or the binder" (K. Sutherland 101).

[12] See, for example, the *Monthly Review*'s assessment of *Waverley*, which points out that "historical utility" will be lost in cases where facts are "coloured according to the dictates of [a writer's] own fancy, and dressed out for ornament and effect" (275). Similarly, Croker, confesses that he has "a great objection to what may be called historical romance" because the mixture of "actual and fabulous events" confuses readers and unsettles the historical record, and wishes that the author had written pure history (377).

[13] It is worth noting that the logic of the plot's ultimate movement toward romance is not simply driven by the metaphorical identification of history as an impediment, but also by the formal demand for a conclusion. With Waverley's education complete and the Stuart cause all but lost, all that remains for the novel is resolution. The story will soon draw to a close, but history, of course, has no closure.

NOTES TO CHAPTER TWO

[1] The best description of the cultural logic of Dickensian representations of authorship remains Mary Poovey's, which contends that Dickens represented novel writing as "simultaneously an expression of self and a gift to others" (101), an activity that was socially valuable because it appeared to offer a perspective from above the fragmented, alienated working conditions in which Victorians frequently felt themselves mired.

² On the importance of sympathy for Romantic aesthetics, see Thomas J. Mc-
Carthy's *Relationships of Sympathy: The Writer and Reader in British Romanticism*.

³ For the purposes of this comparison, it is useful to remember that over the six
months Coleridge produced *The Friend* he lost £200. See Saunders 168.

⁴ As Kathryn Chittick's study of Dickens's early career confirms, "*Pickwick* may
not have been a novel in its original idea or composition, but by the end of its run
nearly two years later [. . .] Dickens had decided that he was going to be known as
a novelist" (91).

⁵ See Engel and King 56-57. *Pickwick*'s first readers had no reason to regard
Dickens as a novelist, since "Boz" had previously become known to the public only
as a writer of newspaper and magazine "Sketches," and critics likewise classified
Pickwick, which appeared in monthly parts, as a sort of periodical; even the subsequent publication of the complete text—bound in only one volume rather than the
usual two or three—implied genres other than the novel. See also Chittick 61-70.

⁶ It was as the editor of *Bentley's* that "Boz" began publishing the articles that
would become *Oliver Twist*, and here too there was some disagreement over
whether or not his production was a novel (Chittick 82). In the original preface to
his next "novel," Dickens describes himself not as a novelist, but as a "periodical
essayist" (*Nicholas Nickleby* 47).

⁷ One of Carlyle's clearest statements on the beneficial effects of hero-worship
may be found in "Signs of the Times": "*one* man that has a higher Wisdom, a hitherto unknown spiritual Truth in him, is stronger, not than ten men that have it not,
or than ten thousand, but *all* men that have it not; and stands among them with a
quite ethereal, angelic power, as with a sword out of Heaven's own armory, sky-
tempered, which no buckler, and no tower of brass, will finally withstand" (48).

⁸ *Heroes and Hero-Worship* 144. Carlyle's influence on early Victorian novelists
was profound, though in practice their claims rarely approached his grandilo-
quence. Still, "friendship" works much like Carlyle's "Hero-worship," since the
friend awakens friendly impulses just as the Hero awakens the Heroic. Though Victorians sensed the continuity between Carlyle's project and Dickens's, many seemed
to prefer the latter's more humble version. A review in *Fraser's* of *David Copperfield* describes a case of the "coincidence of opinion between the two authors"
thus: "it is certain that no one has been more instrumental than Dickens in foster-
ing that spirit of kindly charity which impels a man to do what he can, however
narrow his sphere of action may be, to relieve the sufferings and to instruct the ignorance of his brethren; while Carlyle, on the other hand, treats all such efforts
with lofty disdain, and would call them mere attempts to tap an ocean by gimlet-
holes, or some such disparaging metaphor" ("Charles Dickens and David Copperfield" 709).

⁹ Still worse was any pretension to artistry. Bentham himself had rejected everything artistic as "anergastic," that is, non-functional, unproductive, valueless. See
Altick 133-35.

¹⁰ According to Altick, the entries in the biographical dictionary for just the letter "A" ran to seven half-volumes, "at a loss of £5,000," and the Society fell apart
at the disheartening prospect of undertaking "B" (270). On this and other S.D.U.K.
publishing projects, see Altick 269-70.

¹¹ Louis James has summarized the of the findings of two 1840 surveys of the
circulation of cheap periodicals as follows: "There were approximately eighty

cheap periodicals circulating in London. Two-thirds of this number cost a penny, none cost more than twopence. Nine were scientific—the vestiges of *The Penny Magazine* and its followers. Only four were political, Five were considered licentious, Four were devoted to drama, and sixteen to biographies and memoirs. Twenty-two contained nothing but romances or stories. Large as this proportion of fiction was, it was to increase rapidly in the ensuing decade" (*Fiction for the Working Man* 27). For a more complete overview of developments in the penny press from 1830-1840, see James 12-27.

¹² For a summary of *Pickwick's* serial precursors and imitators, see John Sutherland's *Victorian Fiction* 85-106.

¹³ When Feltes writes of the manner in which serial production allows the audience to be "sensed and expanded," he suggests the same reciprocally (or dialectically) constitutive relationship between audience and text that I pointed to at the outset of this chapter. In practice, though, Feltes lays greater stress on how texts expand the audience by "interpellating, that is, by addressing and engaging an infinity of bourgeois subjects, 'traced' in the text" (9). My own emphasis, as I suggested earlier, is rather on the way the text shows traces of its audience's influence, though it bears repeating that these two aspects should be considered complementary.

¹⁴ Contrast one of Dickens's publishing deals much later in his life for another part-issue novel with Chapman and Hall: "I propose you pay to me £6000 for the half copyright throughout and outright at the times mentioned in your last letter to me on the subject. For that consideration I am ready to enter into articles of agreement with you securing you the publication of the work when I shall be ready to begin publishing and the half share" (qtd. in J. Sutherland, *Victorian Novelists* 79). In this arrangement, for *Our Mutual Friend*, the publishers made substantially less profit than Dickens, who ultimately retained the copyright and its subsidiary rights (such as rights to future cheap editions, to American publication, and to translations). At his most powerful, Dickens could force a publisher to accept only a quarter of profits from publication.

¹⁵ On the "striking reversal" in the stakes of copyright debates between the eighteenth- and nineteenth-centuries, see Mark Rose's *Authors and Owners* 92-112. Rose's work suggests that the concept of authors as privileged creators had been put forward by certain booksellers in eighteenth-century copyright disputes (particularly in the case of *Donaldson v. Becket*), and that writers themselves later used these representations of authorship to support their own property rights: "The booksellers had promulgated the representation of authorship that writers such as Southey and Wordsworth now adopted as their own" (Rose, "The Author as Proprietor" 70).

¹⁶ For more detailed narratives of Talfourd's initiative, see John Feather's *Publishing, Piracy and Politics* 122-148, and David Saunders's *Authorship and Copyright* 126-30.

¹⁷ Saunders cautions against this assumption in his *Authorship and Copyright*. As he asks in reference to the growing personalization of authorship during the copyright reform years, "an author might acquire an elaborate authorial persona, but was it one to be fully and specifically recognised in the sphere of an author's legal existence? Copyright law—in doctrine and in application—remained immune to any such personalising or extra-proprietary development" (147).

¹⁸ See Erickson 39-40.

[19] In this respect, Talfourd's campaign contributed to the formation of what Rose has called a "special kind of commodity, 'the work,'" which had first emerged in the eighteenth century (Rose, "Author as Proprietor" 54). It was only in the nineteenth century, however, that copyright law bound the term of protection to the author's life.

[20] For an overview of the types of agreements writers might make with publishers, see Patten 22-27.

[21] On the relationship of authorship to advertisement in the context of mass-market literature, see Jennifer Wicke's *Advertising Fictions* 19-53.

[22] On the friendship of Dickens and Talfourd, who would later serve as the model for *David Copperfield*'s "Tommy Traddles," see P. F. Skottowe's "Thomas Talfourd and *David Copperfield*."

[23] Hillis Miller has suggested that the "prototype" of the early Pickwick is "the good reporter, such as the author of *Sketches by Boz*, as well as the scientist" (7).

[24] Miller 15. For another description of the recurring fear of the mob in the novel, see Christopher Herbert's "Converging Worlds in *The Pickwick Papers*" 11-12.

[25] For a critique of the linked notions of creating texts and creating audiences, see Pierre Macherey 66-74. Although the emphasis of the present chapter falls on the ideological responses to new market conditions, my own study is informed by Macherey's warning not to "replace a mythology of the creator with a mythology of the public," but to show a reciprocally influential relationship between authorship and changing forms of literary circulation, mediated by larger socioeconomic forces: "the conditions that determine the production of the book also determine the forms of its communication" (70).

[26] See Wicke 25-26.

NOTES TO CHAPTER THREE

[1] Roland Barthes provides one useful (if very sweeping) context for explaining these changes: "the 1850s bring the concurrence of three new and important facts in History: the demographic expansion in Europe, the replacement of textile by heavy industry, that is, the birth of modern capitalism, the scission (completed by the revolution of June 1848) of French society into three mutually hostile classes, bringing the definitive ruin of liberal illusions. These circumstances put the bourgeoisie into a new historical situation. Until then, it was bourgeois ideology itself which gave the measure of the universal by filling it unchallenged. The bourgeois writer, sole judge of other people's woes and without anyone else to gaze on him, was not torn between his social condition and his intellectual vocation. Henceforth, this very ideology appears merely as one among many possible others; the universal escapes it, since transcending itself would mean condemning itself; the writer falls a prey to ambiguity, since his consciousness no longer accounts for the whole of his condition" (*Writing Degree Zero* 60).

[2] For a useful sketch of Lloyd's career, see P. R. Hoggart's "Edward Lloyd, 'The Father of the Cheap Press.' "

[3] These circulation figures are derived from Altick 394-95.

[4] Coverage of crime and legal proceedings was not limited to cheaper newspapers, of course, but as John Sutherland has pointed out, "cheaper prints contained many more crime stories than their 4d. and 5d. rivals like *The Times*" (*Victorian*

Fiction 31). He also notes that the cheaper press was the cradle of investigative reporting, which doubtless influenced the popularity of detective fiction.

[5] To date, the most convincing attempt to contextualize the genre's historical emergence has been Jonathan Loesberg's "The Ideology of Narrative Form in Sensation Fiction," which suggests that the category coalesced in response to growing fears of the erosion of class identity in the years preceding the second Reform Bill. He argues that a particular narrative structure of sensation fiction, especially its gestures towards inevitability and its treatment of the loss of identity (seen in "legal and class aspects") are cognate to, if not exactly caused by, broader ideological narratives in the debates leading to the Bill (117-18). But though his claim that class anxiety informed both sensation novels and critical responses to them is a necessary step in understanding the background of the sensation scandal, it does not sufficiently explain the particularity of the moment of sensationalism as a literary development: anxiety about class boundaries is not new with the 1860s, nor can we claim with and confidence that it was more intense during this period than it had been before. We require a more mediated explanation, one which can pinpoint the translation of contemporary class anxieties (involving general debates about democracy and the breakdown of class boundaries) into the specifically literary context of new relationships between writers, readers, and critics.

[6] It is now generally held that the consolidation of a category of sensation fiction owes less to the novelists who would come to be included in it than to the critics who attacked them. See, for example, Ronald R. Thomas's "Wilkie Collins and the Sensation Novel": "Collins did not invent the sensation novel. Dickens, his mentor and friend, did not invent it, nor did the other most famous and prolific practitioners of the form [. . .]. The 'sensation novel' was a genre invented in the 1860s by the same outraged literary critics and reviewers who condemned it. They coined the term and created the category to describe and contain a disreputable form of literature that they generally regarded as morally diseased, aesthetically bankrupt, and socially dangerous" (480).

[7] Many historians have noted a profound shift in the aims and terms of periodical criticism in the second half of the Victorian period. My argument follows John Woolford's claim that the crucial revisions occurred between 1855 and 1864.

[8] Terry Eagleton has described the difference between the assumptions of mid-Victorian criticism and those of its eighteenth-century forbears in greater depth, showing, for example, that in the later period "the critic is both inside and outside the public arena, responding attentively from within only the more effectively to manage and mould opinion from some superior external vantage point. It is a posture which threatens to invert the priorities of correction and collaboration evident in the *Tatler and Spectator*, where the former was possible and tolerable only on the basis of the latter" (*The Function of Criticism* 51).

[9] "Earlier Type of the Sensation Novel" 460-61. An article in *All the Year Round* went further, suggesting that criticism of the sensational might be applied with equal justice to the New Testament; see "What is Sensational?" 224-25.

[10] Pamela K. Gilbert has described the critical use of metaphors of disease in discussions of sensationalism at great length, linking it with the Victorian anxieties that surfaced in relation to sanitation inquiries and the Contagious Diseases Acts. She concludes that "'Sensation' became a thinly veiled literary euphemism for the action of disease upon the body; spurred by economic and social anxieties, women's popular novels became re-presentations of the grotesque social body and

critical discourse became the speculum with which to achieve surveillance and containment" (80-81). Though I find that her argument ultimately goes too far in failing to see disease itself as yet another euphemism (and she very often takes this critical trope quite literally), her lengthy analysis of mid-Victorian metaphors of reading and circulation remains extremely valuable (15-91).

11 This irony was not lost on the genre's defenders, who were quick to remind their readers that popular acclaim was hardly a new phenomenon. A writer in *All the Year Round*, for instance, pointed out that the critique of popularity, rather than popularity itself, was the anomaly responsible for the sensation scandal: "It is much the fashion now to swell with severity on certain morbid failings and cravings of the grand outside Public—the universal customer—the splendid bespeaker, who goes round every market, purse in hand, and orders plays, poems, novels, pictures, concerts, and operas. Yet this taste for fiery sauces and strongly-seasoned meats and drinks is of a very ancient date, nay, with the public—so long as it has been a public—it has been a constant taste" (qtd. in Taylor 4).

12 See Christopher Kent's "Higher Journalism and the Mid-Victorian Clerisy." More recent studies that have added to Kent's work include Woolford's "Periodicals and the Practice of Literary Criticism," Isobel Armstrong's *Victorian Scrutinies*, and Kelly J. Mays's "The Disease of Reading and Victorian Periodicals."

13 One of the better known journalists who called for the end of anonymous reviewing was G. H. Lewes, whose "Farewell Causerie" made the issue a matter of social influence and individual morality: "I am expressing the views of many serious minds who look on periodical literature as a great civilizing influence very much in need of vigilant control, especially in the direction of earnestness and responsibility, when I say that the first condition of all writing is sincerity, and that one means of securing sincerity is to insist on personal responsibility" (890).

14 On the relationship of the new criticism to university reform, see Heyck's *The Transformation of Intellectual Life* 155-189.

15 Isobel Armstrong's survey of mid-Victorian criticism of poetry discusses the same lapse in the influence of high-romantic doctrine: "A few 'German' terms, such as objective and subjective, are used, but until the sixties, apart from one or two exceptions such as Donne and Masson, it is almost as if Coleridge had never been" (14).

16 The standard exploration of the relationship of Victorian sensationalism in novels to that in the press is Thomas Boyle's *Black Swine in the Sewers of Hampstead*.

17 Mansel 501. The parting salvo at police reports is particularly telling, since it implicates not only the *Times*, but also the many cheaper newspapers in which police reports constituted a more central factor in their appeal. The comparison itself was not uncommon; in 1866 the *Westminster* dismissed sensation novels for having "all the interest, and also the literary power of a police report" ("Belles Lettres" [1866] 126). To be relatively uninterested in the sort of crime reportage that had drawn lower-class readers since the days of gallows broadsides could itself serve as a mark of some literary distinction.

18 Thus Miller's points that "Nervousness seems the necessary 'condition' in the novel for perceiving its real plot and for participating in it as more than a pawn," (150), and that, by extension, the readers of *The Woman in White* learn that to engage with the novel's interpretive strategies they must mirror the characters' intuitive, sensationally registered suspicion (162-64), tell only half the story. One could

argue that the novel teaches just as compellingly—and far more explicitly—that such a panopticonic scrutiny of bodies (including one's own) is powerless to advance anyone's interests in the public sphere. Change is effected in this text only through the suppression of affective impulses in strict accordance with what it calls "professional" self-discipline and the ostensibly unfeeling objectivity of medical and legal ideologies.

[19] Thomas has argued that the recurring concern in novels of the 1860s about questions of social identity is closely tied to contemporary interest in the power of professional discourse to answer them. Writing specifically of sensation novels, he suggests that collectively they "tell the story of the rise of a professional class of lawyers and physicians who established themselves as a powerful elite by taking control of the very terms upon which persons would be recognized and authenticated" (483).

[20] Brantlinger has made this point in reference to the more mysterious of the sensation novels: "At the same time that the narrator of a sensation novel seems to acquire authority by withholding the solution to a mystery, he or she also loses authority or at least innocence, becoming a figure no longer to be trusted" (15).

[21] *Adam Bede* 221. Juridical discourse was not, of course, the only source to which writers turned for metaphors of their work, though the traditional professions appear to have held a particular appeal through the mid-Victorian period. Sheridan LeFanu, for example, drew on medicine and psychology to lend authority (in the figure of Dr. Hesselius) to the narration of his ghost stories. Later popular writers would follow suit: Arthur Conan Doyle's Holmes stories are narrated by Dr. Watson, while Bram Stoker's *Dracula* gives us the heroic Abraham Van Helsing, who is both a doctor and a lawyer.

NOTES TO CHAPTER FOUR

[1] Walter Pater's essay on Wordsworth in *Appreciations* exemplifies the difficulties with which later writers attempted to assimilate Wordsworth. Pater struggles throughout with the question of Wordsworth's moral purpose, first trivializing the poet as a "mere declaimer on moral and social topics" (40), but later assuring the reader that the effect of the poetry is "not to teach lessons, or enforce rules, or even to stimulate us to noble ends" (62). Finally, Pater finds "hidden away" in Wordsworth's poetry the recurring argument of his own work: "To witness this spectacle [of life] with the appropriate emotions is the aim of all culture" (63).

[2] Thomas Strychacz has argued that James's continuing appeal depends in part on the similarity between professional academic authority and James's own: "James's work became central because it adheres to a discourse of obscurity and complexity that happens also to constitute the primary discourse of professional academic studies. Both preserve an identity of purpose and strategy for speaking authoritatively. This would suggest that James is fated to remain as a cornerstone of the literary academic establishment, whatever shape it is to take, much longer than the staunchest supporters and opponents of canon subversion may suppose" (37).

[3] Borus 101. Marcia Jacobson shares his assessment: "Dickens and Trollope had written for audiences that were considerably more homogeneous than at the end of the century. Writers and readers came from a narrower cross-section of the popula-

tion [. . .]. A community of shared assumptions united writer and reader in a way
no longer possible by the time James settled in England" (5).

⁴ On the phenomenon of best-sellers, see Jacobson's *Henry James and the Mass
Market* xxx, and Keating's *Haunted Study* 439-45.

⁵ The long-prevailing myth of James as an artist who soared high above any
petty considerations of sales and market strategies has been debunked by such studies as Michael Anesko's "*Friction with the Market,*" Stuart Culver's "Representing
the Author," and Marcia Jacobson's *Henry James and the Mass Market.*

⁶ "The Question of the Opportunities" 653-54. For longer discussions of
James's interest in the opportunities of market fragmentation, see Richard Salmon
47-61, and Thomas Strychaz 20-22.

⁷ N. N. Feltes argues that the period saw decisive structural changes as late-Victorian society experienced a "transition from a high-capitalist, free enterprise mode
of production to the late-capitalist, monopoly-capital mode," which in turn produced ideological contradictions between a "new literary mode of production and
the residual petty-commodity literary mode of production" (*Literary Capital* 4).

⁸ Among the many studies of politics in *The Princess Casamassima* are Margaret
Scanlan's "Terrorism and the Realistic Novel: Henry James and *The Princess
Casamassima,*" Seltzer's *Henry James and the Art of Power,* and Michal P. Ginsburg's *Economies of Change.* Seltzer describes the novel as "distinctly political" on
the level of narrative technique, while Scanlan argues that "in *The Princess
Casamassima* James fails even to consider the possibility of synthesizing art and
revolution" and that it supports the opposition of the literary and political. Michal
Ginsburg, on the other hand, has argued that Hyacinth can neither choose between
the aesthetic and the political nor synthesize them, but only because his experience
offers no grounds on which to distinguish them as separate categories. The contrast
between these readings suggests not only the difficulty of pinning down the relationship between the political and the aesthetic in the novel, but also the problem
of determining the level on which one should examine this relationship to begin
with.

⁹ For an overview of these stereotypes, see Jonathan Freedman's *Professions of
Taste* 146-49. For an elaboration on James's critique of the aesthetes' immoral detachment, see Freedman's reading of *Portrait of a Lady,* in which, he argues, James
exonerates Isabel from his denunciation of aestheticism by "emphasiz[ing] her own
embededness in historical process, her own participation in the human community" (165).

¹⁰ James recalled that the image that prompted *The Princess Casamassima* was
"that of some individual sensitive nature or fine mind, some small obscure intelligent creature whose education should have been almost wholly derived from them,
capable of profiting by all the civilisation, all the accumulations to which they testify, yet condemned to see these things only from the outside" (34).

¹¹ Among the many examples of limited artist/audience relationships in James's
short stories are "The Figure in the Carpet," "The Middle Years," and "Nona Vincent." In the last of these, the dramatist Allan Wayworth enjoys such a relationship
with Mrs. Alsager, of whom he thinks "she was indeed an ideal public" (70). One
of the things he likes about her, incidentally, is that she thinks his work in writing
the play, "the working out of the thing itself, is pure art," while releasing the play
into the public sphere for production is filled with discouraging complications,
"discouraging, because they're vulgar" (74).

[12] Though I concentrate here on James's response to competing ideologies of authorship as they were represented in the late 1870s and early 1880s, Barbara Hochman has suggested that authorial self-effacement emerged as a "defensive response" to a more general growth in publicity. Though she points to James's ultimate ambivalence about "the optimal degree of a novelist's presence and absence, whether on the printed page or in the public eye" (183), we should also consider that James distinguished between *types* of publicity. Self-effacement within a narrative, for example, did not preclude the flamboyant self-exposure of the New York Edition prefaces.

[13] This estimate is given in T. J. Lustig's introduction to *"The Turn of the Screw" and Other Stories* xvii.

[14] See Seltzer 54-56.

NOTES TO CHAPTER FIVE

[1] As Armstrong argues throughout *Desire and Domestic Fiction*, "novels helped to transform the household into what might be called the 'counterimage' of the modern marketplace, an apolitical realm of culture within the culture as a whole" (48). While Armstrong never forgets that domestic realism plays a powerful political role, she claims that its force derives from its ability to disguise its own political implications, to conceal political problems with sexual ones. Her argument depends on a logic of substitution rather than on conspicuous conflicts or potentially disruptive hybrids, and thus repeats the Victorian gesture of separating the explicitly public and the explicitly private.

[2] While not explicitly mentioned in the preface, friendship is often addressed in the story itself, notably in the narrator's general observations occasioned by the mutual regard of Mary and Margaret: "It is so pleasant to have a friend who possesses the power of setting a difficult question in a clear light; whose judgment can tell what is best to be done; and who is so convinced of what is 'wisest, best', that in consideration of the end, all difficulties in the way diminish. People admire talent, and talk about their admiration. But they value common sense without talking about it, and often without knowing it" (43). Note that the emphasis here on "common sense" is functionally equivalent to the common feelings and common interests discussed in the preface. This description of pleasant friendship, powerful on one hand and humbly common and unobtrusive on the other, stands as a fair illustration of the author's imagined relationship with her readers.

[3] Gaskell's contribution to the inaugural issue of *Household Words*, "Lizzie Leigh," was similar enough to Dickens's work that it was widely regarded, as Margaret Homans has pointed out, as Dickens's own (229). Elsie B. Michie has observed that even though all of Dickens's contributors – male or female – had to accept anonymity as a condition of publication, male writers such as Wilkie Collins could receive compensatory influence and recognition in the journal (88).

[4] Qtd in Foster 140. For a subtle and sustained account of Gaskell's personal struggles with publicity and domestic responsibility, see Foster 136-43.

[5] Gallagher's broader argument about industrial fiction is that it invokes domestic values in order to critique society, but that to do so the domestic must remain untainted by the social: "the association of public and private in realist novels depends on an underlying assumption that the two are separate [. . .]. They make the connection between the family and society one of their main themes and primary

organizing devices, but they simultaneously emphasize that the family must be isolated and protected from the larger social world" (114-15). While true for many novels, this argument fails to account for *Mary Barton*'s contention that isolation (particularly of the middle-class family) is the primary cause of class hostility, and that movement between the public and private (particularly by women) is represented positively. Note that Gallagher's account of Gaskell's evasion, like Armstrong's critique, echoes the earlier and even more influential analysis in Raymond Williams's *Culture and Society*, in which he dismisses Mary's story as a retreat from her father's, which he perceives as more authentically political.

⁶ On the cultural implications of *Mary Barton*'s treatment of prostitution, see Michie 113-41.

⁷ Michie points out that because we "know before the trial scene that John Barton actually committed the murder, we are excruciatingly conscious that Victorian society is *not* looking at its own economic problems" (130). Zlotnick similarly claims that "Gaskell disavows" the interpretation of the trial as a romantic distraction: "To read Mary's story melodramatically is to ignore Gaskell's warnings about the distortions of melodrama" (81).

⁸ Schor affirms that "the 'now' of the book is an essential theme in all of Gaskell's correspondence with Chapman" (27), and she quotes a letter from Gaskell that ties the book's topicality to the potential size of its readership: "I am, (above every other consideration,) desirous that it should be *read*; and if you think there would be a better chance of a large circulation by deferring it's [*sic*] appearance, of course I defer to your superior knowledge, only repeating my own belief that the tale would bear directly upon the present circumstances" (28).

⁹ Consider, by way of contrast, Dickens's most analogous novel, *Hard Times*, which was received with some disappointment by reviewers who expected from its title an examination of the issues raised by the contemporary strike at Preston. Instead, Dickens concentrates on the corrosive effects of Utilitarian philosophy on the middle-class household. Here domesticity goes much further than in Gaskell's work to eclipse immediate political concerns.

¹⁰ Armstrong's understanding of the feminine authority in domestic fiction, mentioned at the beginning of this chapter, certainly contributes to this reevaluation of Gaskell. Terry Lovell's *Consuming Fiction* offers a typical articulation of *Mary Barton*'s feminine authority: "it is women and their suffering in the family which provide the angle of vision in a melodramatic plot in which that suffering can take tangible and heightened forms such as the brain fever suffered by Mary upon Jem's acquittal. It is this angle of vision on the condition of England question which legitimates Gaskell's authority to speak, to write in her authorial persona as educated, womanly sympathizer" (88). Schor's reading of the novel presents a similar, if more nuanced, interpretation, claiming that the novel invents a form of matriarchal authority: the "watching out of sympathetic love [is] the provenance of mothers – or here, mothers turned novelists. Reinstating the authority of the mother also places Gaskell as (maternal) author at the center of her text, and makes the mother the perfect novelistic authority" (33).

¹¹ See Macdonald Daly's note on the text in his edition of *Mary Barton* (xxvii). It is worth noting, in this context, that Gaskell's next publication did appear under a masculine pseudonym, "Cotton Mather Mills," a name that combines the traditionally masculine authorities of religion and industry.

[12] Walter Scott's anonymous deference to the judgment of his readers, described in the first chapter, serves as the most instructive parallel. Scott's construction of authorship was itself mirrored, as I pointed out in the second chapter, by the Utilitarian "useful knowledge" movement, and in that context we may find a more direct antecedent of Gaskell's model in the work Harriet Martineau. Martineau, as Alexis Easley has argued, "actively sought anonymity and objectivity in her work as a means of distancing her gender and identity from her writing. This enabled her to express a more 'objective' perspective on women's issues and to communicate her ideas to a mixed-gender audience" (80). On the relationship between Gaskell and Martineau, see Gallagher 62-67.

[13] Even critics who otherwise honor Gaskell's accomplishments have pointed to what they perceive as a problematic lack of narrative authority in *Mary Barton*. Gallagher, for instance, comments on "the absence of a stable, self-assured narrative posture" (68). Hughes and Lund point to the novel's "fundamental doubts about authority," as exemplified in the "narrator, who begins in uncertainty and only gradually moves toward a more confident stance at the work's conclusion" (35). Their account of increasing narrative authority over the course of the work's composition, however, neglects to mention that the famously self-abnegating preface was written last. Both of these arguments are typical in assuming that Gaskell's narrator *should* exert more authority, and that the lack of self-assured command is a troublesome absence that Gaskell ought to have overcome.

[14] Dickens is the chief target of Eliot's disdain in "The Natural History of German Life," where he serves as the central example of an artist "transcendent in his unreality." Here again, what at first seems to be merely a call for greater psychological realism is specifically a critique of Dickens's idealistic representation of the working poor: "But for the precious salt of his humor, [. . .] his preternaturally virtuous poor children and artisans, his melodramatic boatmen and courtesans, would be as noxious as Eugène Sue's idealized proletaires in encouraging the miserable fallacy that high morality and refined sentiment can grow out of harsh social relations, ignorance, and want, or that the working classes are in a condition to enter at once into a millennial state of *altruism,* wherein everyone is caring for everyone else, and no one for himself" (264-65).

[15] Dianne Sadoff's *Monsters of Affection* helps to clarify the ways in which Eliot's conception of sympathy is limited by her concern for individual integrity. Sympathy for others, first of all, is mediated by one's ability to sympathize with one's self. In *The Mill on the Floss*, Sadoff claims, the "narrator's theory of sympathy depends on an implicit topology of memory in which revival of the forgotten memory-trace reminds us that we too are ineluctably other to ourselves simply by virtue of duration [. . .]. As the narrator tells us in 'Janet's Repentance,' 'sympathy is but a living again through our own past in a new form' [. . .]. Sympathy for otherness exists only in retroactivity" (113). Sadoff's point explains why Dorothea can sympathize with the Lydgates' marital troubles only because of her own difficulties with Casaubon, and it also helps us to see how problems of selfhood distract one from a more immediately intersubjective identification. Sadoff goes on to observe that by the time Eliot wrote *Theophrastus Such*, her sense of the problems of sympathy had grown more acute: "the eccentric and disgruntled old bachelor of *Theophrastus Such* finds himself counted out of desire and intersubjectivity. As a result, he understands the ironic consequences of his hitherto highly touted doctrine of self-sacrifice. Sympathy disallows reciprocity; sympathy annihilates the

self. The cost to the sympathetic self is emptiness, repression of desire, and moral deadness" (114-15).

[16] See Graver 266-73. Graver explains that *Middlemarch* represents a turning point in readers' understanding of Eliot's doctrine of sympathy, and that it occasioned controversy for precisely this reason: "In *Middlemarch* [. . .] she clearly offended a good many people. They took the offense extremely personally" (270).

[17] On the implications of the "Sybil" metaphor, see Beer 26-27.

Bibliography

Abrams, M. H. *Natural Supernaturalism*. New York: Norton, 1971.

Altick, Richard D. *The English Common Reader*. Chicago: U of Chicago P, 1957.

Anderson, Benedict. *Imagined Communities*. Revised edition. London: Verso, 1991.

Anesko, Michael. *"Friction with the Market"*: Henry James and the Profession of Authorship. New York and Oxford: Oxford UP, 1986.

Armstrong, Isobel. *Victorian Scrutinies: Reviews of Poetry, 1830-1870*. London: Athlone Press, 1972.

Armstrong, Nancy. *Desire and Domestic Fiction: A Political History of the Novel*. New York and Oxford: Oxford UP, 1987.

Arnold, Matthew. "The Function of Criticism at the Present Time." *The Complete Prose Works of Matthew Arnold*. Ed. R. H. Super. Vol. 3. Ann Arbor: U of Michigan P, 1962.

Barthes, Roland. *Mythologies*. Trans. Annette Lavers. New York: Noonday Press, 1972.

———. *Writing Degree Zero*. Trans. Annette Lavers and Colin Smith. New York: Hill and Wang, 1968.

Beer, Gillian. *George Eliot*. Bloomington: Indiana UP, 1986.

"Belles Lettres." *Westminster Review* 84 (October 1865): 267-76.

"Belles Lettres." *Westminster Review* 86 (July 1866): 125-32.

Belsey, Catherine. *Critical Practice*. London: Routledge, 1980.

Bennett, Scott. "Revolutions in Thought: Serial Production and the Mass Market for Reading." Shattock and Wolff 225-57.

Besant, Walter. *The Art of Fiction*. London: Chatto and Windus, 1902.

Borus, Daniel H. *Writing Realism: Howells, James, and Norris in the Mass Market.* Chapel Hill: U of North Carolina P, 1989.

Bourdieu, Pierre. *Distinction: A Social Critique of the Judgement of Taste.* Trans. Richard Nice. Cambridge, Mass.: Harvard UP, 1984.

Boyle, Thomas. *Black Swine in the Sewers of Hampstead.* New York: Viking, 1989.

Brantlinger, Patrick. "What is 'Sensational' about the Sensation Novel?" *Nineteenth-Century Fiction* 37.1 (June 1982): 1-28.

Carlyle, Thomas. *On Heroes, Hero-Worship, and the Heroic in History.* London: Chapman and Hall, 1840.

———. "Sir Walter Scott." *Complete Works of Thomas Carlyle.* Vol. 3. New York: Thomas Y. Crowell, 1869. 400-466.

Chapman, Sarah. *Henry James's Portrait of the Writer as Hero.* London: Macmillan, 1990.

"Charles Dickens." *North American Review* 219 (April 1868): 671-72.

"Charles Dickens and David Copperfield." *Fraser's* 42 (December 1850): 698-710.

Chittick, Kathryn. *Dickens and the 1830s.* Cambridge: Cambridge UP, 1990.

Colby, Robin B. *"Some Appointed Work To Do": Women and Vocation in the Fiction of Elizabeth Gaskell.* Westport: Greenwood Press, 1995.

Collins, Philip, ed. *Dickens: The Critical Heritage.* London: Routledge, 1971.

Collins, Wilkie. *No Name.* Ed. Mark Ford. New York: Penguin, 1994.

———. "The Unknown Public." *My Miscellanies.* London: Chatto and Windus, 1875. 249-64.

———. *The Woman in White.* Ed. Matthew Sweet. New York: Penguin, 1999.

[Croker, John W.] Rev. of *Waverley. Quarterly Review* 11 (July 1814): 354-77.

Culver, Stuart. "Representing the Author: Henry James, Intellectual Property and the Work of Writing." *Henry James: Fiction as History.* Ed. Ian F. A. Bell. Vision Press, 1984.

Cvetkovich, Ann. *Mixed Feelings: Feminism, Mass Culture, and Victorian Sensationalism.* New Brunswick, NJ: Rutgers UP, 1992.

Dickens, Charles. *Dombey and Son.* Ed. Peter Fairclough. New York: Penguin, 1985.

———. *Nicholas Nickleby.* Ed. Michael Slater. New York: Penguin, 1986.

———. *The Posthumous Papers of the Pickwick Club.* Ed. Mark Wormald. New York: Penguin, 1999.

"Dickens's Tales." *Edinburgh Review* 68 (1838): 41-53.

Eagleton, Terry. *Criticism and Ideology*. London: NLB, 1976.

———. *The Function of Criticism. From The Spectator to Post-Structuralism*. London: Verso, 1996.

———. *Literary Theory*. Minneapolis: U of Minnesota P, 1983.

"Earlier Type of the Sensation Novel." *Dublin University Magazine* 63 (1864): 460-69.

Easley, Alexis. "Gendered Observations: Harriet Martineau and the Woman Question." *Victorian Women Writers and the Woman Question*. Ed. Nicola Diane Thompson. Cambridge: Cambridge UP, 1999. 80-98.

Eger, Elizabeth, Charlotte Grant, Clíona Ó Gallchoir, and Penny Warburton, eds. *Women, Writing and the Public Sphere, 1700-1830*. Cambridge: Cambridge UP, 2001.

Eliot, George. *Adam Bede*. Ed. Stephen Gill. New York: Penguin, 1985.

———. "Address to Working Men, by Felix Holt." *Selected Critical Writings*. 338-354.

———. "Liszt, Wagner, and Weimar." *Selected Critical Writings*. 82-109.

———. "Margaret Fuller and Mary Wollstonecraft." *Selected Critical Writings*. 180-86.

———. *Middlemarch*. Ed. Rosemary Ashton. New York: Penguin, 1994.

———. "The Natural History of German Life." *Selected Critical Writings*. 260-95.

———. *Selected Critical Writings*. Ed. Rosemary Ashton. Oxford: Oxford UP, 1992.

———. "Silly Novels by Lady Novelists." *Selected Critical Writings*. 296-321.

Engel, Eliot D. and Margaret F. King. "Pickwick's Progress: The Critical Reception of *The Pickwick Papers* from 1836 to 1986." *Dickens Quarterly* 3.1 (March 1986): 56-66.

Erickson, Lee. *The Economy of Literary Form*. Baltimore: Johns Hopkins UP, 1996.

Feather, John. *Publishing, Piracy and Politics*. London: Mansell, 1994.

Feltes, N. N. *Literary Capital and the Late Victorian Novel*. Madison, U of Wisconsin P, 1997.

———. *Modes of Production of Victorian Novels*. Chicago: U of Chicago P, 1986.

Ferris, Ina. *The Achievement of Literary Authority: Gender, History, and the Waverley Novels*. Ithaca: Cornell UP, 1991.

Ford, George Henry. *Dickens and His Readers*. New York: Norton, 1965.

Foster, Shirley. *Victorian Women's Fiction: Marriage, Freedom and the Individual*. Totowa, NJ: Barnes & Noble, 1985.

Foucault, Michel. "What Is an Author?" *Language, Counter-Memory, Practice*. Trans. Donald Bouchard and Sherry Simon. Ed. Donald Bouchard. Ithaca: Cornell UP, 1977. 113-38.

Fowles, John. *The French Lieutenant's Woman*. Boston: Back Bay Books, 1998.

Freedman, Jonathan. *Professions of Taste: Henry James, British Aestheticism, and Commodity Culture*. Stanford: Stanford UP, 1990.

Gallagher, Catherine. *The Industrial Reformation of English Fiction: Social Discourse and Narrative Form, 1832-1867*. Chicago: Chicago UP, 1985.

Gaskell, Elizabeth. *Cranford / Cousin Phillis*. Ed. Peter Keating. New York: Penguin, 1976.

———. *The Life of Charlotte Brontë*. Ed. Angus Easson. Oxford: Oxford UP, 1996.

———. *Mary Barton: A Tale of Manchester Life*. Ed. Macdonald Daly. New York: Penguin, 1996.

Gilbert, Pamela K. *Disease, Desire, and the Body in Victorian Women's Popular Novels*. Cambridge: Cambridge UP, 1997.

Ginsburg, Michal P. *Economies of Change: Form and Transformation in the Nineteenth-Century Novel*. Stanford: Stanford UP, 1996.

Gissing, George. *New Grub Street*. Ed. Bernard Bergonzi. New York: Penguin, 1985.

Goode, John. "The Art of Fiction: Walter Besant and Henry James." *Tradition and Tolerance in Nineteenth-Century Fiction: Critical Essays on Some English and American Novels*. Ed. David Howard. London: Routledge and Kegan Paul, 1966. 243-81.

Graver, Suzanne. *George Eliot and Community: A Study in Social Theory and Fictional Form*. Berkeley: U of California P, 1984.

Hayden, John O., Ed. *Scott: The Critical Heritage*. London: Routledge and Kegan Paul, 1970.

Herbert, Christopher. "Converging Worlds in *The Pickwick Papers*." *Nineteenth-Century Fiction* 27.1 (June 1972): 1-20.

Heyck, T. W. *The Transformation of Intellectual Life in Victorian England*. New York: St. Martin's Press, 1982.

Hillhouse, James T. *The Waverley Novels and Their Critics*. Minneapolis: U of Minnesota P, 1936.

Hochman, Barbara. "Disappearing Authors and Resentful Readers in Late-Nineteenth Century American Fiction: The Case of Henry James." *ELH* 63 (1996): 177-201.

Hoggart, P. R. "Edward Lloyd, 'The Father of the Cheap Press.'" *Dickensian* 80.1 (Spring 1984): 33-38.

Homans, Margaret. *Bearing the Word: Language and Female Experience in Nineteenth-Century Women's Writing*. Chicago: U of Chicago P, 1986.

Hughes, Linda K., and Michael Lund. *Victorian Publishing and Mrs. Gaskell's Work*. Charlottesville: UP of Virginia, 1999.

Hughes, Winifred. *The Maniac in the Cellar: Sensation Novels of the 1860s*. Princeton: Princeton UP, 1980.

Jacobson, Marcia. *Henry James and the Mass Market*. University: U of Alabama P, 1983.

James, Henry. "Art of Fiction." *Literary Criticism*. 1: 44-65.

———. "Anthony Trollope." *Literary Criticism*. 1: 1330-54.

———. "The Lesson of Balzac." *Literary Criticism*. 2: 115-51.

———. *Literary Criticism*. Ed. Leon Edel. 2 vols. New York: Library of America, 1984.

———. *Notes of a Son and Brother*. New York: Scribner's, 1912.

———. "Nona Vincent." *Henry James' Shorter Masterpieces*. Ed. Peter Rawlings. 2 vols. New Jersey: Barnes and Noble, 1984. 1: 68-102.

———. *The Princess Casamassima*. Ed. Derek Brewer. New York: Penguin, 1987.

———. "The Question of the Opportunities." *Literary Criticism*. 1: 651-60.

———. *"The Turn of the Screw" and Other Stories*. Ed. T. J. Lustig. Oxford: Oxford UP, 1992.

James, Louis. *Fiction for the Working Man, 1830-1850*. London: Oxford UP, 1963.

———. "The Trouble with Betsey: Periodicals and the Common Reader in Mid-Nineteenth Century England." Shattock and Wolff 349-66.

Jameson, Fredric. *The Political Unconscious: Narrative as a Socially Symbolic Act*. Ithaca: Cornell UP, 1981.

Joyce, James. *A Portrait of the Artist as a Young Man*. Ed. Seamus Deane. New York: Penguin, 1995.

Jeaffreson, J. Cordy. *Novels and Novelists from Elizabeth to Victoria*. Vol. 2. London: Hurst and Blackett, 1858.

[Jeffrey, Francis.] Rev. of *Waverley*. *Edinburgh Review* 24 (November 1814): 208.

Keating, Peter. *The Haunted Study: A Social History of the English Novel, 1875-1914*. London: Secker and Warburg, 1989.

Kent, Christopher. "Higher Journalism and the Mid-Victorian Clerisy." *Victorian Studies* 13.2 (December 1969): 181-98.

Kerr, James. *Fiction against History: Scott as Storyteller*. Cambridge: Cambridge UP, 1989.

Klancher, Jon P. *The Making of English Reading Audiences, 1790-1832*. Madison: U of Wisconsin P, 1987.

Lentricchia, Frank. *After the New Criticism*. London: Athlone, 1980.

[Lewes, G. H.] "Farewell Causerie." *Fortnightly* 6 (1866): 890-96.

Loesberg, Jonathan. "The Ideology of Narrative Form in Sensation Fiction." *Representations* 13 (Winter 1996): 115-138.

Lonoff, Sue. *Wilkie Collins and His Victorian Readers*. New York: AMS Press, 1982.

Lovell, Terry. *Consuming Fiction*. London: Verso, 1987.

Lukacs, Georg. *The Historical Novel*. Trans. Hannah and Stanley Mitchell. Lincoln: U of Nebraska P, 1983.

Macherey, Pierre. *A Theory of Literary Production*. Trans. Geoffrey Wall. London: Routledge, 1985.

[Mansel, Henry.] "Sensation Novels," *Quarterly Review* 113 (April 1863): 481-514.

Mays, Kelly J. "The Disease of Reading and Victorian Periodicals." *Literature and the Marketplace*. Ed. John O. Jordan and Robert L. Patten. Cambridge: Cambridge UP, 1995.

McCarthy, Thomas J. *Relationships of Sympathy: The Writer and Reader in British Romanticism*. Aldershot: Scolar Press, 1997.

McWhirter, David. *Henry James's New York Edition: The Construction of Authorship*. Stanford: Stanford UP, 1995.

Michie, Elsie B. *Outside the Pale: Cultural Exclusion, Gender Difference, and the Victorian Woman Writer*. Ithaca: Cornell UP, 1993.

Miller, D. A. *The Novel and the Police*. Berkeley: U of California P, 1988.

Miller, J. Hillis. *Charles Dickens: The World of His Novels*. Cambridge, Mass.: Harvard UP, 1965.

Millgate, Jane. *Walter Scott: The Making of the Novelist*. Toronto: U of Toronto P, 1984.

Moretti, Franco. *The Way of the World: The* Bildungsroman *in European Culture*. London: Verso, 1987.

Morris, William. "The Lesser Arts." *News from Nowhere and Other Writings*. Ed. Clive Wilmer. New York: Penguin, 1993. 231-254.

Page, Norman, ed. *Wilkie Collins: The Critical Heritage*. London: Routledge and Kegan Paul, 1974.

Parrinder, Patrick. *Authors and Authority: A Study of English Literary Criticism and its Relation to Culture*. London: Routledge, 1977.

Pater, Walter. *Appreciations: With an Essay on Style*. Evanston: Northwestern UP, 1987.

Patten, Robert L. *Dickens and His Publishers*. Oxford: Clarendon, 1978.

Poovey, Mary. *Uneven Developments: The Ideological Work of Gender in Mid-Victorian England*. Chicago: U of Chicago P, 1988.

Riede, David G. *Oracles and Hierophants: Constructions of Romantic Authority*. Ithaca: Cornell UP, 1991.

Rose, Mark. *Authors and Owners*. Cambridge, Mass.: Harvard UP, 1993.

———. "The Author as Proprietor: *Donaldson v. Becket* and the Genealogy of Modern Authorship." *Representations* 23 (Summer 1988): 51-85.

Rowe, John Carlos. *The Theoretical Dimensions of Henry James*. Madison: U of Wisconsin P, 1984.

Rowland, William G. *Literature and the Marketplace: Romantic Writers and their Audiences in Great Britain and the United States*. Lincoln: U of Nebraska, 1996.

Sadoff, Dianne F. *Monsters of Affection: Dickens, Eliot & Bronte on Fatherhood*. Baltimore: Johns Hopkins UP, 1982.

Sadrin, Amy. "Fragmentation in *The Pickwick Papers*." *Dickens Studies Annual* 22 (1993): 21-34.

Salmon, Richard. *Henry James and the Culture of Publicity*. Cambridge: Cambridge UP, 1997.

Saunders, David. *Authorship and Copyright*. London: Routledge, 1992.

Saunders, J. W. *The Profession of English Letters*. London: Routledge and Kegan Paul, 1964.

Scanlan, Margaret. "Terrorism and the Realistic Novel: Henry James and *The Princess Casamassima*." *Texas Studies in Literature and Language* 34.3 (Fall 1992): 380-402.

Schor, Hilary M. *Scheherezade in the Marketplace: Elizabeth Gaskell and the Victorian Novel*. Oxford: Oxford UP, 1992.

Scott, Walter. "Introduction to *The Abbot*." *Prefaces*. 163-169.

———. "Introductory Epistle to *The Fortunes of Nigel*." *Prefaces*. 40-57.

———. *The Prefaces to the Waverley Novels*. Ed. Mark A. Weinstein. Lincoln: U of Nebraska P, 1978.

———. *Waverley, or, 'Tis Sixty Years Since*. Ed. Claire Lamont. Oxford: Oxford UP, 1986.

Seltzer, Marc. *Henry James and the Art of Power*. Ithaca: Cornell UP, 1984.

Shattock, Joanne, and Michael Wolff, eds. *The Victorian Periodical Press: Samplings and Soundings*. Leicester: Leicester UP, 1982.

Shelley, Percy Bysshe. "A Defence of Poetry." *The Complete Works of Percy Bysshe Shelley*. Ed. Roger Ingpen and Walter E. Peck. Vol. 7. New York: Scribners, 1930.

Skottowe, P. F. "Thomas Talfourd and *David Copperfield*." *Dickensian* 65.1 (Winter 1969): 25-31.

Strychacz, Thomas. *Modernism, Mass Culture, and Professionalism*. Cambridge: Cambridge UP, 1993.

Sutherland, John. *The Life of Walter Scott: A Critical Biography*. Oxford and Cambridge, Mass.: Blackwell, 1995.

———. *Victorian Fiction: Writers, Publishers, Readers*. New York: St. Martin's, 1995.

———. *Victorian Novelists and Publishers*. Chicago: U of Chicago P, 1976.

Sutherland, Kathryn. "Fictional Economies: Adam Smith, Walter Scott and the Nineteenth-Century Novel." *ELH* 54.1 (Spring 1987): 97-127.

Talfourd, Thomas Noon. "Speech on the Motion for Leave to Bring in a Bill to Amend the Law of Copyright." *The Modern British Essayists*. Vol. 7. Philadelphia: A. Hart, 1852.

Taylor, Jenny Bourne. *In the Secret Theatre of Home: Wilkie Collins, Sensation Narrative, and Nineteenth-Century Psychology*. London: Routledge, 1988.

Thomas, Ronald R. "Wilkie Collins and the Sensation Novel." *The Columbia History of the British Novel*. Ed. John Richetti. New York: Columbia UP, 1994. 479-507.

Tillotson, Kathleen. *Novels of the Eighteen-Forties*. Oxford: Oxford UP, 1954.

Trollope, Anthony. *An Autobiography*. London: Oxford UP, 1950.

Vanden Bossche, Chris R. "The Value of Literature: Representations of Print Culture in the Copyright Debate of 1837-1842." *Victorian Studies* 38.1 (Autumn 1994): 41-68.

Rev. of *Waverley*. *Monthly Review* N. S. 75 (November 1814): 275-289.

Welsh, Alexander. *From Copyright to Copperfield*. Cambridge, Mass.: Harvard UP, 1987.

———. *The Hero of the Waverley Novels: With New Essays on Scott*. Revised edition. Princeton: Princeton UP, 1992.

"What is Sensational?" *All the Year Round* 17 (2 March 1867): 221-24.

Wicke, Jennifer. *Advertising Fictions*. New York: Columbia UP, 1988.

Wilde, Oscar. *The Picture of Dorian Gray*. Ed. Peter Ackroyd. New York: Penguin, 1985.

———. "The Soul of Man under Socialism." *The Soul of Man and Prison Writings*. Ed. Isobel Murray. Oxford: Oxford UP, 1990.

Williams, Raymond. *Culture and Society: 1780-1950*. New York: Columbia UP, 1958.

———. *Keywords: A Vocabulary of Culture and Society*, Revised Edition. New York: Oxford UP, 1985.

Woodmansee, Martha. *The Author, Art, and the Market*. New York: Columbia UP, 1994.

———. Introduction. *The Construction of Authorship: Textual Appropriation and Law in Literature*. Ed. Martha Woodmansee and Peter Jaszi. Durham: Duke UP, 1994.

Woolford, John. "Periodicals and the Practice of Literary Criticism, 1855-64." Shattock and Wolff 109-42.

William Wordsworth, "Essay Supplementary to the Preface [of 1815]." *Works*.

———. *The Complete Poetical Works of William Wordsworth*. 10 vols. Boston and New York: Houghton, 1911.

———. "A Poet's Epitaph." *Works*.

———. "Preface to *Lyrical Ballads*, 1800." *Works*.

———. "The World Is Too Much with Us; Late and Soon." *Works*.

———. "The Recluse." *Works*.

Zlotnick, Susan. *Women, Writing, and the Industrial Revolution*. Baltimore: Johns Hopkins, 1998.

Index

For Product Safety Concerns and Information please contact our EU
representative GPSR@taylorandfrancis.com Taylor & Francis Verlag GmbH,
Kaufingerstraße 24, 80331 München, Germany

Printed and bound by CPI Group (UK) Ltd, Croydon, CR0 4YY
11/04/2025
01843992-0016